❦ Grace ❧

Our Ticket Home

Grace

Our Ticket Home

Lesa Scarlett-Grimes

For press inquiries, contact the author at lesagrimes@gmail.com

First printing November 2018.
Printed and published in partnership with BookBaby, 7905 N. Crescent Blvd.,
Pennsauken, NJ 08110
Distributed by Amazon.com, Baker & Taylor, and Ingram.
Electronic edition available through online retailers.

Cover design by Lauren Burgoyne.

ISBN-13: 978-1-54395-281-0

Names and online aliases have been changed in order to preserve privacy.

Contents

Preface

This is my seventeenth trip to Nicaragua in three years. So why am I having such a difficult time packing my suitcase? *Uuugghhh.* I look down at the piles I've made:

- Pots / Pans / Kitchenware
- Medications (including an emergency script of Xanax) (Don't judge me!)
- Towels / Cleaning Products
- My Clothes
- Lucie's Clothes
- Entertainment—books, crayons, DVD player, movies

During previous trips to Managua, the capital of Nicaragua, my husband Tim and I overloaded our luggage with supplies (crafts, clothes, shoes, school stuff) for the children at the orphanage, Puente de Amistad, which for all of my English speaking friends means Bridge of Friendship.

The orphanage is located at the bottom of a canyon, hence the nickname *El Canyon*. The only way to Puente de Amistad is down a curvy, dirt road that is covered in potholes. My first trip down this road was in a bus that cruised at a snail's pace to avoid tipping over. It's one bump after another, and the road is so narrow that turning back is not an option. I thought seriously about getting out and walking, it seemed like a much safer option considering I felt like I was in a bumper car-tilting from side to side. During my first trip there, I recall looking out the window at lush trees and hearing the sound of branches scraping the roof. The smell of the plants and the dust from the road always takes me back to that trip.

As soon as the children heard our bus pull up to the orphanage, they came running to greet us! They are just as curious as we are. The glowing smiles from their caramel complexions always put my anxious heart at ease. Most of the orphanage's visitors are missionaries that arrive in busloads and stay for a week (just as I did initially). Their time with the children consists of crafts, games and field trips to the beach. During these mini-holidays, the children are treated to cake and candy, which is a rarity. The children jump up and down to greet their guests because it's like grandma and grandpa are coming to visit!

There are approximately 40 children (age six months to fifteen years old) that call Puente de Amistad home. The orphanage is made up of two brightly painted green buildings that are covered in murals. The one-story buildings are divided between boys and girls who eat together at long picnic benches that are located between the buildings. It's next to impossible to keep the ceramic tile floors dirt free (believe me I've tried), but the children don't seem to mind. The sound of joyful noise echoes through the halls here.

When I force myself to imagine the trauma and neglect some of these children endured before arriving at Puente de Amistad; I feel the pain cut deep in my mama gut. Some of these children's families just can't afford to feed them. The lucky ones get dropped at the orphanage's doorstep.

My daughter, Martita was not one of the *lucky ones*. At two-years-old, Martita was found abandoned in the marketplace. She was naked and chained up like an animal. The authorities discovered her eating anything she could find off the ground.

(Can you imagine your child like this?) They brought her to the orphanage, where I happened to arrive two weeks later.

My baby girl was starving for more than just a meal when she arrived at Puente de Amistad. The first words I heard out of her mouth were screams. Patches of bald spots covered her curly brown head, and her nose ran like a leaky faucet. The only reason I could physically walk away from Martita and the other children after that first visit was because of the people working there. The orphanage is strapped for resources, but the staff lovingly looks after those babies the best they can.

It's been three years since I first held Martita. While she is in a safe place, she is malnourished like the rest of the children. They eat rice and beans three times a day.

Vegetables and meat are a delicacy rarely found on the menu, yet, these children possess so much joy; it's contagious. You can't have a bad day there.

After spending a few weeks at the orphanage, the children opened up to me with their stories. They confided how desperate they were to be reunited with their families. Some of the kids are shy, some are rambunctious, but they are all in dire need of love they so willingly give. I feel like these children are not only part of my family but part of me; the best part of me.

Visitors play an important role at the orphanage. We become these children's temporary families until they can go to a real home, which sadly isn't always a reality. So that's what we do, we love them as if they are our own.

Only this next trip to Puente de Amistad will be different . . .

After three arduous years of waiting for the green adoption light; we finally got the call. Our spunky, sweet, five-year-old Martita will be coming home with us, on one condition . . . I have to move to Nicaragua to seal the rest of the adoption deal. Crazy! I can barely contain myself. Our baby girl will officially join our family whom I lovingly refer to as a beautifully blended cast of characters. There are five of us: Tim (my husband), his daughter Allie (from his previous marriage), my daughter Scarlett (from my previous marriage), and our daughter Lucie. It's funny, our family never felt incomplete until we met Martita. She is God's glue that connects us all.

My type A brain is in overdrive. There is so much to organize and agonize over in planning this trip. Scarlett, my seventh-grader will stay in the U.S. with my husband who rearranged his work schedule to be home for her. Meanwhile, our six-year-old, Lucie, and I are preparing to hop a plane to Nicaragua, where we will be living for the next few months. (Did I mention this is crazy?!) I'm praying this really is the last step in the adoption process. God, I'm giving this to you.

OK, Les, pull it together. It's time to pack your bags.

Only nothing I threw in my suitcase could prepare us for this journey.

Part I

My First Trip
To Nicaragua

⟨ *Chapter 1* ⟩

Stepping Out of My Comfort Zone

When I was in my twenties, I had this reoccurring dream . . . I was a very large pregnant lady pushing a baby in a shopping cart with two kids running ahead down the grocery store aisle, and a third holding my hand. I felt overwhelmed, sleep-deprived yet somehow, I was in a state of complete bliss. I dreamt of motherhood, but when I awoke, I wasn't corralling toddlers in high chairs; I was chasing promotions in high heels as I climbed the corporate ladder at AT&T. I was living the life of a single gal in San Francisco.

The grocery cart in my *motherhood* dream came to a screeching halt on my 30th birthday. I will never forget that phone conversation with my mom when she said to me, "It's *ok* if you don't have children." Ummmm . . . I never considered life without kids . . . Moms have a gift of turning one sentence into a paradigm shift . . . (I should know, I now have four daughters of my own!)

I hung up the phone and was deafened by the sound of my biological clock. I had to have a baby, and fast . . . and then a second, and a third, and maybe a fourth! So, what would any sane woman do in my situation? That was easy—I gave my current on again, off again, boyfriend an ultimatum; it was time to get married, or it was time to break up. Why he agreed to marry me, I'm still not exactly sure but we ran to the altar, and I got pregnant on my honeymoon. Nine months later, my beautiful Scarlett was born. The End.

Just kidding, it was only the beginning of a life I had never imagined; the life of a single mom. After our daughter was born, my ex and I realized we weren't well matched, so we separated. Divorce was *not* in the dream, and I realized that my life would turn out very different from what I had always thought it would be.

For starters, Scarlett and I left the San Francisco Bay Area and moved to northern Virginia, where we began our new life. I think every mom needs a vice (vices); running was one of mine. I never went to Virginia looking for God, but I felt so spiritual and awake when I laced up my sneakers and hit the pavement. I didn't feel alone anymore and while I had no idea how things would turn out . . . I felt like there was a higher power watching over me, which is a little ironic because up until that point, I had run away from religion.

I have always believed in a higher being but struggled with religion. I didn't grow up with a church and only attended Bible school in the summers when I visited my Dad in Missouri. Quite frankly, I didn't like what I was taught. The lessons seemed extraordinarily judgmental, and honestly, it scared me. "I wasn't good enough to believe. I was going to hell."

So, I shied away from my faith until I *ran* into God during my workouts.

I soon met the man that I was meant to marry, Tim. He was actually my boss at the time (don't judge me), but he turned out to be the man who helped me grow as a person and be my best self. We were in love, but it wasn't all peaches and cream at the beginning. Tim and I had challenging careers. We traveled and worked hard. Our schedules were difficult to coordinate. We had both just ended difficult relationships and shared the biggest challenge of all . . . raising our girls.

I had a daughter, Scarlett and he had a daughter, Allie. Soon after Tim and I got married, Lucie came along, and the children outnumbered the adults. My shopping cart dream was becoming a full-blown reality; I was a mama. We had a few minor bumps (as everyone does) but our blended family was growing beautifully. Since everything was going so well, I guess it was time to shake things up . . .

People often ask me, "What made you want to adopt?" It's a difficult question to answer, but it begins with my spiritual journey.

While in Virginia, Tim and I went on a church hunt . . . or at least that's what we called it. We visited different churches to see where and if our unique family could *fit*. Tim and I wanted to find a place that our girls could grow up in. We found a church made up of members who were passionate about showing us who God really is and the love that is meant for each one of us. I have learned a great deal while attending my church and am part of a family there. It is a place where I feel welcomed and accepted no matter what I have done in my past. I found a place to *lean in* and learn. My spiritual journey is always evolving.

I've never been consumed with being labeled as a specific religion, what matters most to my family is finding a place that we can make a difference in people's lives. It is also a place where my children are thriving. They are experiencing what love is and how they too can positively impact our world. We are learning and evolving together.

Back to the adoption question . . . I was sitting in church one Sunday when a woman made an announcement that our congregation would take a trip to Nicaragua that summer. They were looking for some volunteers to visit a few orphanages. The goal was to find an orphanage that our church could virtually adopt. Sponsoring an orphanage means that our church members would donate clothing, food, and any other supplies needed. However, most importantly, we would create relationships with the children, the orphans. We would be their family in the States.

I remember sitting in the audience and thinking that it would be amazing to go there. I speak a little Spanish and I love children, so it seemed like a good match for me. But then the doubts crept in. I never considered myself a model *Christian*. I'm the more subtle type and to be honest, I was still pretty new to all this church stuff. How could I put myself out there like this? What would my family and friends think? Am I joining a cult? Seriously, what would be expected of me and would I be able to meet those expectations?

I ignored the doubt train cruising through my brain, turned to my husband and said, "I want to go" albeit I was scared to death. This would be my first trip to a third world country, my first mission's trip, and I didn't know anyone who was going. But hey, what's the big deal, right? After church, I spoke with the woman in charge and signed up on the spot. I had no idea what I was getting into but felt a gnawing desire to go. The thought of being able to help these children in any way sounded so wonderful to me.

As a church, we collected donations. I wrote letters to all of my family, friends, and neighbors to let them know where we were going and what we were trying to accomplish. I gave a list of all the things we needed, and the supplies poured in! The tears fell every time I came home and found a pile of donations at my front door. I was so happy to share this with my friends and family. We were in this . . . together!

There are ten women going on this trip. I didn't know any of them since I was so new to the church—but I couldn't think of a better way to bond. We had weekly meetings to prepare in which we organized the supplies, bought things that we needed, and planned activities for the week we would be there. We also had several meetings discussing how to prepare for the trip mentally. What are our goals? What are our questions? Fears? Only there was no real way to prep for this journey. The first trip taught me how valuable it is to just *go-learn-experience* to truly understand.

❨ *Chapter 2* ❩

Nicaragua or Bust!

Disclaimer: You are about to read pages ripped from my diary, which documents my first journey to Nicaragua. It's raw, real, and in some parts a little rough around the edges. I never set out to record this time in my life as I am not a writer, but I felt compelled to pick up my laptop and let the experience flow. Once I got going, I couldn't stop. My three-year love affair with Nicaragua taught me so much about who I am, the people I love, and the person I want to become.

August 9, 2006

My first trip to Nicaragua—*wow*! I am still a little in shock that I am doing this. It started to hit me when the alarm clock woke Tim and me up at 3:00 a.m. "Well, there's no backing out now, I thought to myself" as we waited outside for our group leader to pick me up. The van was so packed with suitcases that there was little room for us to sit. We all loaded our luggage with supplies for the kids and no one seemed to care we were sitting on top of each other.

On the Plane

I am now on the plane to Miami with the rest of our group (a total of ten ladies). You can't miss us, we're the ones in matching white T-shirts that read: *Community Church Nicaragua 2006*. I'm excited to be traveling with these women. We are chatting away like old friends, sharing stories of how we said goodbye to our families and asking questions about the journey that no one can answer.

I can't stop thinking about the kids we're going to meet at the orphanage. The kids! I cannot wait to meet the kids!

I feel like I have so much love to share because I come from such a blessed family; I want to multiply that love while I'm there. Knowing how nervous I was to take this step, Tim wrote me a note and stuck it in my bag. It read: "You are doing this for God, to share His love, how exciting!"

We Made It!

It is now 8:00 p.m., and I am taking some private time to reflect after a long and emotional day. We landed in Managua (the capital of Nicaragua) without any issues. The ladies and I were tired from the journey but fueled with excitement. Customs was a breeze. Our group is here with another church, so after their group arrived, we all took buses to the orphanage we're staying at, Casa Bernabe. It will be our home base for the next seven days as we visit several other orphanages in the city.

Our buses were loud (in color and mechanics)! The bus in front of ours had giant words on the back that read: *Dios es Amor*, God is Love (for my English speaking friends). Translation: We are church ladies on a mission.

When I looked out the bus window, I was taken aback by Managua's beauty. The landscape is a hybrid of Hawaii and Mexico. Hawaii, because of the vegetation; lush green trees, and coffee-colored mountains. Mexico, because of the people, architecture, and overall feel. The climate is pleasantly warm and a little humid (I don't think I packed my hair straightener. Eek!) I think I could get used to this.

People waved and smiled at us during the first leg of our trip; a thirty minute ride to a private restaurant (which resembled a KFC). When we arrived at the restaurant, three young children, approximately nine years old, were begging outside. Our guide asked them to come in and join us. The kids ate the food that was left on our plates. The children were sweet and grateful. They were also patient as they answered our twenty questions in poor *Spanglish*. When we finished eating, our guide asked the kids if they would like to go to the pool with us. The children agreed, so he paid for a taxi that took them to our next stop. They showed up a few minutes after we did, wearing filthy clothes and big smiles.

Can you imagine our kids doing that? Begging strangers for food? Getting into a cab with their friends? Going to a pool without asking their parents' permission, without any swimsuits or towels? What about sunscreen? All kids need sunscreen when they go to the pool!

A little while later, the kids from Casa Bernabe arrived. While the children were excited about the pool, they were shy and distant towards me. I approached the kids and in my most cheery voice said, *"Hola."* Some of the children responded while others completely ignored me. It was so awkward and uncomfortable. I retreated to my shell for a bit and for the first time I felt unsure about being here. I began to miss my family.

After three hours of pool time, we loaded the bus and headed to our final destination, Casa Bernabe. A sweet little girl (probably eight years old) sat next to me on the bus. She didn't talk to me or even look me in the face, so I pulled out some printed pictures of my family. The trip coordinator recommended we share family photos to connect with the children. At first, I was reluctant to do this because I didn't want the children to feel different or left out. However, this little girl loved seeing photos of my girls, husband, and dogs. She now saw me as a Mom and not a stranger. She held the pictures and asked me for everyone's name. I told her she was beautiful, inside and out. Soon she fell asleep on my lap. After a short bus ride, we pulled up to the orphanage. I was sad we arrived so soon.

Since this is my first time staying at an orphanage in a third world country, I had no idea what to expect. Our sleeping quarters are oddly reminiscent of my family's camping trips as a kid. There are two casitas, which house ten women in five bunk beds, sharing two showers, two toilets, (and a partridge in a pear tree). The orphanage only has one water tower, which means water is scarce and showers are freezing! I've developed a handy system for showering. Step 1: Turn the water on to create a lather for the soap. Step 2: Turn the water off. Step 3: Wash as best as you can without water. Step 4: Hold your breath and turn the water back on to rinse off under the icy trickle. It works, and I am clean!

After feeling somewhat relaxed from my shower, I called my husband and completely lost it. This experience is not what I thought it would be. I was disillusioned to think I would come here, and the kids would come running with open arms. I was so centered on the good that I was doing that I was not focused on how these kids would feel meeting yet another group of people from the U.S. How could I be so self-centered?

This is *not* about me!

My prayer tonight is that I have the courage to *be all in* and not hesitate with these children. I know that God has a plan for these kids and somehow, I am blessed to be part of it. Please help me make the most of every moment and focus my energy on them and not me.

August 10, 2006

What a great day! We got up at 6:30 a.m. to have breakfast and hit the beach. The ladies and I got wise. We strategically decided to sit by ourselves on this three-hour bus ride so that the kids would have to sit next to us when we picked them up! Erubea, a reluctant fifteen-year-old sat next to me. I didn't hear much from the sweet young man with the budding mustache, but we made some small talk before he fell asleep. A few hours passed, and we arrived at a beautiful beach that welcomed us with colossal waves and a cool breeze. It was awesome.

On the beach, I met Marlena and her brother Mauricio. *Wow!* Tim and I are sponsoring them through a program at our church. We send money to help them with school, but it was so unbelievable to meet these kids in person. (Before this trip they had only existed on paper.) Marlena and I sat on the beach as she told me how much she loved school (except math). It was easy to observe how close she and her brother are. I made sure to get in some Mama Bear hugs, and I look forward to spending more time with them.

Yesterday, I met a little girl named Marlene, who yelled "get out of my way" in Spanish and then stuck her tongue out at me. It crushed me, so you can imagine the anxiety I felt when she sat next to me on the bus ride home. She settled in by giving me the *evil eye* but softened when I showed her pictures of my family. When she saw Lucie and Scarlett, she said, *Que bonita.*

That was all I got out of her, but since she didn't yell or curse at me, I think our relationship is moving in a very positive direction.

The children are also teaching me some Spanish vocabulary. Today, I learned the word *platicar,* which means to chill and relax while visiting with someone. It is part of Nicaragua's culture, which is why there is such a relaxed pace. *Mas o Menos* is another motto, meaning more or less, so nothing starts or ends on time, which makes me a little *loco.*

August 11, 2006

The electricity went out at 4:00 a.m. The reason I know is that that's when the fans turned off. These are the fans that keep my nine roommates and me from sweating to death, so when they stopped working, we all woke up. Without electricity, the toilets don't work and wait for it . . . wait for it . . . neither does the coffee pot! On the bright side, I think I've shed five pounds from all the sweating. Our outing today could not be more opposite from our beach field trip yesterday. Today we're heading to *la chureca*, which means "the dump" in Spanish. Yes, we're actually going to the local dump where everyone ditches their trash.

The bus came to a halt at the dump's entrance as our leader stood up to warn us about the scene ahead. I felt like I was watching one of those TV shows with the disclaimer at the beginning: "Warning: This video contains extremely graphic and disturbing images, which may offend some viewers. Discretion is strongly advised." Only nothing could have prepared me for this. I looked out the window and tried to see past the endless piles of putrid trash, but I couldn't; garbage covered every acre. There was an indescribable stench that choked the air. Flies seeped in through all the bus windows, and the smell made my eyes water. I covered my mouth and nose with my bandana. Then, right on cue, the sky turned dark, and birds began circling overhead. It was like a scene from a horror movie.

Perhaps the most shocking thing were the men, women, and children that were sorting through the filth. This is what they do day after day to survive. There are generations of families living in shacks made from garbage, yes garbage . . . They never leave. They eat trash for all their meals and drink water from a polluted lake. I cried as I watched naked babies run around with swollen bellies and flies swarming them. This was hell on earth. No one should have to live like this. We drove through miles of garbage until we arrived at a school that sits in the middle of the dump called the Christian School of Hope.

It was the only light that shined in this dark place. Our leader told us all to stop crying. "These kids do not need your tears or your pity."

He was right—I had to pull myself together. So, we all gave each other hugs, wiped our tears and went inside the school. The kids greeted us with love and excitement. The younger ones hugged my legs and reached up with their hands wanting me to pick them up. They reminded me of my own daughter Lucie saying, "uppie uppie" whenever she wanted me to hold her.

These kids were filthy. They were cloaked in dirt, and their hair was slick with grease. Some of their faces were covered in a film of snot, but their smiles were brilliant. They shone so brightly. I quickly got over my *germaphobic* issues and embraced them.

We spent much of the day playing on the swings, talking and laughing. They kissed and hugged me for hours. During our visit, there was a presentation on dental care, in which everyone had to be quiet. As I made my way to the floor, a little hand tugged mine to sit down in the middle of all these kids. There were four on my lap and one on each side. They fought with each other to get my attention. For the first time since I arrived, I felt utterly at peace. I felt like I was exactly where I was supposed to be, and I knew that this place and these children were now part of my life.

Maria was the first little girl that clung to me. I noticed her deformed finger and blistering burns on her hands. Her clothes were filthy, and her body was so dirty that I could actually see bugs in her hair. She was so desperate for me to hold her that when she touched me, I did not hesitate. I wanted her to know that I found her beautiful and I knew that I needed her touch as much as she needed mine. I took a lot of pictures of Maria. I wanted to capture her sweet, beautiful face and etch it into my memory.

Saying goodbye to the kids at the end of the day was painful. I was overcome with such an incredible desire to take all of them home. I didn't want to leave them. I want to help them, care for them, love them but these kids are not orphans, they have parents who love them. It's unfathomable, but these kids don't know how the rest of the world lives. I am struggling with my feelings. I want to help these kids, but I don't know what that looks like yet.

The ride home was sad and long, but I was grateful to share this experience with these women. We talked about how we witnessed God living in this dark place. We saw Him in the kid's smiles. I believe, there is a plan for each one of those kids. I felt blessed to meet them, and to be able to love them. It was an incredible day for me—seeing such poverty, filth, and doom. Then in the middle of this dark place, a school that radiates so much love with these beautiful kids. How can their lights shine so brightly in such darkness?

August 12, 2006

I think my body and mind are on the brink of an emotional and spiritual overload. (Is that a thing?) I woke up with a head cold this morning but thanks to the amazing women (I am here with), I am equipped with vitamin c, multi-vitamins, natural remedies, cough drops, and cold medicine. I think my body is in shock, but it does all seem to be working and I'm feeling much better.

We started our day at an orphanage called Puente de Amistad, which means the Bridge of Friendship. The locals call the orphanage *El Canyon* (The Canyon), because the entire community sits in a canyon and the only way to get there is to travel down a steep road. As our bus thudded uneasily down the steep, rugged road, we slid from one side. At one point I thought getting out of the bus and hoofing it would be a safer option, but the wild ride only added to the excitement of meeting the children. Our group knew that visiting Puente de Amistad would be a focal point of our trip as the orphanage was in great need of support.

The children jumped up and down to greet us as our bus pulled in. Their eyes grew big with curiosity as we settled in among them. We brought flip-flops for the kids to decorate and spent the morning playing soccer and singing songs. We learned that most of the orphanage's visitors are missionaries that arrive in busloads and stay for a week. Their time with the children is like a mini-holiday filled with crafts, games and field trips to the beach. The kids also get to enjoy cake and candy splurges, which is a rarity. That's why the kids flip somersaults when guests come.

There are approximately forty children (age six months to fifteen years old) that call Puente de Amistad home. The orphanage is made up of two brightly painted green buildings that are covered in murals. The one-story buildings are divided between boys and girls who eat together at long picnic benches that are located between the buildings. It's next to impossible to keep the ceramic tile floors dirt free (believe me I've tried), but the children don't seem to mind. The sound of joyful noise echoes through the halls here.

Most of the kids have literally been dropped off at the front door without a story to their name. They have no idea if they have parents, where they are, or what tomorrow holds. Some of these children do have families but because of their dire circumstances, are left at the orphanage so they are fed, cared for, and can attend school. It was a short, yet fantastic visit. When I close my eyes, I can see their caramel complexions and toothy smiles. I am excited to visit them again before the end of our trip. I am so inspired by these children.

Next stop: Church Verbo! This church is incredible and very hands-on with the local orphans and community. We met the staff and had lunch there before heading to our next destination, a refugee camp named *Nueva Vida*, which means New Life. This refugee camp was formed after Hurricane Mitch in 1998. I was shocked to see how devastated the community still was eight years later.

We had a joyous assignment at Nueva Vida today! Our mission was putting on a carnival for forty kids in the neighborhood. We packed all the essential supplies (from home) for the day's events; water balloon throw, big clothes relay, bean bag toss, and sponge races! I was in charge of the clothes relay, which really made me miss my husband because the kids were wearing his clothes in the race. It was no easy task explaining to the kids (in Spanish) how to do the relay while keeping them all in line. However, they caught on quick, and the carnival was a great success.

After the carnival, we fed the kids lunch and I was surprised to see how little they ate. Often, they have days where they don't eat at all. So why weren't they devouring their lunch? I found out later that these kids save the majority of their meals for the rest of their families. How incredible is that?

That evening, when we were all together, dissecting the day, our leader asked a question. "What is the secret of the poor? Why are they so happy when they have so little? Why do they smile, laugh, and love so easily? How can they be so strong? What's their secret?" This was the question that kept haunting me.

He answered the seemingly impossible question.

"They live for today and never worry about tomorrow."

This sparked more questions and discussion . . . Are the rich the ones who struggle? Are we measuring wealth, position, and possessions over all else? Are we centered on what's truly important? Is it too complicated for us to separate what matters most in the world or what matters most to God? It really made me wonder, how is it possible for these beautiful kids to feel so blessed when they are orphans without families? How can they be so happy when they are hungry, live in dirt shacks, and can't afford to go to school? What do they have that I don't?

How do I, a person who has so much, feel as blessed as these kids with so little? This journey is making me question so much and feel so deeply. I just want to love, help and change as much as I can. My newest revelation; it's not just these kids who need my attention, but it's also time I examine my own life and how I'm raising my own children.

August 13, 2006

We slept in today and had a late breakfast at 9:00 a.m. It was wonderful having some time to *platicar,* which was a nice change of pace. We headed to Church Verbo in the morning and attended a beautiful service. The worship was awesome! There were ten people on stage playing all kinds of instruments accompanied by several singers. I felt like I was at a concert. They had at least twelve dancers waving flags as we all danced and sang among them!

On the bus trip to the church, my friend Mauricio (who Tim and I sponsor) sat next to me. We talked and talked (his English is excellent). I really enjoyed learning more about him. Mauricio loves soccer and music and does so well academically that he goes to a special school. His birthday is on Tuesday, and he will be turning 16. Since I knew I would be here for his birthday, I brought him a gift that I hoped he would love. Mauricio is such a polite young man, he waited for me after he got off the bus and we had lunch together. I kept telling him to go hang out with his friends, but I loved spending some quality time with him.

We drove back to Casa Bernabe through Managua and had a chance to see the city. The mountainous backdrop gives way to green trees and lush flowers growing wild. Managua is filled with small homes (made from concrete blocks and dirt floors). *Mercados,* stores selling snacks, line the streets where there are lots of people riding bicycles and walking around. The vibe is upbeat and fast-paced. I am very taken by the people of Nicaragua, they are so welcoming and warm.

After we dropped off the kids at Casa Bernabe, we met with one of Verbo's church leaders. He invited us to his home where he shared his experiences living in Nicaragua. He loves the people here and is so dedicated to them. He feels that God has a purpose for Latin America and that these people are making a difference in the world. He also talked about some of the younger Nicaraguans and their desire for higher education. They want to attend college in the U.S. because our universities outrank the ones in Nicaragua. We also discussed a way to make a genuine difference for these kids, and that is through virtual adoption.

ORPHANetwork, which is the organization that is hosting us, sponsors this program. Virtually adopting these children provides funds for the orphanage to adequately feed the kids, send them to school while connecting them with a family in the states that loves and prays for them. It is an incredible program, and I am excited to support it any way I can. ORPHANetwork is helping me answer the looming question, how can I help these kids?

August 14, 2006

I coughed a lot last night and kept my roommates up. (Sorry!) I am not sure how I am functioning on so little sleep. However, this place invigorates me, and I am overjoyed to be experiencing it. I realized this morning that we only have two days left. The time has really flown by, and I want to make the most of the hours I have. Something in my gut is telling me I will be back with my family. They too need to experience this place and know these kids.

We started the day with the familiar bumpy bus ride down the steep rocky road to El Canyon to see our kids. Many of them were in school, so we logged some quality time with the babies. A toddler named Martita clung to me immediately. She is about two years old and ornery! She refuses to talk; when she wants something, she screams and points.

Martita has only been at the orphanage for two weeks. The lucky orphans are usually dropped off at the doorstep, Martita was not one of them. It hurts me to share this, but I feel Martita's story should be told. The authorities found this little girl abandoned in the marketplace. She was naked and chained up like a dog. She ate anything she could find off the ground. Horrifying.

There are fresh scars on Martita's neck from the chains they found her in and bald spots where hair should be. Looking at her boney body is painful. She is starving, and I'm assuming, abused. She's terrified . . . when I hold her, she grips me so tightly afraid to let go. This little love has such a sweet face and a smile that could melt my iciest mood. She is exceptionally choosy in giving her affections.

Martita needs me, I can feel it. She is different from all the other kids. I feel a strong connection to her that is difficult to describe. It's not a love connection, like the one I felt with Maria at La Chureca, but more of a bond or a need. She seems drawn to me and I to her. I have no idea what Martita's story is or what family she has here but how they found her and the abuse she has already endured in her short two years of life is unfathomable. I asked our leader to check into Martita's story, so I could understand her situation better. I know that somehow my family will support this little girl.

Our time at El Canyon was way too short. We played with the younger kids and then went to the school to give all the kids bracelets. Then we hung out with the kids before it was time to go. On our walk from the school back to the orphanage, I met a girl named Marianna, who was hanging outside the fence. She came up to me and introduced herself. The young teen had a beautiful smile, but she was very dirty. Her clothing was way too small for her and hung in shreds. We talked and walked, and I discovered she was fourteen years old and had never attended school. Attending school in El Canyon costs two dollars per month, which Marianna's family could never afford, so instead of going to school, Marianna hangs off the fence and watches the kids from afar. Can you imagine how it must feel to want something so badly, something we take for granted in the states? Going to school only costs two dollars per month but not being able to afford that for your kids? It's heart-breaking . . . truly. I'm trying to take mental notes of all the kids I want to help; my brain is running out of space.

When I got back to the orphanage, I went to put Martita down because it was time to leave. She started to scream and cry, so of course, I picked her right back up. My team was already on the bus, and it was time for me to go. But, I wanted desperately to keep this girl and love her for a while longer so she wouldn't be so scared. The time I had with her just wasn't enough for either one of us. I blinked my eyes repeatedly trying not to cry when I gave her to one of the ladies that worked at the orphanage. Martita was screaming and crying as tears streamed down my face. I ran to the bus and waved and threw kisses to her as we pulled away.

My heart shattered, leaving didn't feel like the right thing to do. I thought that she truly needed me, not just anyone to hold her but specifically, me. The more you love and connect with these kids, the harder it is to say goodbye.

On the bus ride, our group talked about who we connected with and why. Many of us are considering adoption. It's difficult not to be able to do more to help these kids. I have always had a heart for adoption and a desire to give a child in need, a loving home. I have literally dreamt of having a large family, and now I know that adoption is part of our journey. I'm excited to see where this leads.

We headed to the mall on the way home for some dinner and were pleasantly surprised by the modern vibe and the tasty food court. Nothing says home like burgers and fries, so we ate at Burger King. If you know me at all, I do *not* partake in fast food. However, I have had more fast food this week than I have had for more than a year back home. Fast food here is more of a delicacy than a convenience. We splurged on some donuts for dessert, and I must admit I was proud of myself for doing all the talking. I even picked up a new Spanish word, *docena* (dozen). The guilt I would usually feel chowing down on these calories was replaced with pure delight.

We spent the evening with the older girls from Casa Bernabe with a girls'-night-in slumber party. We braided the girls' hair, painted nails and swapped stories. These young women shared some incredible insights as to what they've endured at such a young age. Storytelling is such a powerful thing. They were so vulnerable to us, and it gave us an even stronger bond as friends. These young women are nothing short of courageous.

August 15, 2006

Our last day here, I can't believe it! I am conflicted. On the one hand I'm so ready to be home with my husband and girls, but on the other hand I can see staying here in Nicaragua for much longer. It's crazy. I love this place. My heart feels full here, and I am so excited for my family to see and experience it all. I know they will love it as I do.

Our day was full of activities. We visited the market and hosted a massive fiesta for the kids at Casa Bernabe. It was an epic celebration with a mariachi band and lots of delicious food. No one went hungry today! It was also Mauricio's birthday, so we had a big cake to celebrate and smashed a pile of spongy frosting on his face (a tradition in Nicaragua). I love these kids so much, but my heart is aching for the children at El Canyon, especially my sweet Martita. How I wish we could have spent more time with her.

The leaders at ORPHANetwork gave strict instructions that there is no crying allowed, a rule I've violated quite a few times. The emotional distress can be upsetting to the kids, which makes perfect sense. If we can't stop crying, we are told to leave the area and return when we are composed again. Saying goodbye has always been a very emotional thing for me, so I ducked out a few times to *pull myself together*. Fortunately, I am not the only baby in the bunch, so I had lots of company in time out.

One of my goals in taking this trip was to grow my relationship with these women, and I feel that I have. We were strangers when we started this journey, and now we share a special connection I don't have with anyone else. I look forward to spending more time with them in the years to come.

August 16, 2006

I am heading home today, and I am overwhelmed with sadness and joy. I cannot wait to hold my husband and be with my girls. I know that I would not be here without Tim's love and support. Every time I talked to him about what I experienced in Nicaragua, it was like he experienced it right along with me. He is such a big part of me.

At the start of this journey, I was concerned that I would not be able to make a significant impact in these children's lives, but after only seven days, I know that I have. What I did not expect, is how much these kids would change me in a week. Being loved by these kids makes me understand how much God loves me. I never knew that this experience would bring me so close to God, but it has.

I think that many people, including myself, ask the question, "Why would God let these kids, and their families, live like this?"

We get angry with God and can't comprehend why we have so much, and others have so little. However, this experience has not made me angry with God but more understanding. I have seen beauty through filth. I have felt pure joy without material things (like a big car or an expensive house). I have experienced authentic love in smiles and hugs that I don't always encounter at home. This trip has given me a greater understanding of what "wealth" means.

This experience has made me question everything, including our big home and expensive lifestyle. Should I change my life entirely and move to Nicaragua? Will Tim and the girls want to bring Martita home and officially make her part of our family? What are the next steps?

Settling in at Home

I was so excited to see my husband at the airport. I couldn't wait to give him a big hug and possibly make out in front of our church group (it has been a week since I've seen him). I walked out of the double doors from security to the baggage claim where all the people are waiting for their friends and family. I saw Tim standing there with flowers and scanning the crowd for me. I walked straight towards him with the biggest smile on my face. He caught my eye but quickly continued to scan the crowd. It dawned on me that my husband didn't recognize me! How is that possible? Yes, seven days without a shower, no makeup, flat hair and a few layers of dirt altered my appearance but seriously?!?! I walked straight over to him and punched him in the arm. It took him a couple seconds but finally the recognition set in and he claimed me as his wife. We laughed until we cried and I think he's still a little embarrassed to be standing next to me.

I've definitely caught the "Nicaraguan bug." It's been a few weeks, and I still can't get the kids' faces out of my head, especially, Martita. I am haunted by the memory of how alone she felt as she clung to me. Would it be possible to bring her home? Would she fit into our family? This was a decision that would take a great deal of thought, discussion, and of course, prayer.

We accomplished our initial goal for our trip. We found an orphanage in Nicaragua that our church has officially adopted, Puente de Amistad. These kids are now ours. We write letters, send packages and financially support them. We are already planning our next trip to Nicaragua with more members of our church, so they too can experience how incredible this journey is. The best part of this news . . . this is the orphanage where Martita lives.

My feelings towards adopting Martita are a bit of a paradox. I don't doubt my love for her, but there is so much more to consider. I feel such an undeniable connection with Martita, but I also know what a massive change this would mean for our entire family. I learned from our contacts at ORPHANetwork that Martita is a true orphan because her parents actually abandoned her. She doesn't have any brothers, sisters or any known relatives, which confirms what I knew in my gut when we first met; she needs me. While I already consider her part of my family; Tim and the girls need to be entirely on board with bringing her home. The next step is having Tim visit Nicaragua to meet Martita. I told him how important it is that he goes alone to create his own experience.

As much as I'd like to go with him, he needs to determine whether he feels the same connection with her.

Adoption can be hazardous to marriage; I wish that were an urban myth, but it's not. Tim and I both had previous marriages, so our chance for staying together is already at thirty-seven percent, *Ouch!* Adopting a child brings down the marriage survival rate to nineteen percent. I cringe at those numbers. My marriage comes first. It comes before my kids. It must if it is to thrive. Divorce is not in our vocabulary, and we need to navigate this decision together to be sure it's something our marriage can handle. I'm a smart girl, and am well aware that many issues come with adoption. That is why I insisted that Tim go to Nicaragua by himself, to make up his own mind. I reassured him that if he doesn't feel the same way I do that we would still continue to support and love Martita from afar. Its' his decision with no hard feelings attached. I trust him and know he will do what is right for our family.

Tim took part in the next trip with our church to Nicaragua . . . without me. I was so excited for him to be in Nicaragua and experience everything that I had. There are so many places I want him to see and people to meet, but I am most excited for my husband to meet Martita. (Obviously!)

I will never, and I mean never, forget the first phone call he made to me from Nicaragua. After we greeted each other, he said simply, "Baye, Martita is ours."

Thinking about it still makes me tear up and lose it. We have no idea what we are getting in to but the decision is made, we are bringing Martita home. Tim and Martita had a great week getting to know each other. He spent most of his time with her at the orphanage, and the two of them became very close. If only Tim could have signed off on the whole adoption and brought her home, but it doesn't work that way. Not even close.

Part II

Three Years Later . . .

April 2009

Chapter 3

My One-Way Ticket

Over the past three years, we have been doing all the necessary things to adopt Martita officially. From home visits to mountains of paperwork, it has been a long and exhausting process. Every document that is requested from the adoption facility in Nicaragua must be translated into Spanish, all our "T's" must be crossed, and "I's" dotted. Now it's a waiting game. Fast forward three years later . . . yes, it has been three long years, and now I am on my seventeenth trip to Nicaragua. So why am I having such a difficult time packing my suitcase? *Uuugghhh*. I look down at the piles I've made:

- Pots / Pans / Kitchenware
- Medications (including an emergency script of Xanax) (Don't judge me.)
- Towels / Cleaning Products
- My Clothes
- Lucie's Clothes
- Entertainment—books, crayons, DVD player, movies

During previous trips to Managua (the capital of Nicaragua) my husband, Tim and I overloaded our luggage with supplies (crafts, clothes, shoes, school stuff) for the children at the orphanage, Puente de Amistad. The orphanage is located at the bottom of a canyon, hence the nickname *El Canyon*. The only way to Puente de Amistad is down a curvy, dirt road that has never been paved. Since the bus is unable to dodge potholes and tree branches on the way down, it's an extremely slow process.

I remember my first trip to Puente de Amistad. I recall looking out the window and seeing lush trees in every shade of green you can imagine. The tropical landscape reminds me of Hawaii, minus the poverty. The stench of burning trash lingers in the air.

I still recall the way I forced myself to imagine the trauma and neglect some of these children endured before arriving at Puente de Amistad; I feel the pain cut deep in my *mama gut.* The only reason I could physically walk away from Martita and the other children after that first visit is because of the people working there. The orphanage has few resources, but the staff lovingly looks after those babies the best they can. While the team is responsible for dozens of children of all different ages, they always are patient and loving with each and every kid.

It's been three years since I first met Martita. We have made so many trips to visit over the past three years but could never take her home. Leaving her just gets more difficult. While she is in a safe place, she is malnourished like the rest of the children. They eat rice and beans three times a day; vegetables and meat are a delicacy rarely found on the menu, yet, these children possess so much joy; it's contagious.

It took many visits to the orphanage and spending a few weeks there, but the children opened up to me with their stories. They confided how desperate they were to be reunited with their families. Some of the kids are shy, some are rambunctious, but they are all in dire need of love they so willingly give. I feel like these children are not only part of my family but part of me; the best part of me.

Visitors play an important role at the orphanage. We become these children's temporary families until they can go to a real home, which sadly isn't always a reality. So that's what we do, we love them as if they are our own. Only this next trip to Puente de Amistad will be different.

After three arduous years of waiting for the green adoption light; we finally got the call. Our spunky, sweet, five-year-old Martita will be coming home with us, on one condition . . . I have to move to Nicaragua to seal the rest of the adoption deal. Crazy! I can barely contain myself. Our baby girl will officially join our family whom I lovingly refer to as a beautifully blended cast of characters. There are five of us: Tim (my husband), his daughter Allie (from his previous marriage), my daughter Scarlett (from my previous marriage) and our daughter Lucie. It's funny, our family never felt incomplete until we met Martita. She is the glue that connects us all.

My Type-A brain is in overdrive. There is so much to organize and agonize over in planning this trip. Scarlett, my seventh grader, will stay in the U.S. with my husband who rearranged his work schedule to be home for her. Meanwhile, our six-year-old, Lucie, and I are preparing to hop a plane to Nicaragua, where we will be living for the next few months. (Did I mention this is crazy?!)

OK, Les, pull it together. It's time to pack your bags. Only nothing I threw in my suitcase could prepare us for this journey.

Three Years in the Making

We were pretty clueless when we signed up for this. The international adoption process is brutal, but I can honestly say that even if we had known how difficult this was going to be, we still would have gone through with it. After Tim arrived home from Nicaragua, we informed the director of the orphanage, Natalia, that we were committed to making Martita a member of our family. She was so happy for us and told us she would do whatever she could to move the process forward.

Okay, so here's how this works: The first step is, Mi Familia (the organization in Nicaragua that oversees adoptions) has to make a declaration that the child is "abandoned." An official search is conducted to ensure that the child has no living relative that can and will care for the child. Officials go to the city where the child is from to determine if there are any relatives. If no relatives are found, then a document is served to a judge who signs it, and the child is officially declared abandoned. Simple, right?

None of Martita's relatives were uncovered in the search. We found out her father was mentally ill and her mother was presumed dead from a drug overdose. She doesn't have any other relatives, so the document was given to the judge and we waited for it to be signed. We waited and waited and waited and waited . . . for weeks. Weeks turned into months, and months turned into years. It literally took two years for a judge to sign a single document!

We did not wait patiently and did everything and anything we could think of to move the process along. We pleaded with the orphanage's director to help and hired a lawyer in Nicaragua. Nothing was happening fast enough, so we connected with people in the U.S. who had relatives in Nicaragua and tried to find someone who could ask the judge to sign the document. However, we were instructed not to push too hard, or the judge could shut down the entire process and deny the adoption. *Uuuuggggg*!

As we waited for the document to be signed, my family spent more than 100 days in Nicaragua visiting Martita. We repeatedly told our girl that we were her family and that we would get her home as soon as we could. When we weren't there, I received regular reports about Martita's health and wellness, and it wasn't always good news. She suffered from scurvy on three separate occasions and had lice several times.

Our biggest concern, however, was her lack of development. At four years old Martita could barely talk. It was challenging for her to communicate. She couldn't hold a spoon or a pencil and needed assistance with the most basic skills. It was a tough time for us. We felt helpless knowing that she was suffering thousands of miles away. We wanted her home now, and we prayed for progress.

Two years later, we received the signed document. Martita was declared abandoned, and we could now move to the next step. Next step: move to Nicaragua and complete the adoption process. After speaking to some missionaries and researching housing options, we decided to rent a two-bedroom place at Condo Allyson for three months. The gated residence is private, and not too far from the orphanage. Other adoptive families are living there also so we will have our own little community. Our lease is week to week and since no one can confirm an actual adoption date, we're estimating how long we'll be there based on other people's experiences.

I'm praying this really is the last step in the adoption process. It will be a challenge, I know, but one we have been looking forward to because it means progress. You know the saying, "Be careful what you wish for?" Well, the long-awaited day has now arrived. Let the adventure begin. When we return home, we will be a family of six instead of five.

Chapter 4

Wuz Up in Nica Lesa?
(The Blog is Born)

Since I'm going to be out of the country for the next three to four months (Ahhh! freak out) I've created a blog to document our adventures in Nicaragua. Lucie and I are moving here to complete the final adoption steps. Tim is coming to set us up and help us get settled. If all goes as planned, Martita will officially be part of our family soon! Since I'm already a little homesick for all of you, I started this blog to keep in touch, while keeping my sanity intact! However, I may be calling out for reinforcements, (e.g., peanut M&M's, wine, Xanax). Don't judge me! I can't wait for you to meet our spunky, sweetheart of a girl!

Saturday, May 8, 2009
Preparing to Leave on Our Big Adventure
This is my first entry (setting up the blog) my husband is *training* me how to download pictures, use the video phone, and how to

blog. What will I do without him? I'm so excited to document our trip! More entries to come.

Monday, May 11, 2009
Hola Nica!

Buenos Dias! It is day three here, and we are so happy to be in Nicaragua! We arrived at noon last Saturday. (Our trip was uneventful and our day went smoothly, which is not usually part of our travel routine.) All of our luggage arrived, which again, doesn't happen too often. We packed so differently from a normal trip. We crammed pots, pans, utensils, cups, plates, bedding, and cleaning products in one suitcase. I had no idea what they would have locally so basically I packed a small house into six bags at fifty pounds each. I arranged for a translator, Manuel (who I've met one other time) to take us to Condo Allyson. Manuel met us at the airport to pick us up. Since I've only seen Manuel one time, I think Tim was a little nervous when I said, "I'm not sure what he looks like!" AAAHHHHH!! But I waved at a possible suspect, and he waved back. We don't actually *blend* with the locals, so we were easy to find.

We went directly to Condo Allyson to drop off our bags and check into the townhouse, where we were pleasantly surprised! It's a very large place (for a two bedroom) with an upstairs. After a thorough cleaning—I feel at home! I am embracing this temporary home; even though it doesn't have any modern conveniences. All of the doors have a big gap at the bottom, which is a little worrisome. There are also armed guards at the gate twenty-four hours a day; I'm still trying to figure out if that makes me feel safe or not . . .

Tim is here setting up my laptop, cameras, phone . . . taking care of me as he always does. He leaves on Wednesday, and I am already dreading it. Just having him here makes me feel safe and loved. I can already tell this adventure will be my greatest challenge. After setting up our townhouse, we went to the grocery store and bought soap, household cleaners, food, water (anything we thought we needed), but I'm sure, we will be back there soon! Then it was time to get everything organized—what a chore! Of course, I had to get it all done before I went to bed. Note: We had been up since 3:30 a.m. (1:30 a.m. Nicaragua time) and in bed by 11:00 p.m. Nicaragua time—so we had put in nearly a twenty-four hour day!

Yesterday (Sunday) was Mother's Day, what a great day to see our little Martita again. It feels so different this time because, at the end of this trip, she will be coming home with us. I feel so blessed to be here with Lucie, Tim, and Martita but on the other hand, I'm missing Scarlett more than I ever have. It seems unnatural to be here without her. It also marks the first Mother's Day since my Grandma passed away. I thought of my mom and her constantly today and reflected on the beautiful women they are. Generation after generation—how we evolve and how we continue to love . . . it's that kind of *mommy* love that changes the world.

My Mother's Day this year is so profoundly different. I look at Martita and think, "Wow, I am your Mommy." When she calls me "Mom" I feel so honored to have that title, and I do not take it lightly. I feel like I was chosen to be her mom even though I didn't give birth to her. My heart explodes with love for my little girl; we are so ready to have her officially join our family.

We went to a church down the street from our condo, which serves a lot of missionaries. I guess we are now missionaries too. The service was in English, which was a plus. We met a lot of people and learned about some church activities (e.g., Bible study, dinners, support groups, etc.) I'm looking forward to hearing these people's stories and getting to know them better. Many of the attendees also stay at Condo Allyson. Yay! More friendly faces in my hood. We have already made some friends like Sheila (who we've known for two years). Having her here is fantastic, albeit short-lived. Sheila leaves on Friday, but it's great spending some time with her. There's also Jack and Beth, who are adopting a little boy named, Ignacio. Since we're going through the same stage in the adoption process, we can totally relate to each other and will have each other to lean on through the weeks to come. Linda is another woman here whose friendship I'm grateful for. She's adopting a little girl named, Marlena. (Marlena is Martita's best friend.) Linda always gives me good advice and is so supportive. Again, I am so looking forward to creating strong bonds with all our new friends!

After church, we went to the orphanage and talked our attorney, Amelia, into letting us take Martita for a few hours. Since we cannot have Martita in our full-time care until the end of next week, we brought her back to the house and went swimming for a few hours. After working up an appetite, we went to a fabulous restaurant called Asada, which means grilled in Spanish. We had amazing food and lovely company—Martita ate and ate and ate. That girl can eat!!! Lucie attempted to clear her plate by putting some of her food on Martita's, and her new little sister was more than happy to take it. The two of them are quite a pair.

I know the truth behind Gracie's large appetite, she's starving. She has been starving for most of her life. Not knowing when the next meal will come and what it will consist of is so difficult to relate to and understand. She thinks this is temporary and she is making the most of every opportunity. Lucie, on the other hand, is a picky 5-year-old who only eats what she wants and knows that there will always be food for her when she is hungry. Two little girls, growing up in such extremely different circumstances, are now sisters sharing dinner. My hope is that soon our Martita will have the same security that Lucie has, she will never starve again.

Keeping the house clean is testing my sanity. We live in a bug motel despite our efforts to sweep and mop daily. Every night, we cover the downstairs with bug spray, but that doesn't deter the red ants, beetles, and lightning bugs from shacking up with us. *Eek!* Did I mention there's not one mirror in this entire house? I don't even want to know what I look like at this point, but we are adding mirrors to our shopping list!

Sorry for the long blog—I had a few days to catch up on. Shorter more entertaining blogs to come. Blessings to all my loved ones . . . miss you dearly!!!

2 Comments:

Alisa said . . .

Lesa, love the blogging! I have been thinking about you all so much and am so happy to know that you are not living in a tent sweating to death. What you and Tim are doing is so fabulous, and I can't wait to see Martita walking the halls of Pinebrook elementary. You don't need a mirror—trust me, you are beautiful! Lots of love, Alisa

Tracy said . . .

Hey Lesa! Love the blog—not sure if I successfully signed up as a "follower" or not but will definitely be checking in with you as often as possible. Sounds like you're all settled and I'm sure the place is as clean as you can get it—saw the photos of your place on Facebook—nice digs! Give all the kids a hug and a kiss for us . . . can't wait until you have Martita with you at the end of the week but glad you got to get some time with her today. All our love, Tracy & Kevin

Wednesday, May 13, 2009
Good News . . . Bad News . . .

Good Morning! I am still on east coast time and up by 5:00 a.m. every day. It gives me a lot of extra time in the morning to get things in gear, but I'm sure as time goes by, I will get on track. Yesterday was a big day for us, we had a meeting with a social worker at Mi Familia. (This official meeting kicked off our fostering time with Martita.) The social worker went over Martita's health and behaviors (as if we haven't known her for three years).

The whole scene was a little comical, but the fact that it's official is beyond comprehension!

We were also granted permission to have Martita spend the night, so we came home, and I made dinner for the four of us. It was Tim's last night with us (since he leaves today) and so it was very nice to hang out together as a family. Our friends, Linda and Brenda, came by with a key lime pie to say "goodbye" to Tim. (FYI: They bought the dessert from Price Club, yes, we have a Price Club here, and it kicks butt!) These ladies are so sweet and invited me over for dinner after he leaves. They know that I am sad that Tim is going and so I am so grateful for the pick-me-up. Linda and Brenda have experienced the same thing, their husbands leaving, their kids leaving. It's tough.

Everyone has to sacrifice to make adoption a reality. It's difficult to stay here, and it's difficult to be at home. While I'm here working on the adoption, my husband will be at home taking care of our daughter Scarlett, working full time, and managing all the things that I usually do, which believe me, isn't easy.

I'm happy to report that we are getting settled thanks to people like our taxi driver Norman. Somehow, we are communicating although his English is about as good as my Spanish, and he is already helping my vocabulary, which is such a blessing. I'm grateful for this sweet man whose taxi rates are beyond reasonable. He charges five dollars an hour, so when he picks us up at the condo and takes us to the orphanage (for two hours), it's only ten dollars, not bad.

Remember I told you about my mission to find a mirror? I don't consider myself too vain, but seriously, I want to see what other people are seeing before I leave the condo. We ventured to several stores but still couldn't find one, until one evening Norman showed up at our house (carrying a mirror) with his wife. He hung the mirror for us and wouldn't let me pay him. It is so comforting to have some allies here.

I also do not know what I would do without our interpreter, Manuel. He has a solid relationship with our attorney, so he'll bring up our case to her and report back to us. Every evening my phone rings, and it's Manuel on the other end, usually with an update and to say, "good night." I am so thankful for the people of Nicaragua that are getting us through this process.

We are supposed to have full custody of Martita today or tomorrow, which means she will not have to go back to the orphanage. Woohoo! Today we have to submit two letters to Mi Familia. One of the letters gives a detailed account as to why my husband isn't here. The second letter outlines how long we have known Martita and documents the time spent with her. In this letter, we are asking the adoption agency to shorten our time fostering Martita. This is a *Big Deal*! If we're granted our request, she can come home sooner. We'll be praying for that.

How am I feeling? I'm excited about our adventure. I know that I am really getting back to the basics, hand washing our clothes, homeschooling my girls, lots of time alone, which is completely freeing for me. How often do we get a chance to escape our busy lives and experience another part of the world (literally)? While it's crazy that I'm living in Nicaragua, I feel I'm escaping a lot of craziness by being here. I know this process will continue to challenge me but the simplicity of it all is attractive.

I'm sad that Tim is leaving. Who will I talk to? He is my partner in this, and I wish he could stay and experience every moment with me. He is also in charge of cleaning up the bathroom. This is a big job because Martita is not potty-trained even though she is five years old. This is not a pleasant job especially without my husband helping. I'm nervous about being here and taking care of the girls on my own. I always pride myself on being strong, but this is a little scary. There are no down times or breaks. I will be with them every minute of every day.

An update on the bug situation: I'm already sick and tired of the ants in this house! Last night, we asked Linda: "What do you do about the ant situation?"

She replied, "I name them." *Love* her! I guess I can keep my sense of humor intact while I am stepping on them, smashing them, killing them! Tim says if he sees me on Skype with my hair out of control and a strange look in my eye . . . he will know that I've lost it.

Well, Tim is about to take Martita to school with our friends Jack and Beth. I will go for a run, and then we will get Tim packed and ready for the airport. We leave at noon, and his flight is at 3:00 p.m. His time here has flown by, miss him already. :(

1 Comment:

Timothy said . . .
Hola Mi Esposa!
Well, this is my first entry on your blog, and I LOVE THAT YOU ARE ABLE TO SHARE WHILE I AM NOT THERE! Love you and know that I am with you in spirit (think about that with the potential bathroom messes ;-) XOXOXOXOXOX

Thursday, May 14, 2009
Edward, Chester and Bubba

Lucie and I have a few reptilian housemates (geckos) that I'd like to introduce to you. Their names are Edward (big *Twilight* fans here) Chester and Bubba. We thought one of our scaly friends could perhaps be a girl, but since girls *never* eat bugs, we're pretty confident they're boys. We love our gecko friends even though they keep me on my toes (literally) as I try to dodge their every sprint when I walk into a room or turn on a light. In exchange for rent, they're providing a free extermination service (as they eat all the bugs).

What's even more exciting than our lizard housemates is that we'll be gaining a new roomie today, Martita! *Big Day!* We are heading to the orphanage to meet with the social worker who will sign off on our girl's foster period at our home. We will still visit the orphanage to see all the other kids we love but having our girl with us will be fantastic. Mi Familia will follow up with two site visits at our home to observe how Martita is adjusting to her new living situation and how she interacts with Lucie and I. We hope to get our two site visits nailed down before the next Consejo meeting. (The Consejo is the governing group that will approve our adoption.) The group members are supposed to meet monthly, however, sometimes meetings and decisions are delayed without warning. That is why timing is so critical. If we complete our two home visits before the Consejo's meeting, it could really speed up the adoption process.

We are also going to Mi Familia to deliver some paperwork today. I just hope that everyone who is supposed to be there, is there, and that all goes smoothly!

While I'm anxious about getting Martita under our roof, I think having an adjustment period to settle in is good for us. Being here is a *huge* adjustment. The most time I have ever spent with Martita in Nicaragua is a week, so I cannot imagine what she must be thinking and feeling. She has been living at the orphanage for almost three years, and that is about to change. It will be a major transition for her.

I cannot even believe I'm typing this, but after today, we will actually have her *forever*! *Amazing* and *Unbelieveable*!

In other news, I've started a list of things that I'm grateful for that I used to take for granted. Focusing on gratitude keeps me centered and puts everything into perspective. My window air conditioning unit tops the list today. Lucie and I can handle the heat and the humidity during the afternoon, but at night it's a sticky beast. I'm still trying to figure out the best setting. I turn the AC on about an hour before I go to bed and it's nice and cool in my room when I lie down, but then after a couple of hours of sleep, I wake up shivering, so I turn it off. Then a couple hours later, I turn it on because I'm hot, hot, hot! (Repeat.) It's like having a newborn who never sleeps more than two hours at a time. Tonight, I will try the lowest setting to see if that works. (I'm also comforted by the noise.) Well, these are the big decisions I am making in Nicaragua! :D

Love to you all from Lucie, Martita, Edward, Chester, and Bubba. Blessings and talk to you tomorrow.

Friday, May 15, 2009
All in a Shoebox

Buenos Noches! "*Hoy es una dia muy importante para mi familia.*" Today is an important day for my family! We had the official *legal exit*, and Martita is now in our custody from this day forward! Pretty awesome . . . I still don't think it's hit me yet but every time I look at her—I smile :D

As you may recall from my last entry, this was supposed to happen yesterday. The schedule got pushed back, and so we had to wait one more day, but as they say, it was so worth the wait!

The adventures at Puente de Amistad never cease to surprise me. Today was no exception. We had a mini-spa day, and I was the lucky recipient. Sofia gave me a back rub, and Camila did my hair. After my treatments, I caught up with little Marina over lunch. Although we're taking Martita with us, we will continue to visit the kids at the orphanage that we love so much.

The happy chaos that typically fills the halls of the orphanage was disrupted by a strange commotion. Several men were running through the compound. Gabriela (the orphanage director) looked worried as she observed the situation. She told me the horse, Pancho got loose. We watched in bewilderment as one of the guards tore through the kitchen and retreated with a knife. (*A very large knife!*)

"What does he need a knife for?!!" I asked.

"I have no idea," Gabriela replied.

The next thing we knew, the horse was dead. I was somewhat relieved to learn he died from a disease rather than bludgeoning. (Still, I can't believe the horse died while we were there!) The older boys and men workers dug a big hole at the far end of the property for the horse's burial. They looped a rope around the horse and pulled him towards the big hole. The scene made Lucie very upset as she thought they were hurting the horse. When I explained that the horse was already dead, she thought for a minute and said, "Well God made him so God can take him back." Brilliant.

The day seemed to drag a bit (even with all the drama) as we waited for our 2:30 p.m. appointment. I was anxious, this was a big day for our family, and I wanted everything to go smoothly. They kept delaying us. Then, I found out that they didn't have our paperwork. Since it was admittedly their fault, they said we could still take Martita home with us. We would just have to come back the following Monday to sign the document. This stuff happens all the time. *Más O Menos*. Appointments get pushed, records get lost, rules change. It is *very* difficult to get your hopes up because nothing is ever guaranteed. I just sat and cried, thinking we were not going to be able to take her. When I found out Martita would be able to come with us, I sat and cried some more. It's such a flippin' emotional roller-coaster.

Our cab driver waited out front as I rushed around trying to get Martita ready to go. When I asked the director to get Martita's things together, she took me to the office and handed me a shoe box. I didn't understand and asked her what it was.

She said, "This is the box with Martita's things."

I was so shocked I didn't know how to respond. I'm not sure what I expected, but I thought about all the things that I packed for Lucie when we were coming to Nicaragua for only a few weeks. The toys, the pictures, the clothes, the books . . . And so many of her things were left at home.

Can you imagine leaving your home after almost six years with only a shoe box?

I opened the box and found stickers, a small doll, and a plastic necklace. I just held it close to me and realized how little Martita had. I'm not just talking about possessions but what her lack of belongings means. There are no family photographs, birthday cards or special gifts from loved ones. There was nothing about who she was or where she lived for the past three years. I gave the box to Martita, and she was thrilled. I was devastated.

I thought about that shoe box for a long time. Then something clicked. I realized that Martita has and always will be part of our family. Her things, her pictures, her loved ones are in Virginia. She will have so much room to fill up her life with the love that's been missing. Starting today, she will no longer live off beans and rice, or develop rashes from not washing (poor baby has one now on her bum). She will have her own space, her own things, but most importantly, she will have her *own* family whose love could fill up the contents of a trillion shoe boxes.

3 Comments:

mck4099 said . . .
Hola Lesa!
What an exciting week you have had! You are all well on your way—adjustments and all! I know there will be some challenges, but you have so many friends here and in Nicaragua praying for you. How is Lucie adjusting to Nicaragua and Martita on a full-time basis? Did the children at Puente de Amistad enjoy the cards and photos? Please tell everyone there that Matthew, Meagan and I said hello. Happy Mother's Day and Happy Birthday! We are "following" you so we will blog again soon.
Love, Donna

Timothy said . . .
It truly is/ was an amazing day. I am still in awe that this is happening. How this little girl named Martita . . . has been taken from dire circumstances, placed in an orphanage, meeting two people that really didn't have adoption at the top of their list so that SHE could enter our hearts . . . and then almost three years later . . . leave with a shoe box not even full . . . to live with dignity. If that doesn't convince you there is a God and that there is hope in the world . . . well what can I say. Thanks to God for this blessing.

Tracy said . . .

What a great birthday present—we are so glad Martita is with you! What an amazing journey you all have been on. Keep being strong! Can't wait until you all are back home in VA! Have a great birthday today! Love ya, Tracy

Chapter 5

Nica Birthdays

Saturday, May 16, 2009

I was brought up to play up birthdays as much as possible. It is my day! For the past thirty years (ha ha ha), my mom has told me about the day I was born, and it makes me feel special. I don't want anyone else to have this day . . . it's mine! To be completely honest I wasn't totally jazzed to spend my birthday here, knowing I won't have Scarlett and Allie with me, I won't get spoiled, cards, and gifts. I thought to myself, this kind of sucks, so yesterday I started to think, I can still make it special, right?

Birthdays are a celebration of one's life. I have the husband of my dreams, gorgeous children (on the inside and out), a precious addition to our family that we have worked so hard to receive, and friends and relatives who love me dearly. God has been so very good to me.

I started my birthday the best way I know how, with a run. I listened to Chris Tomlin blasting through my headphones as I hit the pavement. If you don't know Chris Tomlin, check him out! My spirit was so high. Nothing could bring me down today, not even that pile of laundry I had to do.

Remember that list of things I took for granted that I am now grateful for—add washing machine and dryer to the list. I don't have either here but I have a sink outside and a washboard (I'm basically camping). It's a pretty simple process, you scrub the clothes against the washboard with some liquid soap and then rinse with cold water. (There is no hot water.) To dry, just hang them up on the line with clothespins. Voila! *The Little House on the Prairie* method works fantastically unless of course, it rains. Nicaragua's climate is a bit like Florida so when the afternoon showers hit we have to make sure there's no laundry on the line.

Well, today, laundry time was rather enjoyable as I had a special little helper named Martita. My girl is a big talker; however, it is challenging to understand what she is saying most of the time. Martita is scrubbing and gabbing away when I hear her say "*chi chi's.*" I looked over, and my youngest daughter is washing my bra and giggling. Lucie and I start cracking up. One of the best things about Martita is her laugh—it starts in her toes and vibrates through her entire body. It was a fun moment for the three of us.

The rest of the day was busy. While Tim was here, he did some birthday scheming in my honor. (Mission accomplished Baye!) I had a great day out shopping and sight-seeing. We got in some pool time as well. My little fish, Lucie, swam up to me at the end of the pool, kissed my leg and said, "Happy birthday my beautiful Momma." Ahh, my heart is full. I also enjoyed a cook-out and a cake with my new friends who live here.

I also felt the love from home. My family sent the wackiest video, and I received some calls from close friends, whom I cherish. So, I leave you with this thought, celebrating our birth is something we should do more often, not just on our special day. Celebrate your life! What are the good things that happened to you? What are the good things you did? Who are the people you made smile, brought joy to and celebrated? Who did you show love and kindness to throughout the year? Then at the end of an ordinary day, you can say, "I celebrated my birth today."

1 Comment:

mck4099 said . . .
You are so inspiring Lesa! Happy Birthday!
Donna

Sunday, May 17, 2009 & Monday, May 18, 2009
Reason, Season, Life

This blog is all about the long and beautiful day I had yesterday. I couldn't write to you last night because I was up late Skyping with Tim, that sneaky minx. He organized and paid for a surprise birthday dinner party for me and invited all of my friends. Jack and Beth, Linda, Rachel, Amanda, Norman (our taxi driver) and his wife, Manuel (our interpreter) and all the kids. It was awesome!

It amazes me how close I feel to these people that I just met a week ago, but since we're all going through a very unique and powerful life-altering experience, it makes sense that we're bonding through our adoptions. We all have our stories, our challenges, our successes, but we are all in support of each other. Most importantly we can be real with one another. I honestly can't imagine what it would be like to try and navigate the adoption by myself, without any support. What a blessing it is to have these special souls in my life.

Today, we went to church, and the blessings continued after service. I got to hang with Linda and Rachel. We read scripture, swapped stories and vented. We talked at length about our support systems or lack thereof. It was very emotional for my friends to discuss the lack of support they are receiving as time goes by in Nicaragua. They're surprised that some of their closest friends don't appear to be *there* for them during this trying season. They're frustrated when their friends say things like, "This time will go by fast, and then your entire family will be together." But when you are here just trying to get through each day, it's hard to be positive sometimes. Although they mean well, that statement can feel dismissive.

I look back on my life, and I definitely have had all types of friends. I think the saying goes "Some friends you have for a reason, some friends for a season, and some friends for life." (I always mess up idioms, so that may not be exactly right, but you get the gist.)

We have such high expectations of our loved ones. I already feel let down by some of mine. Is that fair? Why are some of our friends/family there for us and some are not? Do they love us less? If the roles were reversed, would I meet their expectations? Am I a friend for life? How do I, or should I, set this experience aside and continue my friendships when I get home?

How is it possible for our friends and family to know how best to support us? I often do not communicate what I need, which is part of the problem. I hope I come out of this experience feeling truly supported and loved, even though my friends and family may not "show up" the way that I want. In a few months (gasp) when I'm home from this journey, I know my family and friends' support will mean even more. I just pray that I receive what I need while I'm here so that I am not sent straight to the funny farm on my trip home. While I am questioning some of my relationships, my faith has never been stronger. God always provides the security and love that no one else can.

Last night my husband asked me, "How are you *really* doing?" It made me laugh. I cannot "lose it," at least not yet. I can honestly, say that when I looked around at the faces of my new friends at dinner tonight and thought about my dear ones back home, I can confidently say, I am doing just fine.

Ciao for now . . .

4 Comments:

CTGoodyear said . . .
Hi Sweetie, I hope you know how many people love you. We are not always the best at showing it, but I know how much I love you and cannot imagine that everyone you know doesn't

feel the same. If they don't, it is their loss. Remember one day at a time. Love, Mom XOXOXOXOXO

Sandy said . . .

Hello my beautiful, amazing, inspirational cousin. This morning I received an invitation to join Facebook from Aunt Carol, now remember I don't get on my personal email often, so I decide to join which of course leads me to this incredible daily journal of yours. My friend and I begin reading and of course, share a cry and sit back and reflect on how maybe we need to simplify our lives. Believe me, you are making a difference in more than just Martita's life, you are making a mark in many. Mine for one . . . I am so VERY PROUD to say you are "*mi familia*," which I fail to say often. Please know that I love you VERY MUCH. I will be checking in daily to follow your journal. Can't wait to meet our new addition! Love your favorite cousin ~ Sandy

Amy said . . .

Hi Lesa!!! I miss you. I have been following your blogs. It is so awesome to hear how God is showing you Himself every day. I know this must be a tough time, but you are not alone!!! Love you, girl.
Amy

Tracy said . . .

Hey Lesa—I'm just getting to the blog today (Monday at 10:20 p.m.)—it's been an up and down day for me here (I'll fill you in later but all work-related stuff that's got me in a tail-spin). I love that you're updating this and hope you know how much we love and support you—we did get a camera set up and tried to Skype you around 9:15 p.m. our time, but don't think you were online. We'll catch you on there soon! We think of you every day, and Sydney includes you in her prayers every night (as do I). Stay strong and give Lucie and Martita a kiss from us! XOXO to you too!
Good night. Tracy

Monday, May 18, 2009
119 Minutes Too Long!!!

Happy Monday! We had a jam-packed day! We went to Mi Familia first thing this morning to sign off on some paperwork (they were supposed to deliver last Friday). We also wanted to take the opportunity to meet with Diego. Diego is the manager at Mi Familia who is our point of contact. Diego meets with the Consejo, and submits our paperwork as we weave through this process. We had presented a letter to him asking to waive our fostering time. Since our adoption has been lengthy, we proposed to drop the standard six-week fostering period.

The Grimes' girls arrived at Mi Familia at 9:00 a.m. sharp, signed our document and then waited for Diego to come back from a meeting. It was so hot today that they shut the doors and actually turned on the air conditioning! When it's that hot for locals, you can imagine how hot it was for us.

Martita, Lucie, Manuel (interpreter) and Amelia (lawyer) and I sat in chairs in the center of the office. The girls were so sweet to each other for about two and a half minutes. I remember thinking, "Aren't they the sweetest thing?" Then minute three began, and Lucie decided she didn't like Martita.

Lucie began yelling, "*No mas* Martita."

Martita thought that was funny and started to pull Lucie's hair. I tried to solve this silently with my "drop dead eye look," but they didn't even glance at me. Before the situation could escalate, I reasoned with them like those perfect TV mothers who say things like, "You're not making the right choices."

It is a challenge to discipline Martita because she had very little structure at the orphanage. I also don't have all the right words to explain to her what I expect. If she doesn't like what I say, she turns her entire body around and ignores me. I don't know how to threaten her yet (I'm sure I will come up with a few options very soon . . . a couple ideas are coming to me now) or communicate that her behaviors have consequences.

As we waited for more than two hours, the behavior climaxed but not without a fight. I took everything away from Lucie that I could think of. When that didn't work, I even started to threaten to go buy her new toys and then give them away to the kids at the orphanage. Honest mom moment: Her tears were in some way comforting to me because she was driving me absolutely *crazy*. (I know, "Mother of the Year Award" over here.)

In their defense, what five-year-old can sit in a hot box with almost nothing to do for two-and-a-half hours and behave politely?

Our meeting with Diego went well. He is a very nice man, but we have a very short time-frame to get a lot of details to him. I want to do everything possible to ensure that our case is presented to the Consejo when they meet in May. This would ensure that we could be home by mid-July. I would love to have time to get Martita home before school starts.

Coming here, I knew that Martita would be a challenge, but I didn't give much thought to my Goose (Lucie's nickname). Lucie has always been so close and sweet to Martita and secure in her relationship with me. I think she can sense that something has dramatically changed, that Martita really is her sister now, and that she doesn't know where she fits in anymore. She's not at home, she misses her Dad and her sister and her dogs. She always has this look on her face like, *Can someone get me out of here?"*

Then I get her back to the townhouse and to the pool, and the Lucie I know and love is reborn. I need to be sure to take extra time with her and make sure she is okay and that she can talk to me about how she's feeling, which is a much better alternative than punching her new sister.

So, I have to come up with some alternatives during these meetings because our wait time was about 119 minutes too long!

Buenos Noches

2 Comments:

CTGoodyear said . . .
I am so sorry for what you're going thru. It has to be so hard on all three of you. Lucie having to share and put up with all the inconveniences, Martita not understanding, and Momma (supposed to have all the answers and keep your cool.) I can't imagine how hard it must be. I love you so much Lesa. I hope you know . . . My love to the girls and tell them that Gramma said no more fighting. RIGHT . . . I love you Lesa, Mom XOXOXOXOXO

Tuesday, May 19, 2009
I Love Lucie!!!

Doesn't that title conjure images of a certain fiery redhead running around her 1950s apartment trying to get out of her latest pickle? Today I laughed so hard when I heard our own Martita saying, "Come on Lucie—come on Lucie."

Her Ricky Ricardo accent is so spot on; it makes my gut hurt from howling. Now I need to teach her to say, "You got some explaining to do!"

The Lucie I love and adore was back today. She woke up with a smile and a big kiss for her Momma. She wanted a big breakfast and told me that she felt GREAT today. I told her we were going to Puente de Amistad, which thrilled her! While at the orphanage, she quickly made friends with all of the children as she helped them do their chores. They get quite the kick out of her because of the funny faces she loves to make. She helped me serve lunch to all the kids, picked the little ones up from school and played so well with her sister. Lucie shined so brightly today.

We submitted some additional paperwork to Mi Familia today to back up our request to limit our fostering period. The paperwork included copies of our passport pages and a letter from the director of the orphanage, which supported our claim of how many days we have spent with Martita over the past couple of years. 104 days! This includes nine trips to Nicaragua and Martita's visit to the states. The numbers jumped out at me on the paper and made me realize just how lengthy a process this has been.

We capped the evening off with some friends sharing dinner at the pool. The thunder and lightning added to the excitement of the evening as Lucie shared how much she loved telling scary stories at night. Lucie was quite the chatter bug sharing all sorts of fun facts (she likes to swim and dive and knows how to do well in school and that she can make pizza). Lord, I must have told her three times "Okay honey—eat your dinner!"

Then she looked up at me and said, "Mommy I want to go home *now* before the storm hits here."

She was so nervous, she just kept talking and talking! We got home way before the storm hit and she told me that she might have to sleep with me tonight (if the storm rolls in). So, we shall see.

Today, we not only survived but enjoyed each other so much. Martita had the biggest smile on her face when she caught me looking at her. Our little girl is such a loving daughter and sister. She is bringing out the best in Lucie and me.

Now we play the waiting game as we wait to learn when the Consejo will meet in May and *if* our case will be heard. *Please* keep us in your prayers and of course, I will let you know as soon as I hear anything. You are all such a blessing to my family and I. Thank you for following my blog, for your love and support. (Your comments keep me going, *Thank You*!) I cannot survive without it and knowing you are experiencing this with me is a blanket of comfort during this unpredictable and scary process.

Blessings and Love, Lesa

Wednesday, May 20, 2009
Journey of Change

My very dear friend, Donna, gave me a bracelet before I left on this trip. On one side it reads "Life is a Journey" and on the flip side it reads "Not a Destination." I have heard this saying many times and thought that I understood the meaning, but I think only now am I starting to understand what it means genuinely.

Change seems to be a common theme in my journey. Sometimes change is welcome and sometimes it can't come quick enough. Other times it feels unfair and out of our control.

Sometimes change happens all of a sudden.

I just heard that a very dear friend of mine, JJ, got in a horrific motorcycle accident. It's times like these I feel the farthest from home. Each mile that we're separated feels like a punch in the gut. I wish I could click my heels like Dorothy and be there to hug him and help his family. Thank God JJ will be fine. It's just crazy to think that one moment he's cruising on his cousin's new motorcycle and the next he's skidding across pavement, wondering if he'll walk away alive. Change-happened in an instant.

While JJ's change was not a welcome one, my family has been working so hard to make change happen. Our adoption has been dotted with hours of work and punctuated with mounting piles of paperwork, frustrations, commitments, and broken promises. Just when we thought a change would never happen, we got the call, our adoption was approved, and we're moving to Nicaragua. The change occurred in an instant.

People often gripe and grumble about change and yet we talk about it all the time.

"I'm going to get in shape this summer."

"I'm going to finish that course in Spanish."

"I'm going to stop all my bad habits." (I won't go into detail about my bad habits, may shock a few people, but you get the point.)

We see ourselves as someone different from who we are today—someone thinner, smarter, prettier . . .

I too, fall into this trap. My goals for going to Nicaragua were to become a better Mom, lose weight, speak fluent Spanish . . .

Change happens whether we're expecting it or not. I've been reflecting on my first mission trip to Nicaragua. I had never planned on meeting a two-year-old who would change my life forever, but it happened. This adoption process is both a joy and a struggle, and some of my greatest happiness has been realized through the most trying battles. The challenges opened me up to meeting incredible people who are sharing in my story. Through the joy and the struggle, I've felt an out-pouring of love and support from my family and friends that I could never have predicted.

My journey of change has been a journey of personal growth. I am learning to be patient and more understanding. I have learned that God has a plan for me. All I have to do is follow it. The payout is indescribable (although I'm trying to document it through this blog). I am now the official Mom of our sweet Martita, and as a result of change, I am experiencing a sacred place and cherished people.

I am going to do my best to enjoy each day of this journey of change.

Love and Blessings!! Lesa

1 Comment:

Tracy said . . .
Thank you, Lesa for letting us share your journey with you. We are in it with you for the long haul and keep you, the girls, Tim, and the process in our prayers daily. We love and miss you! Tracy

Thursday, May 21, 2009
Cold and Dry

Well, today was a very *interesting* day for us. We started off Thursday with our typical morning routine; a run/walk for Mom (to keep my sanity throughout the day), and some fun in the park for the girls (to burn some energy, which aides in Mom's sanity.) Condo Allyson has become my *track*. All of the condos are perched on a steep drive. At the end of the driveway, there is a small park with a couple of swings. It is about a fourth of a mile long, and so I usually run intervals (running up the driveway and walking down it) while Martita and Lucie play at the park. This set-up allows me to watch them while getting in my workout. This is a big deal for me because I don't function as well without exercise. My running time is therapy. It keeps me clear headed, and I can listen to my music while enjoying some "me time." At the beginning of this process, I was concerned about how I would make this work. The girls are with me (literally) twenty-four hours a day, so this driveway is one of the best things about living here.

We made a trip to the orphanage from 10:00 a.m. to 2:00 p.m. and then made it back to the townhouse to meet our property manager who was scheduled to look at our refrigerator (again). Ever since we moved in, our fridge has been a little troublesome. It would occasionally make an obtrusive motoring noise, which looking back meant it was actually working. When I gave a little kick or punch to the front of the refrigerator, the sound stopped. So that's how we functioned . . . loud, obnoxious noise, strong kick, quiet again. Repeat . . . Repeat . . . Repeat . . . until about three days ago I realized the noises were gone. Then I also noticed that my ice didn't freeze, my milk spoiled, and all the frozen meat had thawed, so immediately I asked our manager for *help*! He came with an assistant, checked it out for a while and told me he would be back today at 2:00 p.m. His goal was to look at the refrigerator again and hopefully fix the problem.

I was home by 2:00 p.m. and my driver Norman stuck around to help me communicate with our property manager since his English is non-existent, and my Spanish doesn't include *frozen* or *loud rumbling noise* or *all my meat has gone bad*. Well, actually I think I can say the last one. Norman talked to the manager and explained, "No, coming back tomorrow and bringing a different guy to look at it would *not* work."

Thank you, Norman!

We began the search for another fridge by scavenging through vacant apartments (with permission) on the hunt for a working refrigerator. When we found the new addition to our appliance family, we lugged it down the long road to my townhouse. I am *not* kidding! Why fix something if you can just swap it out?

After we plugged it in, Lucie took one look at it and said, "Wow Mom, it has a light when you open the door."

Obviously, our first one didn't because it was a piece of crap. Am I allowed to say, "crap" in a blog? Anyway, we are in business.

Another significant change in our lives today . . . a new shower curtain. When Tim was here, we bought two shower curtains for the bathrooms. Little did we know they were made of paper and hung from the top of the shower to the middle of the shower (basically to your knees). So, when you get out of the shower—you step into a puddle of water in the bathroom. The pool is just about dried up when you take your second shower of the day, in the evening. It's nasty and swampy. I had been to three stores and had yet to find a shower curtain. My friend Linda gave us one that might work, so I hung it in my shower today, and it hangs to the floor! I am so happy. No more wet floor, no more soggy feet, thank you Linda!

So, I am dry (at least for five minutes after getting out of the shower), and my food is appropriately cold and frozen. What an *awesome day*!!!

Love and Blessings to you all!!!

Friday, May 22, 2009
Handsome Boy

Today was a lazy and relaxing day for us—we had one action item
... find the waterman (he typically shows up at any time during
the day on Tuesdays and Fridays) and get our water dispenser
from him. We have two big jugs of water but no machine. So
every other day, I have to buy more water. Due to my paranoia,
I use bottled water for cooking, coffee, washing food, and brush-
ing my teeth, so water goes very fast in our casita.

After our run and park time, the three of us headed to the
pool for a little relaxation. I would get out of the pool and look down
the street every fifteen minutes to see if the waterman had arrived.
After several hours, I finally saw him and attempted to communicate. He told me they won't have the dispenser until next week,
which is what they told me last week. *Mas o menos*. I explained this
to the water boy's manager who said as soon as he has one, he will
bring it. It will be interesting to see how long that takes.

The overwhelming realization I've had today is feeling just
how much I miss my husband. It's officially the longest chunk
of time I've been away from him and while I'm managing to
have some fun without him, being without him leaves a large
hole in my heart. I am a strong person and can put on a good
front, but I miss my handsome boy (this is how Lucie greets Tim
every morning, "Good morning handsome boy"). I miss so many
things about him ...

I miss telling him every detail about my day and how he
just completely gets me and thinks I'm funny. I miss how he
listens to me so intently and truly respects my point of view. I
miss my parenting partner and how he makes raising our girls
so much more fun. I miss how he laughs at me when I cry, which
makes me laugh. I even miss the way he chews, which is very
loud. Martita chewed her food quite loudly today, and I looked
at her and grinned because it reminded me of her Papa.

I think it's hit us both that we will be separated for a very
long time. I am two weeks in and cannot really imagine two

more months of being a part (maybe longer). We are both aware of why we're doing this and agree the payoff is going to be worth every second apart. However, today the clock seems to be ticking away a little too painfully.

So, this blog is dedicated to my "Handsome Boy." Thank you for being the love of my life, my best friend, and my one true partner. You are the best thing that has ever happened to me, and I miss you more than words can say. I love you with all my heart. I thank God for you every day. Good night Handsome Boy. I Love You.

2 Comments:

Timothy said . . .
So how does my hair look?

Everyone knows that in our family, I am just a little outnumbered in the sexes category. Pre three years ago, the count in our family was five females (Lesa, Allie, Scarlett, Lucie, Stella), one male. Then comes along Martita . . . then Esme (the latest member of our family . . . an English Bulldog which all my girls say has a striking resemblance to me)!. So the count today is seven females, one male! To say I am outnumbered is both an understatement . . . and a complete blessing.

As you might imagine, my "girls" . . . all of them . . . require just a little maintenance. But that is okay because they are all beautiful women. On any given day, I dole out lots of compliments . . . all of which are well-deserved mind you. OCCASIONALLY, I get the compliment returned, and as an attention-starved male (LOL), one compliment is usually not enough for me (they have trained me so well)! So I ask additional questions. The scenario goes something like this . . .

> **Scarlett:** "Eddie, I really like the tie you are wearing

Eddie: "Thanks Scarlett . . . can you tell I have been working out?"

As Scarlett's stepdad she wanted to call me something besides my first name—my middle name is Edward, so my girl Scarlett calls me "Eddie."

Another scenario . . .

Lucie: "Good Morning my handsome boy."

Lesa: "Yeah Lucie, doesn't he look handsome?"

Me: "Thanks, girls . . . and how does my hair look?"

And then a blog entry like this one comes along . . . completely unconditional and completely from the heart. And it is humbling, to say the least. When Lesa and I started this journey, we knew the day was coming when we would be separated for a while. We really took it in stride knowing this final stage was in the future. Then we got the call and reality set in that our separation was really going to happen. Thank GOD, THIS separation was based upon blessings and not a broken relationship . . . something that we both have painfully experienced in past lives. It is this fact alone that encourages me to get through it. Yeah, it did hit us both on the same day and yeah it is much, much harder than what I thought it would be . . . but knowing I get Lesa back, in the end, keeps me going. She is my true partner in every way and in everything we do AND I get the added benefit of her being beautiful, intelligent and extremely hot (okay, I just wrote that about my wife on a public blog)! From a guy's perspective, this makes her the gold standard when it comes to wives! I am one lucky man!!!! Watching her go through this process (process is an understatement) while maintaining a great attitude has been incredible . . . knowing how humble she is about the whole thing . . . completely inspiring. We are on day fourteen and knowing that we have somewhere between forty to seventy-six more days to go (not that I am counting or anything) means that we are not really close to the end of this saga. We both anticipate a number of breaking points in the future, and we will get through those times. That said, I could not think of anyone I would rather have on my side than Lesa. Baye, keep the faith and keep being who you are . . . the best wife in the world! Can't wait to see you in June for a few hours! Love you beyond words . . . XOXOXOXOXOXOXOXOXOXOXOX

ctgoodyear said . . .

Lesa, I think maybe you'd better keep him. I love you so much and am so thankful that you found each other. I'm proud of you both. I can't say I know how hard it is for you, only that I can't imagine. But I know you'll come through this, and bless you both, you've given us another beautiful granddaughter. I love you . . . Mom & Tom, XOXOXOXOXO

Chapter 6

There's No Place Like Home

Saturday, May 23, 2009

I grew up watching *The Wizard of Oz* and fell in love with the music, those dancing munchkins, and the "Somewhere Over the Rainbow" storyline. I remember the film being broadcast on TV once a year. This was way before TiVo and movie rentals . . . Lord, I am aging myself. My mom bought me Toto (the small cute dog) stuffed animal, and I remember bringing it everywhere with me. It was my favorite toy. I think what I loved most about it was the adventure that Dorothy went on . . . she was a little bored on the farm and followed the yellow brick road to the most exciting experience.

I never gave too much thought about her obsession with wanting to go home. (I mean seriously, she just got there, right?!) She kept saying how long it had been since she saw Auntie Em and how desperate she was to get home. She literally got there and wanted to click her ruby slippers and return home.

I'm totally feeling you, Dorothy. I am having the adventure of a lifetime but want so badly to go home. I am grateful to have some of my family here, and I am enjoying this special time with the girls, but there are so many instances throughout the day, I hear and feel things that I want to share with home—it's all so difficult.

Every day Martita becomes more of my daughter. I heard Lucie and her belly laughing today, and I thought, "We are so blessed to have her in our lives." So many people tell us how unselfish we are to adopt our girl, but our sacrifice is so small compared to the daughter we are receiving.

This time, right now, in Nicaragua—away from my husband and daughter is the sacrifice. This is what we are willing to pay for our girl. I want so badly to click my flip-flops together and be home (my fashion sense has dramatically changed in this country). But I'm following my mom's advice, and I'm taking it one day at a time. Lesson learned Dorothy, "There is no place like home."

2 Comments:

Timothy said . . .
Puuut em up . . . puuut em up . . . errrr rough! Wow, I can't believe you even remember when *The Wizard of Oz* was on only one time a year! I thought the first time you saw the Wizard was on DVD ;-)

ctgoodyear said . . .
You used to think that your Pop actually played the part. I'm loving your blogs. I love you, Mom XOXOXOXOXO

Monday, May 25, 2009
Crazy Busy Sunday!!

Since we arrived in Nicaragua, I have been attending a church down the street. The service is in English, and many of the missionaries and adoptive families who live at Condo Allyson attend this church together. Yesterday, we switched things up a little and went to church at El Canyon, right across from the orphanage. While I've attended service here several times, I will never forget what happened here today. I can guarantee it is nothing like you've experienced in your pews at home!

First, let me describe the church's aesthetics. The small building is made of cement and a tin roof (why tin, I don't understand because every time I look up, I can feel the heat radiating from the ceiling on my face). The interior consists of a red tiled floor and two doors that are closed by a gate, so plenty of air can get in which, is a blessing because it's always hot. I sit next to the door to suck in any breeze that trickles in.

The members of the church are made up of the impoverished people from the community and the kids from the orphanage. I know many of the people and all the kids. As soon as I walk in, four-year-old Esaul (who is very animated and wild) says, "Lesa, Lesa, *mirame, mirame!*" (Lesa, Lesa, look at me, look at me.)

He runs across the church and finds two armchairs that are against the wall. He climbs on top of them, sneaks a glance at me, to make sure I'm watching, then poses with one leg in the air. This is all happening *during* church while someone is speaking, and we are *supposed* to be paying attention. Of course, I cracked up, so Esaul comes running over to me, laughs with me and then takes off again saying, "Lesa, Lesa, *mirame, mirame.*"

This went on for quite some time! Keep in mind, I also have two girls sitting on my lap, Victoria and Martina who are drawing all over my notes and playing with my hair. Mario, our other sweet *angel* (ha, ha) decided to outdo his buddy Esaul and climbs up the door like a monkey! Surprisingly, he actually got in trouble. I looked over as someone picked him up and took him out of the church. I have never seen that type of discipline here before . . . busted!

In the midst of this chaos, I feel like a Rock Star. I am sweating like a pig, surrounded by kids I love, and understanding about every fifth word in Spanish. This moment is reminiscent of my recurring dream as a twenty-year-old as this is exactly what I thought bliss would feel like. I am in heaven.

As soon as church is finished, we walk across the street to the orphanage and make ice cream cups for everyone in the community. We also passed out little bags filled with small stuffed animals and candy for all the kids. It was only noon when I realized I was covered in ice cream. I looked over at my two children who were even dirtier than me! The heat was relentless, so we decided to head home and hit up the pool. I asked if I could take five of the older girls back to our house to go swimming.

Gabriela, Sofia, Camila, Arlen, Catalina, and Samantha came home with us to go swimming. Our cab driver, Norman had his wife with him when he arrived and picked us up. Norman sat in the front with his wife, and the rest of us sat in the back seat. We had eight girls in the back, and ten passengers in total! This is quite normal in Nicaragua as there are no laws as to how many people can ride in a car. There are no laws about car-seats either. However, you can get pulled over for not wearing a seat belt in the front seat (crazy laws). It's a short ride to Condo Allyson (thank goodness), and we made it safe and sound.

We changed our clothes and spent a couple hours at the pool. Pool-time was very refreshing, and it was so good to spend some time with the older girls. They found a mango tree and picked some sweet, golden fruit. They topped the mangos with salt and ate them skin and all; it was a real treat.

It was very hectic in our small house with all the girls running around, asking questions, laughing and checking out all our stuff. I often think of how difficult it must be for them. They are very seldom considered for adoption and often witness many of the younger ones going to families. In the meantime, they are trying to navigate the bitter-sweetness of growing up, with all the challenges and emotions that come with it. They are beautiful girls—inside and out. I am grateful for this time to really get to know them. It's a real blessing.

After the fun time at the pool, the girls had to return to the orphanage while my girls and I went to dinner with the Linda's and Rachel's family. Lucie and Martita fell asleep in the cab on the way to the restaurant. (They were wiped). The food was tasty, but we were ready to be home.

Sunday nights are when my neighbors get together. There are four of us—Linda, Rachel, Beth and I. We are all adoptive moms leaning on each other through this process. I love just to hang out and hear about each other's struggles as we support one another. These women are so vital to me; we are forging true friendships that I believe will continue to grow as time goes on.

I had a much shorter Skype with my husband and Scarlett, only talked for a couple of minutes, which was the only negative of my day. Well, let me correct that I have one more negative... while Camila played with Lucie's hair, she informed me that my daughter has lice. *Eeek!* I will have an entire blog dedicated to that one but not even those gnarly little bugs could steal the love, encouragement, laughter, and fun that belongs to us today. The end of the day is always a bit sad because I am away from my husband—but it was a good day!

Love and blessings to you all and I hope your Sunday was as good as mine!

2 Comments:

Timothy said . . .
Lucie is officially Nicaraguan! For those of you reading the blog, you have to have at least one case of lice to enter this distinguished group! GO LUCIE!!!!
XOXOXOXOXOXOX

P.S. And if you don't think this trip is life-changing for Lesa . . . consider the fact that she is taking Lucie's lice in stride. Also, consider that the other night they went out for pizza . . .

a bunch of them, one of the boys found a huge bug baked into his slice . . . Lesa stated, "WOW . . . OMG, that is a big bug" and then continued to eat. LOL Love you, Baye!

Kristl said . . .
Lesa, I've been reading about your journey from the start, but I don't know if my comments are getting through. I will try again. Hang in there, all my love, Kristl

Tuesday, May 26, 2009
That's a Four Letter Word!!!!

It's official . . . we now have a representative from every insect family living in my townhouse! We didn't have lice—but hey, Lucie decided they belonged here too. Apparently, all are welcome . . . *Bienvenidos*!!! L I C E !!! Ewwww!!!

Lice is a big issue at the orphanage. The four-letter word is the main reason Martita never has long hair because about three times a year, there's a lice infestation and with forty plus kids, it's just easier to cut hair than to clean it. Now I understand, after spending an hour combing through Lucie's mane. I use a tiny little comb that I comb through each hair from root to end. It's a long and painful process (for both Mom and Lucie).

Camila, one of the girls from the orphanage, was playing with Lucie's hair (everyone here is obsessed with Lucie's hair because it is long and blond, which is rare in this country) and showed me the little "nits." I couldn't see anything. I am always looking for the little black bugs, but I guess that comes later. If you are completed *freaked out* at this point, I don't blame you, I am too! Simply writing the four-letter word gives me the chills. Eeewwwwww!!!

The lice may outnumber me, but they've never had to deal with this *Mamacita* before! This. Is. War. I hand washed every sheet, pillowcase and stuffed animal that the girls sleep with. The zero hot water situation is posing a challenge. Hot water is kryptonite for these little suckers, so my alternative is washing each item repeatedly. The detergent is made with bleach, so I'm praying that when the laundry bakes in the sun, it will destroy all the pests for good! I did a thorough comb through of my hair and Martita's (just in case) and sprayed every surface with disinfectant spray.

This is what I'm supposed to do to avoid getting lice in the future.

- Do not lay on any of the beds at the orphanage.
- Do not use any of the girls' combs and brushes.
- Hugging the girls poses a risk because when your heads touch the lice can jump from one head to another. *Yes*, they jump!!!

Well, I'm willing to give up a lot here, but I am *not* willing to stop loving on our kids and having a blast at the orphanage. So, albeit, I have avoided getting lice all these years something tells me the war may not be completely over. I know . . . Eeeww!!!

3 comments:

CTGoodyear said . . .
Bless you my darling and brave daughter. What else can I say but BLESS YOU!!!! I'm so proud of you and wish you didn't have such a hardship to bare, thank God for the blessings that come with it. Thank you for all you are doing so we can have Martita in our family. I love you, kiss the girls. Love Mom XOXOXOXOXO

ivaniam97 said . . .
Hay No . . . *PIOJOS*!!! Lol I know it's not funny but the way you put it just cracks me up. Hey but whatcha gonna do but laugh, right?!?!. I don't blame them, even the *piojos* love being around you girls. Hope you got rid of those little suckers.

Timothy said . . .
I LOVE MY WIFE . . . SHE IS "TROOPER EXTRAORDI-
NAIRE!!!" GO BABY GO! We are going to film your *Survivor*
audition tape while I am down there in a couple of weeks (well
and maybe a couple of other things as well ;-) . . . you are a
shoe in for that show for sure! And Ivania is right . . . *piojos* are
not funny, but you have me cracking up! XOXOXOX

Tuesday, May 26, 2009
"Don't Judge Me" Volume I

A very good friend of mine has said to me a time or two, "Don't
judge me" when she may be indulging in a vice or two (or three).
Well, this is Volume I of Lesa's, "Don't Judge Me."

We had an appointment with our social worker Renea at
8:30 a.m., so I got up at 6:00 a.m to prepare. This is our first
home visit. I cleaned the house, (as best as I could around the live
insects) got the girls and I cleaned up and then prepped them for
who was coming and why. Basically, my instructions were, "Act
like you love each other and smile all the time." During my tidy-
ing, I received a call from another adoptive mother who lives in
our little community. (She was over at our house the night before.)

She called to give me a little advice, "It would probably
be a good idea to remove the bottle of white wine on top of
your refrigerator before the social worker arrives." Don't judge
me. I actually thought it was *excellent* advice, and it hadn't even
crossed my mind. Okay, now I was completely ready for our visit!

At 9:15 a.m., (yes, forty-five minutes *after* our scheduled
appointment) I received a call informing me that our social
worker would not be able to meet with us today and would call us
later to schedule an appointment for Thursday. I lost it. I already
had the translator at my house, and the girls and I were ready to
go. I was most upset because this appointment was our best bet
to allow the Consejo to hear our case this month. After I hung
up, I searched the house for those little pills my doctor gave me

to take when I get my annual Mammogram. It's a generic form of Xanax to calm me down. When I found the magic pill, I popped one (yes, just one) in my mouth. *Don't judge me!*

Then, I called my translator to vent. He must have caught on to how upset I was because he cut me off and said he would take care of it. Twenty minutes later, they arrived! I know . . . I am bad to the bone!!! ;D

The visit went great. We answered some very basic questions, and I think our social worker got an honest picture of how our family interacts, even though in today's version we are clean, on our best behavior *and* Mom is taking some prescription drugs. *Don't judge me.*

Love and Blessings, Lesa

3 Comments:

Tracy said . . .

I'm smiling the entire time I'm reading this and 'not judging' you!!! I'm so glad the meeting did happen, and it went well! Can you pass on the name of your doctor who gives you pills to calm down? :) Love ya—hope today is a good one!
T

Timothy said . . .

STONE HER! STONE HER! The crowd chants ;-) Hey at least they didn't find Lucie's pack of smokes! HA HA HA. Glad it all worked out for you my love.

ivaniam97 said . . .

Girl ain't no judging here, mom has gotta do what mom has gotta do, shoot! Ain't no shame in your game ;) LMAO Glad it went well.
I LOVE YOU LESA!!!
XOXO

Wednesday, May 27, 2009
I Give Up . . .

Okay, I think I've earned a slow and boring day, but it's apparently, not in the cards yet. We had an appointment at 8:30 a.m. today with Diego at Mi Familia. Diego is a very genuine man who wants to help with the adoption. He really seems to have some authority in determining how often the Consejo meets and how the process works. He was our last chance to state our case with the hopes of getting into the May Consejo, which is happening tomorrow.

Well, if caffeine isn't enough to get you going in the morning, I suggest moving to Nicaragua. For a slower paced, third—world country, this place can be extremely stressful. Norman had car trouble and picked us up at 8:30 a.m. instead of 7:30 a.m. The girls and I waited for about twenty minutes before I called him and asked, *"Donde esta?"* Where are you?!

Many apologies and twenty minutes later, he showed up. Then he proceeded to drive faster than anyone I know (including myself) down the beat-up roads (without lanes) in which people and livestock (chickens, cows, and horses) are continually crossing the street. It was like driving in a video game! Earn double points for a quick left turn to avoid the cow in the road—watch out for the pothole and earn an extra turn by speeding around the broken-down car. The girls kept saying, "Whoa" and I did my famous *"uuuggghhhh"* a few times. Lord, no more caffeine for me. And by the way, why didn't I take another pill this morning?!?!?

We arrived ten minutes late, which is entirely acceptable here in Nicaragua. Thirty minutes late is also acceptable (I'm not kidding). We went directly into our meeting with Diego. Tim gave me some good suggestions for how to state our case, and while I gave him the best pitch I could, I didn't close the deal. The agenda was set, and we were not on it. I held it together until I got out the door and then I started to cry. Martita began to rub my leg and kept looking at me. Lucie paid absolutely no attention to me (she is used to her mother crying).

Well, what does this mean? It means we wait until the Consejo meets in June to give us an official court date. We have another month to wait and worry about when and if the Consejo meets in June. I made a decision today—my husband and I have done everything we can to make this happen, and there is nothing more we can do. So, I give up . . . Jesus take the wheel! Seriously, it is all in God's hands, and I feel much better letting him drive than myself or my cab driver!

4 Comments:

ctkmichele said . . .
Amen and Amen =)

ivaniam97 said . . .
hahahaha . . . .waaaa . . . hahaha . . . waaa. That's me while reading your entry today. OMGoodness . . . you're killing me Lesa!!! I swear it's so awesome to read your blog not only do I get to hear about your journey but I get my laughs and cries for the day too, and we both know I can cry. We were always the first ones crying at small group! Alisson always looks over at me while I'm watching, Oprah, the news or one of my favorite shows because if it's a happy story I cry, if it's a sad story I cry . . . I always cry. So I can relate to what you said about Lucie. It's so sad Alfred and Alisson don't pay attention to my tears unless there's been a death or severe illness within our family or close friends. I get you girlfriend, I get you ;) Oh and I sooo get what you were saying about your cab driver. The roads in the countryside are exactly the same in Costa Rica. Man chica one time on our way to the market from our hotel my uncle was driving so fast I almost sharted my pants! BTW just in case . . . sharted, definition—when you fart so hard that a little piece of shit comes out! Okay . . . laughing uncontrollably right now!!! Hmm . . . LOLOL

No seriously now, one thing is for sure, you're right, let go and let God! Just go with the flow and ask God for peace in those moments of desperation. I know it's easy for me to say, I'm not there walking in your shoes right now, and I can't imagine being able to withstand what you are going through. I truly admire you, you are so strong and so brave! I do know a bit about letting God drive though. I have had, no, I mean I still have those moments in my life where I just want to control and do all I can to make a certain situation happen, run smoother or faster. It's only after I've struggled with myself, I'm at my wit's end and broken down that I finally say, "Okay God, help me I can't do it anymore." I lay my burden unto his feet, finally surrender and allow his precious peace to fill my heart. Then change begins and what I had desired begins to happen if it is His will and if it's not then I begin to have peace and patience.

Wish I was there to give you a big hug, I may not be there in body, but my heart is with you always! Now chin up, enjoy Nicaragua, eat some bugs have a glass of wine!?

Love you

xoxox

Timothy said . . .

SHART . . . .LOL . . . VERY GOOD!!!!

mck4099 said . . .

Hi Lesa,

We were out of town, but I am now caught up on your journey to date. Like others, I have smiled, laughed, and teared up when reading your blog. You have your good days and those that are more challenging, and God is with you through them all. Ivania is so right about handing your challenges over to God, knowing that He will take care of matters at the right time. He must have something wonderful planned for you between now and the June meeting!

Thank you for sharing your thoughts and emotions with us through your journey. I know it is therapeutic for you, but also for me. Your experiences and words help me to slow down, reflect, and appreciate what I have.

God Bless,

Donna

P.S. On a less serious note, I have two thoughts—1.) You should consider writing a book at the end of this chapter of your life. You are a regular Erma Bombeck. If you don't know who she is, ask Tim! :D 2.) I have to meet Ivania—"sharting"—too funny!

Thursday, May 28, 2009
Through Her Eyes . . .

Hello, loved ones!!! I had a fantastic day today, a friend of mine, Rachel asked me to go to a local mall with her to shop yesterday's blues away. I was so in! We loaded up the cab and set out for the Galleria mall, which is about a thirty-minute ride. I have learned that if I let the girls know what the day will entail; they do a little better making it through. I explained to them, "This is a day for Mommy to relax, a day for a little patience, a day to not ask a bunch of questions, and to just go with the flow." (This was not easy to communicate with my Spanish speaking daughter, but I think she got the main points.)

We arrived around 11:00 a.m., and the deep fried, finger-lickin' good aroma from the food court took me back to the first time I had been here. On my very first mission's trip to Nicaragua, we had stopped at this mall for a fast food feast. As I recall, the dining options are to die for! Chicken, pizza, Burger King, *Yes! Yes Yes!* Now I was really excited. Bonus: I remember how happy I was to use the bathroom in the mall (it was clean, and there's actually running water).

I wasn't the only one excited. Our sweet Martita giggled every time she went up the escalator. I realized, when she was apprehensive about taking her first step, she had never seen or been on a motorized staircase before. When we walked into the toy store, she talked non-stop, "Momma, Momma, Momma..." She even learned the assumptive close (I too, am very good at this). She would grab a toy and say, "Thank you Momma" before I even said she could have it! Well, I had told her not to ask questions today. Needless to say, she went home with a few new treasures.

She used the same assumptive close when I tried on shoes. (I found the cutest pair of sandals.) She would copycat me, try on a pair of shoes she liked, pose in front of the mirror and smile. We ate lunch at Tip Top (much like Kentucky Fried Chicken). I bought her a kids' meal of chicken nuggets and fries, which came with a plastic watch. She was so excited and kept saying, "Thank you, Mom. I love you, Mom." She was so proud to show me her watch to which I would play along and ask her, "What time is it?" And she would say one o'clock. Then two minutes later, she would show me her watch again, and I would ask the same question, and her face would light up as she said, "One o'clock!"

She is so excited by the things that I take for granted; a free toy, an air-conditioned mall, riding an escalator, wanting something and actually getting it and being part of a family. Martita's enthusiasm is contagious, and both Lucie and I enjoyed our day with our girl.

Tonight, I told my husband that I catch myself watching Martita. I get so much fulfillment in observing her happiness. I will never tire of seeing her glowing grin, and I am amazed at her relentless *wanting to please attitude*. She has the most loving heart. I look at this little girl who once belonged to nobody, and now I can't believe that she's ours. Martita is our daughter!

This time in Nicaragua is tough. It's challenging, but it is a small price to pay for our precious treasure . . .

Friday, May 29, 2009
What's the Plan?

I am the lady with a plan. I *love* my phone with its calendar, bells, whistles, and alarms that alert me to meetings, lunches, to do's, birthdays. Bottom Line: If it makes it easier for me to plan: I'm sold! While I enjoy my R & R, I have to plan relaxation time in my calendar. There's such a comfort in knowing, who I'm meeting, where, when, and why—isn't that the way life is supposed to be?

How is it possible to function in a place without a plan? How will I get by using a phone without a calendar? There's no plan for next week. I have no clue what, when, where, who, and why is next.

Right now, I have plans for next Thursday. I'm going to the beach with the other adoptive families and then saying good-bye to Linda and her family. Tomorrow, I am supposed to do something with Natalia (director of the orphanage), but I have no idea what or when or where. She was supposed to call me but hasn't. There is no plan! My calendar is empty, but my days are full . . . I don't know when I'll leave this place, when I'll see my husband next, or when I will look back on all this and laugh. There is no plan.

To keep my sanity, I plan out the most basic actions. I planned on doing laundry today, only because the garbage bag that is home to all the dirty clothes is stinky and nearly full. My *little helpers* are more for amusement than for assistance, but I love having my girls flittering about as I scrub a dub on the old washboard. After laundry, I cooked dinner on our gas stove, and then we retreated upstairs to relax.

As soon as we sat down to watch *Transformers*, I heard a loud clap of thunder. I asked Lucie "Is that rain?" She said, "I think so Momma." Never fails! I ran downstairs and out the door to the laundry room . . . it was pouring! I quickly grabbed all the clothes off the line, handed them to Martita (Lucie was still upstairs watching *Transformers*—Ummmm Hello) and was thoroughly soaked. I wrung the clothes out again in the kitchen sink and started to hang them to dry in different spots around the house (dining room chairs, the railing of the stairs, and any knob I could find).

Minutes later my friend Manuel is at my door asking to borrow a bottle opener. (Don't judge him!) Then Lucie yells down that Daddy is trying to Skype—she answers the Skype but can't turn off the movie—*Chaos*!!!

I talked to Scarlett and Tim, put the girls to bed and then the electricity went out. I only brought *one* small flashlight and some candles on this trip so I *feel* my way downstairs to find the flashlight and the candles and creep back upstairs to witness both girls out of bed, completely freaked out. When the electricity goes out, the air conditioner units stop working. So about five minutes after the power shut off we were hot, uncomfortable and a little cranky. I put some candles on the floor outside the girls' room, in hopes they would go back to sleep. Then I waited patiently for the lights and fans to come back on. Why is it so scary when it's dark? I guess I will never get over that fear—but I continued pecking away on my laptop and within an hour . . . BOOM! We were back in business! Who is this calm, chill, relaxed Lesa who waits patiently for the power to turn on when all of her plans are foiled?! Next thing you know I'll be wearing hemp and smoking hookah. I smiled when I saw my husband online and heard that *Transformers* was still playing. I laughed at myself and thought, what will happen to us tomorrow?

I may not be as successful of a planner that I thought I was, but I am learning and evolving. I'm learning to go with the flow, learning that nature doesn't always cooperate and that whatever my plan is, very well may *not* be the actual plan!

1 Comment:

mck4099 said . . .
Once again Nicaragua wins! Although once you are back in VA for a while and scheduled up to your eyeballs with meetings,

outings, etc., you'll probably look back and think a few dull days involving no planning would be great! It sounds like you'll be hugging your appliances when you get home too—scrub boards are "hardcore" (as you say).

Matthew is in the process of completing a family heritage project at school about my dad's life. This blog just makes me think of the great stories that your girls will be able to write about as they progress through school. Like I said a couple of days ago, you've got to write a book!

Enjoy your day with Natalia (tell her and the kids I said, "Hi")!

Chapter 7

Feliz Dia de Madres

Saturday, May 30, 2009

Today is Mother's Day in Nicaragua. There was no forgetting it because I actually received a text message from the telecommunications carrier that said, "*Feliz Dia de Madres.*" We stayed at the house for most of the day but celebrated with a little dinner out. Norman told us how he cooked breakfast for his wife and made her a cake. During our chat, he explained that Mother's Day is a *big* deal in Nicaragua compared to Father's Day. I told him that it's the same in the states.

I know this holiday is wrapped up in shiny paper and bows that make mucho marketing dollars for all the companies that profit from the cards and gifts that we moms, grandmas, sisters, and wives cherish. But still, it is a day I always look forward to. My husband and girls take excellent care of me on my special day. This day is not to be confused with my birthday which is another special day that belongs to me. ☺ We celebrated Mother's Day before we left for Nicaragua because we knew I would be here for Mother's Day. Honestly, it felt rushed. Don't get me

81

wrong; it was terrific to hang out with my family and receive cards and lots of love, but it wasn't the same. I feel the day more today because it is celebrated here and it has made me very homesick. Missing my husband, Allie, and Scarlett.

This is my first Mother's Day without my Grandma, which is weighing on me, too. I miss her so much. I'm so thankful she had a chance to meet our Martita when she came to the States to visit. Even though Grandma thought Martita was a boy at first (don't judge her, she was 92) she warmed up to our girl and had a twinkle in her eye when she watched her. I think my Grandma is looking down at her crazy granddaughter while laughing at all my experiences in Nicaragua.

Okay, I'm equal parts happy and sad because although I am missing home, there is much to celebrate here. This is my first Mother's Day with Martita. What a milestone! I think about her future, and I am so at peace knowing she will grow up with a family that loves and supports her. Our little girl's world is so different now; she has so many opportunities that she can actually be whatever she chooses to be. I wonder if she will like math—be a Daddy's girl—go to college? Would she return to Nicaragua and have an impact on her country? Will she move far away from me, as I did to my own Mother? (Okay I'm already trying to make her feel guilty, and she doesn't even speak English yet!)

My mind always returns to the same question. How can I best give Martita what she needs to feel totally loved and part of our family? Lucie has said a couple times that she wished she was adopted. She witnesses the love these families have for their adoptive children, and I think she wants to be celebrated like that. Hopefully, that's the case, and she's not actually wanting a different Mommy. But it won't always be this easy. Martita will have challenges and may struggle with not knowing who her birth parents are and what happened to them. She may wonder why she was abandoned? I pray that both Tim, the girls and I can give her what she needs to become her best self. To know she is wanted and loved.

I guess these are thoughts all moms have about their kids. I have such a beautiful family, and I am so blessed. *Feliz Dia de Madres* all my dear loved ones. I hope your day was as special as mine and that you're able to focus on the true gift of how amazing it is to be a Mom.

Sunday, May 31, 2009
Your Spanish is PERFECT!

Sundays are becoming my favorite day in Nicaragua. I *love* going to church at El Canyon. Today was special because Pastor Martin led the service after returning from a trip to Germany. He is an amazing man. There is no nodding off in his sermons as he preaches with heartfelt passion. He talks about how it doesn't matter where we live, what we have or who we are because we are all God's children. He makes me feel like I am home—so wholly welcome.

Pastor Martin is known to let out a few tears from time to time (actually he cries pretty much every time he gives a sermon). As a fellow crier, I relate entirely and never let him cry alone. He cried once today when he said he could picture Lesa (me) walking hand in hand with Martita and Lucie at our home in Virginia. He gets me every time!

I was so happy to catch up with Pastor Martin last Friday. He only speaks Spanish, so our talks are short and to the point. However, when I saw him, I was on a Spanish speaking roll. I told him how much he was missed and shared what was going on with Martita, Lucie, and my husband. I said to him that we're counting down the day to go home.

At the end of our conversation, I asked him "Me *tiendes*?" "Do you understand what I said?"

He smiled and said, "*Si, su Espanol* is *perfecto*."

My Spanish is perfect!

We both laughed at that. Being here has forced me to speak Spanish even though I feel very self-conscious about each word.

I want to sound intelligent and communicate effectively and not like a 2nd grader. However, as true with anything in life, I have learned the only way to get better is to keep practicing. Everyone is so patient with me, and my Spanish has dramatically improved. I was feeling pretty good about my progress until . . . we went to church service that Sunday. Pastor Martin started to tell everyone my story during the service. He explained how I was here to take Martita home and he asked me to come up and talk to the congregation in *Spanish*!!! I was shocked and felt completely unprepared. (Who knows if today is a good Spanish speaking day for me or not!?) I walked up to the microphone and got very emotional and said, (in Spanish) "I love the people of Nicaragua. You are so good to my family and me. You are all family to me. I am so happy to be here in the final steps of our adoption. I thank God for making this work and ask that He blesses us all. I wish you all a happy Mother's Day and thank you."

Not too bad—right!? Then Pastor Martin prayed for us with his hand on my shoulder and asked that we are taken care of, watched over and to give us strength for our entire family. There was a lot more said, but I only caught a few words.

"Wow," I thought. "We are so blessed to have this man and this community praying for us. I am so glad I came today."

After church, we served lunch to the community, and then I hung out with Natalia and all the kids. It was a Sunday I will replay in my mind for years to come.

Later we went out to dinner with several families from Condo Allyson, and Natalia and Amanda and Pablo from the orphanage. We went to a restaurant called *Asada*, which means grill and the food was *fabulous*! As we enjoyed delicious bites and each other's company, I overheard Lucie ask our friend Beth (who happens to be a pastor's wife) "Do you like alcohol?" (This could only go bad.)

Beth replied, "Well, not really Lucie."

Lucie didn't miss a beat and said, "My Mom *loves* alcohol!"

Of course, everyone at the table heard my middle daughter throwing me under the bus and howled with laughter. I really didn't know what to say. I had thoughts of killing my daughter or screaming "Don't judge me." But what I actually said was, "Well, I savor it, that's for sure." I thought I had answered truthfully without saying too much. Next topic please, but Lucie wasn't finished. "Well, Mommy, you drink beer upstairs every night!" Can someone seriously shut this kid up?! Albeit my daughter tells exaggerated tales of my drinking patterns in Nicaragua, I do so enjoy a glass of wine or a beer at the end of the day. It is because of *her* that *I love alcohol*!!!

Next topic, seriously. In adoption news, the Consejo did not meet in May, which means we have two foreseeable options. This delay *may* buy us the time we need to get into the next Consejo in early June *or* we may be pushed back until July. Tomorrow, it starts again. We will sit and wait at Mi Familia to meet with Diego to attempt to convince him (again) to consider us and then beg for another home visit before the Consejo meets. So please, keep us in your prayers that we are heard in June.

I want to thank you all for reading my blog—you have no idea how much it means to have my loved ones support me from afar. Your comments bring me so much joy, and without them, I don't think I could keep my positive attitude and find the blessings in this process. So, keep those comments coming and happy reading.

Love and blessings to you all!!

3 Comments:

Timothy said . . .
Ha ha ha . . . so Lucie is your conscience now? UGH . . . SHE is a character. I heard the story of Pastor Martin when we SKYPED but rereading it was really cool. For those of you in blog land, you read many blogs ago about what the church looks like (remember . . . Lesa, Lesa *mira mi mira mi* !)

The building doesn't matter when it comes to a church . . . What matters is the people on the inside. At El Canyon, they are a community of great people that have NOTHING from a material side but EVERYTHING spiritually. It's cool because everyone is equal at the core. I am now going to go have a beer for breakfast . . . don't tell Lucie ;-) LOL

CTGoodyear said . . .
Bless our children for they know not what they do. Tom & I laughed so hard we had to wipe the tears. We'll have a glass of wine tonight, and you can tell Lucie. :) We love you sooo much. Mom XOXOXOXO

fourirvines said . . .
I am rolling on the floor girl!! Lucie is a mess! God bless her :O) You have to keep all of this and show her when she is much older. Give both girls a big squeeze for us. We love and miss you guys. Kim

Monday, June 1, 2009
Feliz Dia de Niños!!

Happy Children's Day?! Yes—they actually celebrate Children's Day in Nicaragua! I love children like anybody else (why else would I continue to grow my family) but *Ppplllleeeaasssee*!!! It's Children's Day *everyday*!!! Of course, we joined the festivities, but it got me thinking . . . seriously, why should kids have a day?

My daily schedule is centered on serving my kids (like every parent). I wake up and love on them, feed them, clean them, dress them and make sure they have enough activities to challenge themselves and to leave me alone. At noon, the process starts all over again, feeding, cleaning and grooming! What would you girls like to do? How do you feel? Are you Okay? Be careful. Don't hit your sister. Yes, that is a beautiful picture. Wow, you are such a great swimmer. Yes, honey, I'm watching.

Are you hungry? Let me make you some dinner. Dinner is its own circus. I have to be as creative as possible to have my children consume vegetables without shoving it down their throats or threatening to keep sugar away from them for a few hours. It's Children's Day every day!

In honor of Children's Day, we headed to the orphanage armed with three giant cakes, (enough to feed fifty kids). I stuffed *piñatas,* handed out drinks, cake, and candy, and smiled the entire time. For some reason, it's easier to serve other people's kids than my own. After Martita had binged on cotton candy, orange Fanta and several Spanish labeled candies, I said, "enough." She stared me straight in the eye and said, "No." After I got over my initial shock, I looked back at her, smiled and said, "Please listen to Mommy and you can save the rest of the candy for later." She gave me her ugly look, and I set off to find Lucie so that I could fulfill my role as the evil queen who robs children of their sugar contraband. I looked back at Martita, and she was (as fast as she could) shoveling more candy in her mouth. This time I took it away from her and said she was not to have any more. She played tug-of-war with the candy bag and continued to scream "no" at me. I looked up and realized that the Grimes' girls were, the center of attention (yet again) so today was Martita's turn to humiliate her Mommy.

Being at the orphanage is a blessing but also a challenge as Martita's mom. I think she gets confused and the lines blur as to how she is expected to behave. This was her home for three years, and these amazing women took care of her so when she's here, I think it's a challenge for her to see me as her Mom. It's frustrating. This is going to be a process and not a fun one.

We made a quick exit to the cab waiting out front. Once we arrived home, I immediately started cooking the girls a balanced dinner with lots of vegetables. I watched them suffer as they stuffed their mouths with leafy greens, which made me a little happier. It was the highlight of my day. Strike that—putting them to bed was the highlight.

So, here's to all the children in the world—Happy Children's day and I hope you don't choke on your candy!

1 Comment:

Timothy said . . .
HA HA HA . . . okay so I thought you were building up to this really inspiring ending to this entire story . . . and then the punchline comes "I HOPE YOU DON'T CHOKE ON YOUR CANDY"?!?!?!? HA HA HA HA. Hang in there my love . . . just a few more days!

Tuesday, June 2, 2009
Three More Days

Today was a pretty *ordinary* day. I got in some therapy (AKA went on my run this morning) and made a delicious breakfast of eggs and pancakes for the girls and me. After refueling, I called my translator and lawyer and was very stern asking for a progress update. Then we were off to the pool. We splashed and played for a short while before it was time for lunch and then off to the orphanage. We had dinner with friends and hung out for a while and then I came home and Skyped with Tim and Scarlett.

All day, I thought about how in three days (but who's counting) my husband will be here!!! *Yyyeeesss*!!! It has been three weeks since I saw him and let me tell you . . . that is too long. I am soooo looking forward to having him here. I can't wait to hang out with him, make out with him (my girls would say, "gross" right now . . . you might be too) sharing everything with him. I can't wait to have my partner back.

We only have a very short time together—Tim flies in Friday late afternoon—and I leave the next day in the afternoon. Tim is coming to watch the girls, so I can fly home and go to my nephew, Casey's graduation in Vermont. My Dad and my sister will fly into Virginia to meet me, and then we'll all travel to Vermont together. I know this is a very special day for Casey, and I would never want to miss it, but this is very difficult for me to go since I have such little time with my husband.) I also feel strange leaving this country and my girls for any length of time. I will be home with Scarlett, Allie, and my dogs and able to love on them since I've missed them so terribly but again, it's difficult to leave.

All this being said, I think this will be an amazing experience for Tim. Albeit he doesn't speak any Spanish, I know he will soak up all the adventure Nicaragua has to offer. It's totally out of his comfort zone, but every time I step out of my comfort zone, I'm *amazed* at the mind-blowing things that happen. I want Tim to experience *it all*. It's a little scary not knowing what I would encounter or how I would communicate or function living in a foreign country. Tim's already gotten a taste of it reading my blogs. I am sure he's thought more than once "Better her than me!" But the girls will show him the ropes. They are so excited to have their daddy here. I know this will be an incredible bonding experience.

So, in three days, I will have my husband in Nicaragua. We will have a wonderful evening, and then I'll be home for a week. And the best part is when I return to Nicaragua Scarlett will be flying back with me! I feel so lost without my girl; we are so close in so many ways; she just gets me. She also has developed a love for Nicaragua, so I'm excited to experience the rest of this journey through her eyes and observations. I feel that having her in Nicaragua will make everything (including me) better. She is my love.

I'm not sure I've successfully communicated just how long three weeks feel without my husband. In short, it's been three weeks too long. I am praying we can see each other more often as the process continues—and I am sure I will have a very interesting blog after we are together. Here's to time going by very fast these next couple of days and my husband's safe arrival in Nicaragua.

3 Comments:

Timothy said . . .
So this is how I read this blog today (and I am borrowing a little bit from our friend Steve) . . . Blah Blah Blah Blah AND MAKE OUT WITH HIM . . . blah blah blah blah. LOL. I LOVE YOU AND CAN'T WAIT TO GET THERE! XOXOXOXOXOX

Donna said . . .
Hey Lesa-Your husband is showing me how to blog, comment or whatever this is called. I just want you to know how much I am enjoying reading and following your adventures every day. As a mom, wife, and adoptee—you are really touching my heart. You are an awesome writer. Thank you for taking the time to share.

ivaniam97 said . . .
Hi Honey!!!
So happy you will be home for a few days and will be bringing Scarlett back to Nicaragua with you. Enjoy your time with the hubby ;)
xoxo

Wednesday, June 3, 2009
That's Right . . . I am a U.S. Citizen!!!

Today I had to go to the U.S. Embassy. I was a little nervous, mainly because it was a new experience. I have seen the Embassy from the street many times but never been in before. From all the movies I've seen, I have always thought of the Embassy as a place to go if I was in big trouble and or running from the authorities! Exciting . . . but a little scary.

Well, I needed to do a couple of things while I was there.

1. Get my fingerprints renewed because it doesn't look like we are going to make our July 7 deadline, which

is when my fingerprints expire (yes, it has taken much longer to get through this process as you all know).

2. I had to be sure that they have documents verifying that I am adopting a girl that is five-years-old.

Today, my friend Linda went to get her Visa to go home on Saturday, and they had her written down as adopting a four-year-old boy with special needs, which she is not! Now, they are scrambling to get everything corrected.

Well, the girls and I arrived at 1:30 p.m. (They allow U.S. citizens to *walk-in* between 1:00 p.m. to 3:00 p.m.) Several people were waiting outside (all Nicaraguans) so I walked up to the door and knocked, and the security guard immediately waved at me and started for the door. Then a man came and walked right in front of me in line, he was a local and quite rude. Let's call him Mr. Rudo! When the security guard got to the door, Mr. Rudo tried to enter in front of me, and the guard told him he had to wait to check his papers and let me walk right in. I, of course, realized that albeit I have a little bit of a tan since I have been here, it is obvious that I am not from Nicaragua and was ushered in without any precautions. I think Lucie helped our case as well.

Then, I had to go through a security line. After guards dug through all of our bags, we were allowed to put our things on the conveyor belt and walk through the metal detector. Right on cue . . . Mr. Rudo appears, cuts in front of me (*again*) and places his bag on the belt. Immediately, the guard told him to get behind me in line and let me go through first. I was like, "That's right buddy—I'm next!!!"

Then it was on to another security line where I was given a number and had to wait for it to be called. The Embassy reminded me of a DMV office. It was very clean and had excellent air conditioning.

Lucie even said, "I could stay in here for a long time Mommy!"
And I thought, "Me, too!"

We were called within five minutes, and I was treated with respect and courtesy. It dawned on me how often I'm not treated this way. Usually, I am cut off, pushed around and when I don't understand what someone is saying, the person will roll their eyes and laugh at me. I too laugh because I know my Spanish is not good, but I am doing the best I can. Usually, it's men that treat me this way. It is my understanding that women are seriously looked down upon here. I didn't realize how much that impacted me until I was treated with respect.

Well, I got my fingerprints done very quickly and was assured that yes, I am adopting a five-year-old girl. So, we made some real progress today. As I left the building, I looked back at the waiting area, and Mr. Rudo was still waiting for his number to be called.

I am very proud to be a U.S. citizen. I know our country has a bad reputation (sometimes rightly so) in many countries, but I am proud to live in a country that treats women with respect and has processes that work. I am grateful that our country views adoption as an act of love not as a crime. My experience at the Embassy was also a lesson in empathy. In Nicaragua, I am the foreigner. I don't belong here in many people's opinions. How often do we, as U.S. citizens treat visitors of our country like this? How do we treat people who *look* like they don't belong? With respect? With compassion? I know that experiencing this type of hostility makes me want to be more compassionate towards others. I know first-hand how difficult it is to live in a country where you don't speak the language. Does that make me stupid? Am I not welcome?

The compassion I am searching for here is what I will give to others once I'm home. Something, I believe, we should all strive to do. I am walking a little taller today feeling that I belong and look forward to my next experience at the Embassy. Hopefully, I will not be running away from the authorities!

2 Comments:

ivaniam97 said . . .

You go girl! I too am so proud to be a U.S. citizen. In my opinion this is the greatest country in the world.

xoxo

Donna said . . .

Hi Lesa,

It sounds like perfect timing for you to take a quick trip to the U.S. to visit the country and folks that you love! Enjoy your twelve hours with your wonderful husband and your trip to Vermont! I just dropped off some notes for Tim to deliver to the kids and Scarlett is excited about traveling back to Managua with you. As always, you are in our prayers.

Love,

Donna

Thursday, June 4, 2009
Surf's Up!!!

Today, the girls and I went to *Los Cardones* Surf Lodge with our friends. *Los Cardones* is about an hour drive from our house down a very bumpy, dirt road. We saw cows, horses, goats, and other animals (I couldn't really even say what they were). The trip was a little challenging, but it was worth every minute.

Los Cardones is a beachfront property with cabanas and bungalows. It was created for surfers but is also open to the public. We arrived around 10:00 a.m. and paid ten dollars per adult to enter. The cabanas are right on the ocean, and the breeze was so awesome! It was breath-taking, and the water was so warm and beautiful. It was a little slice of paradise.

As soon as we arrived we took off running towards the ocean, all except for Lucie, who cried at the shore and acted like some child I did not give birth to. Martita, who is afraid of the pool held my hand and got swept away with the tide. She loved every minute of it! We played in the water, gathered a bunch of shells and then had a superb lunch in the cabana. I ordered the catch of the day and was told the fish I ate was alive and swimming at 6:00 a.m. that morning. It was delicious. I wandered around and checked out one of the bungalows. It was gorgeous and had hardwood floors and enough room for a bed that was adorned with mosquito netting. I was delighted at how clean the bungalow was. The one major set-back: there wasf no electricity. Initially, I thought, "So what, I can live without electricity as long as I can look out my window and see the ocean." But as some time went by, I realized no electricity means, no Internet, no blogging, no TV, no lights . . . Okay, well I know I could do it for at least one night, right?!?!?

Decision made . . . we are going back there! This is only the second excursion we've taken since we have been here. I need to lie in a hammock and watch the sunset. After experiencing this utopia, it hit me just how beautiful this country is. Being outside of Managua was the little get-a-way I needed. It felt so good to escape, walk the beach, listen to the ocean, and feel the surf playing with my toes.

Today, I made a very important decision. We are no longer going to torment ourselves wondering whether the Consejo is going to meet. We're getting out there, exploring this new exotic landscape and all the beauty it has to offer. I am not going to be a victim, waiting by a phone that never rings. I want to explore, taste, and experience this country with my daughters.

Drum roll . . . today is also the last day I'll spend without my husband and Scarlett! I smiled all day wishing they were with me, but soon they will be. This is my last day of doing this alone. Tim will be here for a week (while I am home) and then I'll return with Scarlett. She is such a love. Albeit, I am her mother, my oldest is always a big help and her love and support bring me comfort and peace.

I'm looking forward to showing her our temporary home; having her meet all our new friends and watching her enjoy this country and its people as I know she will. Yeah, I'm so happy she will be here!

As for my handsome husband, I have a narrow window of time with him tomorrow evening and Saturday morning. Not sure if I have the time (or energy) to write so for the next few days, Tim will take over the blog. I am sure he will entertain you with his witty observations so please stay tuned for his entries. I will be back on the fifteenth. We still have a long road ahead so please stay with us—keep the comments coming and know how much I love you all.

Your love and support keep me going!

Blessings, Lesa

〈 Chapter 8 〉

A Week with *Papi*

Sunday, June 7, 2009
Charades

Hello everyone out in *Wuz Up in Nica Lesa* land! As you are already aware, Lesa is hopefully back in the United States at this point having slept at least a few hours in our soft bed, in the AC, after a warm shower, *and no bugs*! How happy she must be right about now! Hmmm . . . Well, I don't know for sure. Nica is definitely her second home . . . one that actually runs a very close second to Chantilly, Virginia. She blossoms in Nica, and while it is a daily challenge, she *loves it here*!

As you might expect, writing for her blog is going to be a real challenge. First, I am not a great writer, *and* I am not disciplined to the level she is regarding journaling. But I am going to give it my best shot to keep you guys up to date and informed.

Yesterday the girls and I dropped Lesa off at the airport to say our goodbyes and start our week-long adventure together. Not speaking Spanish is a complete challenge for me especially when I'm trying to communicate with Martita. This all became apparent as I tried to explain to her why Momma went through the big glass doors and disappeared into the security area. I quickly pulled out the *helpful Spanish phrases* Lesa had prepared for me . . . and scanned it for *"Momma will be back soon."*

I saw:

"Be nice to your sister."

"Wash your hands."

"Be careful."

"Put your pajamas on."

"Go to bed."

"Don't pull your sister's hair," but nothing on "Momma will be back!"

Hmmmm . . . I hope this isn't some sort of contrived plan by *mi esposa* (my wife)! So, my only thought was to chain together my bad Spanglish and my charades skills and start communicating. I am not sure what I said and did with arm, leg and head gyrations but it seemed to satisfy Martita's questions. Lucie jumped in to help, and it was probably her Spanish that finally made Martita stop asking the question. Either that or she has learned to be embarrassed by her Papa! We were all quite the sight! I decided it was best that we just leave the airport and get into the *safety* of the taxi and head home where we would not continue to be viewed as the wacky *gringos* from the United States. Lesson learned . . . *Stay out of public places for at least a couple of days!*

To say the least, I was a bit exhausted by day's end. Martita went to bed at 7:30 p.m., Lucie at 8:30 p.m., me at 8:31 p.m. So, it's off to El Canyon and the orphanage today! Today or tomorrow; it's a little confusing. Thanks for reading everyone and being such excellent support for our family. We love you guys!

4 Comments:

ivaniam97 said . . .
Hi Tim!
Have a wonderful week. I'm sure it will be filled with great stories for you to share with us.

ctgoodyear said . . .
Hi Sweetie, this is the first time I've been able to read the blogs for about a week. I know that this will be an interesting week (to say the least) but I'm sure you're up for the challenge. Hope we'll be able to get online at our next stops. Kiss the girls for G&G. Love you, Carol XOXOXOXO

mawyer said . . .
Here's to a great week Tim—I know you'll do great! You have our full support, love, and prayers. We can't wait to read how your next few days go! Please give our love to all the kids—we miss them so much! *Adios mi amigo!*

wuzupinNicaLesa said . . .
Hey love!!!
Well, you were always pretty good at charades! I can picture you attempting to communicate using English words (loudly and slowly) and then Goose (Lucie) *helping* you. I'm imagining what's going on in my Martita's mind . . . "Momma—come save me!!!" Seriously, I know you will do great—and the bonding experience you will have with the girls . . . Priceless!! ;) (I'm sure you are not thinking that way right now!) Your writing is great and I am so so happy that you are there blogging and I am here commenting. Albeit, being with my husband is what is missing in my life—I am happy to be home with Scarlett and in our soft, awesome bed—taking hot showers and feeling like myself again.

My first day home included a stop at my nail shop where I held up my Nicaraguan feet and said, "Save me!!!" Now that I have freshly painted toes and nails, I feel almost normal again.

I want to thank you again, my love, for being my partner in this adoption process, for giving me the opportunity to come home, go to my nephew's graduation, and recharge. This is so needed and so appreciated.

I love you with all my heart and wish you a fabulous week!

Sunday, June 7, 2009
Rock Star

It has been said that when Lesa is in Nicaragua, she really doesn't *blend* in that well. I mean really, I think the tallest Nicaraguan I have seen on *all* of my trips here is 5'8," and that was a woman. On average most Nicaraguans are about 5'2" or shorter . . . with jet black hair and very dark skin! To say Lesa doesn't blend in is an understatement!

And neither does our daughter Lucie!

In fact, Lucie is starting to reach Rock Star status in Nicaragua. I mean everywhere we go, people point, touch her hair, (yes total strangers do this) and whisper about her . . . Seriously, she might as well be Miley Cyrus with the attention she gets everywhere she goes. Yesterday morning we were at the orphanage . . . Lucie gets out of the limo . . . I mean taxi . . . and the crowd goes crazy. I went to Church in El Canyon and for two hours . . . yes two hours . . . I listened to Pastor Martin preach in Spanish. No less than twelve times he said Lucie's name and asked me *in Spanish* how old Lucie was . . . Lucie Lucie Lucie! Her momma ran a close second with her name being mentioned at least eight times! The coup de gras was at dinner. The only couple here with a car (Jack and Beth and their adoptive son) and another friend Rachel with her adoptive daughter, asked Martita, the Rock Star and I to go to dinner . . . at McDonald's! LOL.

I digress for a minute. Lesa *hates* with a capital "H" McDonald's. She has even converted me to the non-super-size side, but hey, we are in Nicaragua . . . and what goes on in Nica . . . stays in Nica?! Anyway, since taking up residence here in Nica, Lesa has *not* been asked to go to McDonald's! Then, less than forty-eight hours *after* she leaves the country, *we* get asked to have *dinner* at McDonald's! Makes me think there really is such a thing as "All on God's time!"

Okay, back to the Rock Star . . . so we walk into McDonald's, which just happens to have a playground, and immediately, the crowd begins *the stare*. Lucie is once again the center of attention and loving it! We get our Happy Meals . . . Lucie scarfs it down and asks if she can go to the Playland. Now, remember, in Nicaragua, you are always just a little on guard from a safety standpoint, so I did my fatherly duty and began to scope things out . . . looking for the exits, the entrances, looking at the people (all of which looked like the upper class in Managua). I guess McDonald's on Sunday night is a big night out? Things seemed safe albeit a little crowded. There were about thirty kids in the tunnels, space capsules, slides, etc. I tell Lucie the place is safe, and she can go play. Lucie immediately kicks off her shoes, runs across the McDonald's (ugh . . . sorry Baye, I know this whole running barefoot in a McDonald's is freaking you out) and into the crowd of kids disappearing into a tunnel! I was a little freaked out, but then it hit me . . . Lucie is a Rock Star and doesn't blend in at all! And boy did that come in handy! Every few minutes or so I would see this VERY white kid with VERY white hair moving through the apparatus and a feeling of peace would allay my fears . . . *There was Lucie!*

On the other hand, I lost Martita at least five times . . . *Just kidding Baye!* She stood by the two kids that were holding puppies while they ate chicken nuggets. I guess that could be a blog all by itself. Yes, puppies in the McDonald's!

Okay, on to full day number two!

2 Comments:

Donna said . . .

Hi Tim! You're doing a great job blogging. Not quite up to Lesa's level, but very entertaining. (Insert smile icon here.) I am sure that Bill would be very interested to hear about your trip to McDonald's. (Insert frown icon here). Take care!

wuzupinNicaLesa (Lesa) said . . .

I really don't know where to begin . . . Yes, it amazes me that after a month living in Nicaragua and never stepping foot into a fast food restaurant—you have my daughters in McDonald's within forty-eight hours. (I don't think this is a God thing . . . maybe a Daddy thing?! ;)

Secondly, our Lucie is a Rock Star, but that doesn't mean that you can check on her every few minutes (in Dad's language -that's about ten minutes at a time) and be sure she is still in the building!

What may surprise you—No shoes . . . in Nicaragua . . . in McDonald's—guess what, not that big of a deal anymore. I have grown to understand that my children's feet are *always* filthy in Nicaragua—that's just what happens no matter where you go.

My final point . . . losing Martita several times, well that really isn't good my love. Please remember that albeit she blends in with all the others . . . She is one of us! ;)

Monday, June 8, 2009
The Nicaraguan Gods

To be honest, I was a bit apprehensive about today. Other than a *short* meeting at Mi Familia scheduled for 10:00 a.m., the girls and I had absolutely *nothing* planned. There was a good reason for this actually. Given my experience with Mi Familia and Nicaragua in general, I've learned nothing happens when it is supposed to, so I was prepared that our *short* meeting could actually last hours. Also, Lucie and Martita can be wild cards relative to their ability to stay focused, polite, and not be complete *hellions*, so we left the day open allowing a lot of room for error.

The day started on track. We told our taxi driver (yesterday) to be at our casa at 9:30 a.m.; this would get us to Mi Familia with plenty of time to spare. He was there at 9:20 a.m.! We arrived at Mi Familia at 9:50 a.m. and were escorted in to see our caseworker at 10:05 a.m.! Okay, so it was five minutes later than planned. This is still an absolute miracle. Our caseworker immediately put three documents in front of me to sign. It took me literally ten seconds to sign them!

At this point, I am thinking I overslept, and this is all a dream . . . *Nothing* goes this smoothly. Then as Lucie attempted to sit in her chair, she flipped it over and with a loud *bang*, a "Sorry Dad," and a goofy giggle from Martita, I realized I was actually awake, and everything *was* going very smoothly!

I handed the documents back to our caseworker, and she said thank you and goodbye . . . I said, "Come on *ninas*, *vamonos!*" (let's go) and we were out in the street, into the waiting taxi and home by 10:35 a.m..

As we pulled up to our casa, we saw Ignacio and his family wearing swimsuits heading towards the pool so immediately the girls said, "*We have to go to the pool . . . now!!!!*"

Well, actually Lucie said it, Martita said something in Spanish over and over, but she kept hitting me on the shoulder and pointing towards the pool, so I figured she was agreeing with Lucie! Don't you love the way kids can craft a simple thing like going to pool into a life or death situation? I of course said . . . Sure! I mean what else were we going to do . . . read books? Do a little homeschooling? Some crafts? Maybe make Mommy a nice picture for when she *gets here in less than 132 hours*?

Not on your life . . . Pool means Daddy gets a break! I don't even have to keep an eye on them because we are gated in, Lucie swims and Martita . . . well, I attach anything that holds air on to her arms and chest, give her a shove, say, "*haste la vista*" and then find a lounge chair! We spent the entire day at the pool. The girls swam, I did some work and talked to the people from our little community who came and went throughout the day. And the bonus? By 7:30 p.m. *both* Martita and Lucie asked me if they could go to bed! Leave it to a guy to figure this whole *fostering period* thing out in a couple of days!!!

Okay, I am laughing at myself right now knowing the Nicaraguan Gods are reading this and maybe even laughing because they know our luck won't last. Well, it better last because we are heading to the Masaya volcano tomorrow! The last time it erupted was in 2001. Ahhh . . . What are the odds?

Love you guys!!!

3 Comments:

mawyer said . . .
Tim,
Sounds like things are going great and you're handling things with ease! I so enjoy reading your blog and taking this journey with you and Lesa. Have a great day at the volcano—can't wait to see pictures and hear all about it.
Love,
Tracy

ivaniam97 said . . .
Wow, what a day . . . NICE! You're such an awesome daddy. :) Have a blast at the volcano, don't forget to apply repellent before you leave.

wuzupinNicaLesa (Lesa) said . . .
It's funny how when I go to the pool—it's quite a different experience! I pack lunch for the girls, put on sunscreen (make sure they wait until it is all soaked in) watch Lucie like a hawk

because she just barely has learned to SWIM in the big pool, and have to constantly answer to Martita's *"Mire Mire Momma"* (watch me, watch me Momma) with "Aaahhhs and ooohhhs!"

Maybe . . . and that's a big maybe . . . My husband DOES HAVE THIS ENTIRE FOSTERING SYSTEM DOWN!!!

I love and miss you all so so much!!! Please be sure my girls are alive when I get there!! ;)

Tuesday, June 9, 2009
DIE You Little Bast$%ds!!!

Peaceful co-existence is no longer an option!

Darkness covers the battlefield once again . . . the remnants of prior casualties litter the floor . . . a leg broken in four places . . . a head smashed beyond recognition. The smell of death is still in the air from last night's skirmishes. It is on these hot, humid nights that the enemy knows we are at our weakest. They have excellent night vision and always control the combat zone.

We hunker down in any spot that has a breeze. We try to relax, stay together and yet are always wondering, "Where are the enemies? What are they doing? What are they are eating?"

For some crazy reason though, tonight is different; I decide to venture into the darkness, into their world; the enemy zone. I'd had enough, and I *really* needed to get something from the refrigerator. (Don't judge me either!) Slowly I head towards the stairs. I peer down the steps into the darkness moving my head from side to side, attempting to focus. I look for movement of any kind. Nothing . . . total darkness, but I sense the enemy is there. I move down, one step at a time, slowly. I reach the bottom step and peer around the corner towards the kitchen. I sense them. I know they are working the countertop, the sink, even the silverware drawer.

I extend my arm out into the darkness trying to find the light switch. Up and down, up and down . . . my hand searches the wall. Beads of sweat drip down my face. Finally, I feel the switch! With one quick finger brush the fluorescent light flickers in an attempt to be my ally. A few more glimmers before the bright light shines. Now the battle is on! They are everywhere!!! Having spotted me, the enemy starts to form into groups. There are five on the microwave, ten on the counter, a brigade of twenty marching on the wall. There are fifteen to twenty lone fighters running in circles on the floor trying to distract me while the others move into position! I hyperventilate . . . I know this is going to be my shot; my chance to cause mass casualties. Maybe even send them into a retreat . . . to our neighbor's house!

I run for the cabinet under the sink picking off three or four in my bare feet! I start searching desperately for my only weapon . . . a big can of insect repellant. There, I have it in my hand! Oh No! False alarm this is the can of disinfectant spray! I reach deeper in the cabinet knocking over the fabric refresher, sticking my hand into the bleach wipes, wondering if the enemy has moved the insect repellant . . . some sort of trap! How did they know I was coming?!? Ah ha! Another can . . . the right one this time! *Yes!!!*

I lean backward, off balance at this point and roll across the kitchen floor! I start to spray anything and everything that is moving! (The kids were already in bed thank goodness.) Adrenaline pulses through my veins . . . I scream *"Die you little bastards!"*

I arch my back and then flexing my six-pack stomach I spring up . . . into a standing position! Spraying, spraying, spraying! Two dead on the wall, five running in circles; the poison stings their little brains. I think to myself, "They are on the run!!!! *Yes Yes Yes!*"

My eyes are watering, and my lungs are burning from the poisonous gas that hangs in the air. The death rate continues to climb . . . twenty-five, thirty, fifty! Bodies are scattered across the floor! I run for the stairs hitting the ones trying to retreat under the front door. Seven more dead! One last spray and I am back on the stairs. I look back to see mayhem everywhere! Completely satisfied I *spike* the can of Raid like a hall of famer after scoring the winning touchdown! *Victory!* I am a complete stud!

Do you think Nicaragua is getting to me? Please hang in there with me . . . I promise two things. First, Lesa *will* be back blogging next Monday! Second, I promise some mushy stuff very soon! Love you all a ton!

1 Comment:

wuzupinNicaLesa (Lesa) said . . .
OK my love—keep your day job!!! ;) I love you so, so much and this is quite the descriptive story! Believe me . . . I know EXACTLY what you mean, and yes, I will be there soon to help minimize the bug population.
I love you!

Wednesday, June 10, 2009
Who's Got Your Back?

This morning at the pool, I overheard this conversation between two ladies . . . we will call them Caroline and Sally.

> **Caroline:** "Hi Sally, hey, I have been meaning to ask you something . . . "

> **Sally:** "Hey, what's up?"

> **Caroline:** "I am trying to find out the status of your house this summer."

> **Sally:** "What do you need?"

> **Caroline:** "We have some people that will be here on and off all summer long . . . and I am wondering if you have any spare space?"

Sally: "Oh yeah . . . I forgot about your visitors. Sure, let's see. There are two extra beds in the one bedroom, and we can move another spare bed into our master bedroom. No worries, you can use any part of our house you need for as long as you want."

Okay, so I don't know if this seems just a little over the top to you, but it shocked me to hear this conversation and for *Sally* to basically offer up any part of her house to these unknown guests for an unlimited amount of time? I mean I certainly didn't get the sense that Sally was going on some sort of extended vacation or anything. This was going to be an inconvenience regardless of how you look at it . . . but it was being offered up.

After having read the blogs about our adventure here in Nicaragua, you already know that our "home away from home" is a compound of apartments, townhouses (not South Riding type for sure) and duplexes. You have also gotten to know a few of the people that live here. You also know that there's a swimming pool, armed guards, guard dogs and lots of bugs. However, what might not be so apparent is the *real* community that exists here at Condo Allyson.

Here in our little neighborhood of about fifty families, you witness real community being lived out. If you are in the market and don't have enough money . . . your neighbor offers it up. You *always* get asked over to people's homes for food and conversation, and you share rides and cabs. When someone is moving from Condo Allyson, they offer up their stuff to those of us staying . . . water stands, left-over food, detergent, fans (ahh the one luxury we love), etc. Groups of people get together at least once a week in smaller groups, to talk about life and issues. The people with washers and dryers allow others to use theirs. (People are so gracious that I have not asked to use a washer and dryer. I did laundry this morning on the washboard LOL!) And by the way, all of this community happens even though everyone has jobs, care for young kids and make sure the older ones get to school on time. These people are living their lives, cooking, cleaning the house, arguing with their spouses, etc. It really is rather remarkable to watch and to be part of as well!

In short, *everyone has each other's back!* It doesn't matter who you are, where you came from or what kind of belief system you have . . . you are part of a community. If there is one thing that I hope I can take home with me (*besides Martita . . . heeellllo*) it is this sense of community. Not community that has to be organized for me, not one that has to have structure . . . just one that works on a daily basis, the way this one does at Condo Allyson.

1 Comment:

Nicely said, my love!! It's so true, we are all part of a family. Why at home do we not speak to our neighbors? We are gracious when it's easy but make a minimal effort to extend a hand across the street! This is a great thing to take home with you—to open our homes—our hearts really . . .

Thursday, June 11, 2009
O Ma God *Senor*

The Spanish language and I don't mix. Seriously, my Spanish is really bad. No, let me restate that, *It's terrible!* I read somewhere the more you expose a young brain to new ideas, thoughts, and skills, the more flexible it is to adapt in the future. Really smart people say that our brains, before ten years of age, are continuously mapping to new things and ideas. It's called "mind mapping." The idea here is to expose young kids to as many diverse things as possible, like foreign languages, so that their brain can "map it" and have the capacity to learn these things in the future. Okay, maybe you are thinking I should watch a bit more TV and put down the books!

Actually, I find this whole mind mapping thing pretty interesting. I think it is the reason we try to protect or overprotect in some cases, our kids when they are young. I also think it is why we really need to expose our kids to a lot more things in their early years (like foreign languages), even if we don't think they understand what we are sharing with them. If the theory holds true, they will be mind-mapping like crazy!

Now back to my Spanish. I am convinced at this point that my brain *never* mapped foreign languages when I was young. At this point, I am sure my wife is saying that I must have been exposed to a lot of things that are *geeky* and *nerdy!* I bring *all* of this up to try and explain why it is that Martita is learning more English than I am Spanish! Seriously, as my Spanish vocabulary has increased maybe ten words this week, Martita's English vocabulary has increased by at least thirty! And the Rock Star (Lucie) you might ask? She's leaving me in the dust putting entire sentences together in Spanish.

Now granted, Lucie's sentences are things like "Martita, don't touch my stuff," or "Martita come here," or "Martita you need to go to bed."

(She tries to be the parent . . . maybe she thinks I should do a better job, but she is really accelerating.) The other day as we were leaving the volcano we headed down the road pretty fast. The taxi was rattling, brakes squealing and smoking, as the smell of burnt rubber invaded the back seat.

Lucie says to our taxi driver, "Uh Norman? *No mas rapido por favor. Comprendo?*"

(Don't go fast or please slow down!) I guess her survival mechanism really kicked her mind map into gear!

To give you a feel for Martita's English . . . she has learned "You are crazy."

"I'm hungry." (*Ok*, that phrase may, once again, be a reflection of my parenting!) And,

"What the heck?" *Yes*, she said heck! *That* is *my* parenting. If it were Lesa's the word heck would have been . . . well, you know where I am going with this one!

She also says in a Ricky Ricardo accent, "O ma God!"

Ok let me explain this one. Our regular taxi driver, Norman, says, "O ma God" *all of the time*! For example, he will say in broken English to me, "Jo wife Leeza, she no come back por *uno* week? O ma God senor!!!"

Or, "Dat Luucie . . . che is clazy . . . ha ha ha . . . O ma God!"

Note to self . . . don't allow your child to interface with Nicaraguan taxi drivers. (Just kidding, we love Norman.) All of this said, there is one Spanish word I learned this week that will stick with me as my "special" Spanish word. We all know that mothers are special people. When it comes to Lesa and Martita or for that matter Lesa and our other girls, *she* is their support structure, their security blanket, their comfort.

It has been very difficult for me to get close to Martita given Lesa's *mom skills* and Martita's background. She wanted and needed a Momma. For almost three years, I have lived at arm's length from Martita. This didn't discourage me, but it did get me down more than most people even know. This week Martita has apparently gotten a little closer to her Papa (okay maybe she had no choice)! She actually only started calling me Papa in the last year, but at the pool the other day she started calling me Pa Pea (phonetically). Confused, I asked one of the folks at the pool about this change in vocabulary. I was told this is a very, very good thing. It means she went from calling me Dad . . . to *Daddy*! If that is the *only* Spanish word I learn this week, or for that matter the rest of my life . . . I am good with it!

Thanks for *hangin* with me this week. Love you guys!

2 Comments:

ivaniam97 said . . .
Sweet Lucie, she's such a riot! Please tell her how proud Miss Ivania is of her for being such a great sissy to Martita! That is awesome that Martita is calling you *Papi,* that is the term

we Central Americans use to mean daddy. It speaks volumes about what a great job you are doing and that she not only sees your love but feels it, too.

Keep up the great job, *El Mejor Papi en Nica*! :)

wuzupinNicaLesa (Lesa) said . . .

My love . . . this post makes me cry!! *Papi*—I guess you are doing Ok! I know we both have had mixed emotions about this week—you being in Nicaragua without the basic skills (Spanish is only one of them) and me . . . here at home without the love of my life! I kept telling you "Baye, it will be a good bonding experience for you and the girls!"

Not to say this yet once again, but I WAS RIGHT!!! ;)

My love, your words about me are so sweet—and true! ;) OK just kidding, but I am cracking myself up! Seriously, without Momma being there—Lucie has to step up, and Martita gets to know her *Papi*.

I know we have continued to struggle without each other this week—knowing that I have two more months without you is almost unbearable. But I will say that after reading this blog—I wouldn't change this week at all my love. Thank you for being such an amazing Daddy to our girls—thank you for being such an amazing husband—I love you!!!

Please tell Goose to continue to keep everyone on their toes!!! ;) xoxoxoxoxoxxo

Friday, June 12, 2009
HEY I Know It's a Table!

Late this afternoon we went to the movies to see *UP* . . . in Spanish! To know how good a movie really is, try watching it in a foreign language. This movie kicked butt, and I have no idea what was said. Well, I think the film kicked butt. Maybe, just maybe, it was enhanced by the movie theater itself.

Since the movie is playing at the Galleria mall my girls and I ventured to the *other side of the tracks* to see it. I knew something was up when we got out of our taxi, and I saw a GUESS store! This more elite part of Managua is not big . . . trust me. *Our* side of the tracks is where most people live.

The people walking around the mall were very well dressed. There were several very nice restaurants and a multiplex theater that puts Brambleton to shame (sorry for the local reference *out of towners.*) The first shocking feature was the fact it had a VIP Room, yes, VIP room! I looked at the price for the VIP room, and it was seven dollars for *adultos* and five dollars for *niños*. In Managua that is a lot of money for a movie but hey, we are *Americanos*, so I sprung for the seats.

We walked into the actual screening room and were struck by the *very* large screen and about fifty *chairs* and by chairs, I mean *big, leather* chairs that I would buy for our house. These chairs were, well unbelievable. Then I saw the waiters. Okay, was I at FedEx Field in the sky suite section? You want food? They get it for you. You want drinks? They get it for you. You have to go to the bathroom? Well, I didn't try that out, but I am betting you that . . . oh never mind! Oh yeah . . . *Air conditioning*!!! And the fact that it was about 100 degrees here today, I thought maybe I had died and was sitting in the *Big Guy's* home theater! There were also side tables between each chair for your food and drink.

Side note . . . when I first went in, it was kind of dark. I put Martita in one seat, skipped what I thought was another seat, and put Lucie in her chair. I was planning on sitting between them. I sat down, and it seemed a little hard on the tushy. But for about five minutes I sat like a proud *Papi* between my girls . . . eating my popcorn and settling in for the movie. When I looked over and saw a waiter put food on a *table* across the aisle, I realized I was sitting on the table! I am sure the local *other side of the track* Managuans thought, "What is that crazy *Americano* doing?!"

So, I stood up, acted like I was stretching, and then scooped Lucie up and basically threw her one more seat over and flopped into my cushy armchair. The only bad thing about the movie was finding out *after* the movie was over that the chairs had kick-out foot stools . . . they were recliners . . . *Heelllooo Ugh* . . . I missed out on that one.

Through this whole experience, what struck me though was the fact that my sitting on the table was not the only thing that made people stare. After the movie, we walked out into the food court. Boy, did we get some looks. We were out of place for sure. Here we were, interracial families (two other families went with us) clearly from the *other* side of the tracks. The people were nice, and everything but the stares made me feel like we didn't fit in.

At times I wanted to go up to people and say, "*hey*, you should see my neighborhood back in the states."

Or, "Yeah I have a job and so does my wife."

But mostly, I just wanted to say, "Please don't make us feel so different."

I want my girls to keep their innocence about our world. I want them to believe we are all equal . . . men, women, black, white, brown. I want them to know that even if we don't have what you have, or all look the same, we are good people. This experience really made me think about how many times *I might* have made other people feel uncomfortable, how many times I stared, how many times I felt like I was better than others. Hey, I am not saying I meant to do it . . . *ever* . . . but I am not sure that matters to the *people* on the receiving end. So maybe not only did I see a great movie tonight, but maybe I learned how to be a better person in the process. For the kids of the families I interface with on a daily basis . . . I sure hope so.

Only one more day without the love of my life . . . *Yes!!!* Thanks for always supporting us with your prayers and words of encouragement . . . you guys are *awesome!*

3 Comments:

wuzupinNicaLesa (Lesa) said . . .

Not fair! Not fair! Not fair! I have been talking with Rachel about going to that movie theater since I first arrived in Nicaragua and never went! Isn't it just like my husband to blaze the trail (is that the right saying love)? Before me?! Typical!

Well, I am very happy to hear it is so nice and cannot wait to check it out myself. I find it hard to believe that your skinny butt was on a table and you didn't realize it—even when the girls were sitting in the comfy chairs (my husband is a natural blond). Seriously, if it were me (with my bom bom) it would be a little more believable! But I'm glad my love that you enjoyed the theater.

Being a minority is a humbling experience. I am just realizing—our family will forever be . . . a minority. We are a mixed family! Cool, isn't it? Funny, how we haven't given this much thought. In our world, Martita was born into our family with physical features that look like her *Papi* and a personality that is so much like her Momma. I think it is so important to be humbled from time to time.

Well, love, I must say that my reasoning for getting on your blog first thing this morning was to be sure that you and the girls had survived the *isleta* "island" with the monkeys. I have been worried about you all since yesterday morning and have not received a call from you yet! I have been holding my phone in my hand—waiting. I don't know if you changed your mind or if you haven't had a chance to blog about it yet but PLEASE CALL YOUR WIFE!!! I want to be sure my girls and my husband are in one piece.

Oh—one more thing . . . I GET TO SEE AND LOVE ON YOU TOMORROW!!!!! XOXOXOXOXOXOXXOOO

Donna said . . .

Hey! Welcome to the cool "Mixed Families" club! So glad that the Grimes have joined the Mines. Love you guys!

Saturday, June 13, 2009
Getting Your Heart Dirty

This week has been a challenge for sure. Yes, being Mr. Mom has given me a whole new appreciation for mothers! Funny, I had to travel more than a thousand miles, to another country to grasp the real value of these blessed women! God Bless all of the mothers reading this blog . . . *Let me say it again . . . God bless all of the Mothers reading this blog!* But a close second to getting clarity on motherhood is learning a little more about our world. What's crazy is that I have been to Nicaragua many times, and each time I go, I discover something new.

Lesa and I calculated that we have spent between ninety to 100 or more days in Nicaragua over the past two-and-a-half years. While coming here to see Martita is one of our main priorities, we are also fortunate to be part of different missions. We're on teams made up of groups and organizations. Witnessing people experience Nicaragua for the first time, the orphanage Puente de Amistad, El Canyon the community where the orphanage is located is utterly awesome! Each time I learn so much from the other team members; their perspective and insight are invaluable.

People change when they get out of their comfort zone . . . out of their *box.* They get a different perspective when they visit Nicaragua or any other country for that matter. *Yes,* we have issues in the United States . . . issues that we should all care about and try to help resolve. But something about getting outside the walls of the U.S. is powerful. You just see things that you can't and maybe don't want to ever see in the U.S. And the crazy thing? *Outside our walls* is normal to the rest of the world.

Okay, hang with me here . . . this is not a political rant, I promise.

What hit me this week is how difficult it is to step out of your comfort zone. Yeah, just deciding to step out is hard . . . but once you get out there and become engaged in people's lives, people that have needs, and lots of them, the intensity steps up in a big way.

For almost three years now, we have been going to *Puente de Amistad*. The sole purpose of going was *not* to build things or do projects. Our sole purpose is to build relationships with kids that have been rejected their entire life—to show them complete and unconditional love . . . *Now that is a radical idea!* What? You aren't going to build a school, a road, or some outhouses? Aren't you going to get your hands dirty? Try unconditionally loving someone, especially a kid that you may never see again, or one whose fate is to end up on the street begging or becoming a prostitute. What about the seventeen-year-old who is forced to leave the orphanage because they are too old to have government provided assistance anymore. *That* creates a whole different kind of dirt. I call it getting your "heart dirty."

There is a boy who used to live at the orphanage; *the* model kid. Lesa and I have known him since we first started coming to Puente de Amistad. He is smart, extremely polite (he could be a mentor to any kid), engaging in conversation, and very spiritual. A couple of months ago, he turned seventeen and wasn't allowed to be at the orphanage anymore. Today he is on the streets of Managua begging while he tries to wash windshields at a busy intersection.

Last week he called a friend of ours in Managua and said, "I am starving can you get me some food?"

Okay, so you all may have many different thoughts and emotions running through your heads and hearts at this point . . . and I have heard and had them all. I have heard everything from, "Hey, people that end up on the streets are innately lazy" or "They are just looking for government handouts."

I've also heard people say, "How can our God allow this to happen?"

And you know what? I have the same question, and I don't have the answer and probably never will. *This* is what happens when you get engaged, when you get your "heart dirty" and it hurts badly. But I am pretty sure it's not an excuse to not do anything. The story about the boy, the "perfect" kid is not over so far as I am convinced. Yeah, call it "naive hope" but maybe that's what we need to keep us going.

What I do know is that there was a little girl at that same orphanage that came from a not so good life (huge understatement). There were times in her life when I am sure the people around her asked the same hard questions about God. What no one could have possibly foreseen is the way her story continues. Who could have guessed, the amount of unconditional love she has given a set of parents she really didn't know and who really didn't deserve it? Perhaps, they couldn't have imagined the impact she is having on total strangers thousands of miles away. Or what about the future impact she may have on our country, her native home or world? I think it would have taken a lot of "naive hope" for people to have predicted this about Martita.

Throughout this process, Lesa and I have been asked some really tough questions.

"Are you doing this for your own self-gratification?"

"Are you trying to impress people with your 'foreign adoption?'" (I guess Madonna and Angelina have made it *en* vogue?)

"Do you think you win favor with God by doing this?"

"Don't you know you can't fix these kinds of problems?"

And on and on.

We have also been asked, "When do you throw in the towel?"

In fact, we have been asked this multiple times given the lengthy process we're still going through. After this week I will probably ask Lesa that question again!!! Believe me, Lesa and I have asked ourselves *all* of these questions repeatedly! I think it really comes down to this simple fact. Regardless of your belief system . . . Christian, Muslim, Hindu, Atheist, etc., there is something inside all of us that drives us to help others in need. It is just the way we were created. There are a lot of reasons we don't act on this drive, but I am convinced it is in all of us.

The problem is that getting engaged in someone else's problems is messy . . . getting your *heart dirty* is not fun . . . in fact most of the time it can be downright heartbreaking. But I am not sure, at least for me, that it's a valid reason not to act. What about that one-time things actually work out? All of the dirt seems to wash away; it's all somehow worth it.

Maybe this is what we need to keep in mind when we venture out of our "comfort zone" and do something . . . anything to make a difference.

Again *Wuz up in Nica Lesa* readers . . . it has been a blast sharing the ups and downs of Nica this week. Lesa will be back and hopefully, just a little rejuvenated next week while blogging her heart out. I really don't know what I would do without her . . . she is an amazing woman and one that I am proud to call the absolute love of my life.

Adios mi amigos! Te Amo! (Did I say that right?)

2 Comments:

ivaniam97 said . . .

Thank you so much for sharing today's blog. It's nice to be reminded how the world needs us and no matter how big or small the need is we must do all we can to reach out and help our fellow brothers and sisters. This journey that you, Lesa and the girls have taken is so inspiring to Alfred and me. We know the Lord sent us to Virginia just so we could meet the Grimes' family. You two are such an inspiring couple that we admire so much. We only wish the Lord had given us more time with you but even though we are no longer living in the same zip code, He still somehow manages to use you as an example of a strong couple who love Christ. We don't see that in anyone else we know. Everyone in both our families is divorced, except our grandparents but they are not Christians. You are an awesome Daddy and husband, and you were amazing with the *chicas*. I am so happy the Lord gave you this past week with the girls, and I'm so happy Martita has a *Papi* now!!!

God bless you and again, thanks for blessing me with the opportunity to follow your journey through this marvelous blog. I pray that soon I will see you all and meet Martita!!!
Big Hugs!!!!!!!!!!!

bduffy5469 said . . .
Tim—you are a good writer—funny, sincere, fascinating. Thanks for sharing your insights. Glad you had such a good experience!

(*Chapter 9*)

Momma's Back in Nica

Tuesday, June 16, 2009
I'm Back . . .

Yes, the rumors are true . . . I am back in Nicaragua. And I have *Scarlett with me*! *So happy.* Many of you thought that I would get a taste of the "good life" and leave my husband stranded in Nicaragua with my two youngest daughters . . . I would be lying if I said the thought never crossed my mind! ;) It has been a hectic, fun, few days . . .

One of the first things I did on American soil was head to the nail shop where I had some major work done on my feet and hands. This is the number one modern convenience I am really having a hard time living without (don't judge me). Next, on the list, my hairdresser came to my house to "Wash that gray right out of my hair, I'm gonna wash that gray right out of my hair . . . "and gave me a little trim (*ok*, I guess that's number two on the list of modern conveniences).

I met up with some friends at Red Robin, where I enjoyed a colossal Cobb Salad, dined at Coastal Flats and Sweetwater and had a blast with some of my friends. (I guess you could count this as number three on the modern convenience list . . . but that's a stretch . . . a girls' gotta eat, right?) I went on walks in my neighborhood, shopped for some Nicaragua gear and spent some great quality time with my Dad, sister, and niece. (My Dad drove me crazy as he loves my husband much more than me . . . Tim *must* be present for all future visits with Dad.) The trip was jammed with travel and airport excursions as I ventured to Vermont and back to Virginia. Then it was on to Nicaragua!

What did I enjoy the most about being home? *Finally* seeing my girl Scarlett, hot showers, room to turn around in my bathroom, not having to put toilet paper in the trash can (future blog), sleeping on a bed that is so comfortable it's almost orgasmic. (Is that *ok* to say online?) The list goes on . . . being with some of my closest friends, sitting on my deck drinking coffee in the morning, loving on my dogs, Starbucks, wearing high heel shoes and *doing laundry with a washer and dryer*!!! Yes, it was good to be home!

As you know, my purpose for returning home was to see my nephew Casey graduate from high school in Vermont. My sister Vicki, niece Taylor and my Dad flew into Virginia, and then we all traveled to Vermont for a quick two and a half days. Casey is joining the Air Force in a couple of months . . . I cannot believe how grown up he is. I always think of the first time I held him, I wouldn't put him down because he was so sweet and smelled so good . . . My poor sister; we all spoiled him! Now, he towers over me and relates to me on the same level. Casey has so much drive and is so excited for the future. I love him more than the first day I met him (which I never thought possible) and being a part of his graduation was a true blessing.

This blessing would not have been possible without my husband. He agreed to take off work and take care of the girls for a week during my absence. So, let me just go on the record by saying how much I *adore* my husband and how appreciative I am of what he does for our family. None of this would be possible without him.

Now, let me give you some scoop . . . I know that many of you read Tim's blogs (just so you know, he purposely tried to *out-do* me). Ha ha! While his Spanish speaking skills barely moved the needle, his sign-language has dramatically improved. He ventured out, had a lot of fun and won the hearts of our cab driver and the other families. My husband's most significant accomplishment; both my *girls* were *alive* when I got home! This was the only requirement . . . keeping the *girls* alive. Admittedly, I worried this would not be the case when he told me on the phone that he planned to take the girls to an island populated with wild monkeys . . . I calmly explained that he was in a third world country, doesn't speak Spanish and doesn't know any first aid . . . Hellooooo! I worried all day until I read his blog that he had skipped the wild monkey island. (He opted for the local zoo.) Praise God! He also took the girls to an active volcano. Later, I learned that Lucie was so nervous she didn't want to get out of the car at first, crying and screaming. She channeled her fear into perfect Spanish telling the cab driver, *"please slow down!"*

Even at five years old, Lucie has no issues with speaking her mind, and I think this helped her Daddy in keeping everyone safe.

When I arrived back, I really felt a sense of peace. I had my three girls and my husband with me. The only one missing was Allie (Tim's daughter). It has been a long time since we have all been together and I realized that being in Nicaragua is *ok* with me, as long as I have my family. Also, having a break did me well. I needed some time to pamper myself and love on some friends and family. I am renewed.

My husband is leaving today, and I am not holding it together very well. I broke down a couple of times, totally surprising Tim. For some reason, he believes that I am the strongest most independent woman and that I am doing so well on my own. That is so far from the truth. I could not do this without him and when he leaves a big part of me longs for him. Besides the great sex (don't judge me), I really do love my husband's company, his sense of humor and his unrelenting faith. He gives me strength and peace . . .

So, it's just the Grimes' girls once again, but this next chapter is going to be different. My goal is to *thrive*, not just *survive*! When will I ever get the chance to have my girls all to myself? No distractions . . . no modern conveniences . . . no friends . . . no husband . . . no time to myself . . . (Oh sorry, back to thriving.) Seriously though, there are countless adventures to be had with my *three* daughters. Together we will taste, touch and see more of the culture and wonder Nicaragua has to offer. I honestly, cannot wait!

Tuesday, June 16, 2009
Another Step Forward

While we're certainly here to embark upon the adventure there is a reality hanging over our heads; we can't leave Latin America until we settle this adoption. Reality check set in on Monday afternoon, during our second home visit with our social worker. This was Tim's last day in Nicaragua and it was important that he was present for our home visit. During our fostering time, it is her job to "observe" our family to see how Martita is adjusting. Our first visit was several weeks ago, and while I thought it went great, she was concerned about Martita and Lucie's relationship. Our social worker had observed a little disagreement between our two girls. Martita wanted Lucie's toy, and Lucie basically had a mild temper tantrum . . . yes, right in front of our social worker. Again, I thought, "Hey kids will be kids." Later, I found out that because of this disagreement, our social worker thought that the girls need some more time to adjust.

Before our social worker's second visit, we explained to all the girls why she was coming over and then proceeded to tell them why it is so important they "get along" and show how they honestly feel about each other. We talked to the girls individually and as a group. I felt very confident that everyone understood what was at stake. (Yes, there was some bribery involved—don't judge me!)

We had some last minute issues arise, which is a common theme here. There were problems with transportation, no translator, which is why our social worker asked if we could change the date of the visit. This was the only day that Tim would be here, so we needed to proceed as scheduled. In the end, it all worked out, and our social worker showed up.

We began the meeting in the kitchen, sitting together; it was picture perfect. Martita sat on my lap (we didn't have enough chairs for everyone) and the social worker started asking questions. She asked Scarlett what she thought about the adoption and followed up with some basic questions about Martita's eating habits and sleeping patterns. The elephant in the room showed up when she asked how Martita was getting along with Lucie. About twenty minutes into the interview, Lucie got up from her chair, came over to where Martita and I sat and put her arm around Martita! I smiled and listened to the social worker while my insides did handsprings with anticipation.

(What would my daughter do next?!) One thing I know about Lucie . . . she is very unpredictable. Well, Lucie looked at Martita and then gave her a kiss on the cheek! (The finish line is near!) I avoided my husband's eyes because I didn't know if I could keep a straight face.

Lucie then took Martita's hand, and they both went upstairs to play, hand in hand. (Victory!) There was no screaming, yelling or running . . . just quiet! As the interview proceeded, I pictured Lucie loving on Martita. My smile was real this time.

The social worker then asked us some excellent questions. She asked how Martita felt about both Tim and I, was it the same? I explained how incredible the last week was for Tim and Martita, how this time without me gave them a chance to bond and really get to know each other. I told her that Martita called Tim *"Papi,"* which is a great indication of how she feels about him.

She also asked me if I ever thought about calling it quits and going home. I hesitated for a couple of seconds and answered yes; I have thought about it a couple of times. I told her how difficult it was for me to be here without my husband and Scarlett. I shared how much I missed home and all the people who love and support me. I explained that not knowing when I can go home is extremely difficult, much more difficult than I ever thought it would be. I was nervous about her reaction. She scribbled notes while I poured out how I really felt. But I explained that the reason I didn't leave is that *I know* that Martita is a part of my family; she is our daughter. I know that we are destined to adopt our little girl and that is why I don't quit.

Then the social worker told me that she thought I was a very strong woman and that she admired my strength and faith. She went on to say, she knew I would continue to be strong and be a good mother to Martita. My response (as a strong woman) was to cry and hug her at the same time!

The best news came when she told us that we were finished with our fostering period and that we would definitely be in the June Consejo. Of course, we don't know when that will be, but we have finished this step in the process. Progress!

There are still so many items to check off the list, and the question remains as to when we will return home, but none of that matters right now. The moments I will relive over and over from today are Scarlett telling our social worker how excited she is to have Martita as a sister, and Lucie taking her little sister's hand without being asked. I will think about what I said about how much I love and miss my husband when he's away and how this is a challenging and difficult process. Sometimes admitting your vulnerability shows real strength. It's hitting me just how proud I am of all of us right now. We have sacrificed so much to be a family and will always do so to remain one.

This was a good day . . . Another step forward!

4 Comments:

mawyer said . . .
Yeah Lesa! I'm so thankful the visit went well! As I read the blog my eyes started tearing up—nothing wrong with a strong woman crying, right! I truly love reading your daily blogs and am so glad you're doing it. We think of you every day and keep you guys in our prayers. We are so looking forward to the day you bring your entire family home! Love ya! T

Amy said . . .
Hi Lesa!! What an answer to prayer!! I can't imagine how stressed you and Tim must have been through that meeting. God has and will continue to "have your back" through the next month or so. Isn't it so awesome to know that HE is right there with you . . . every step.
    We can't wait to see the entire Grimes family.
Love you,
Amy

CTGoodyear said . . .
Hi Honey, finally able to read your blog again. Hopefully I'll be able to catch you on Skype. I love you so much and am so proud of all of you. Give my girls a big hug and lots of kisses. Mom XOXOXOXXO

ivaniam97 said . . .
WONDERFUL NEWS!!!
XOXO

Wednesday, June 17, 2009
The HUGE Cockroach!!

First, let me warn you that I have become a little feisty these past few weeks. I guess it's because of what's going on in my life right now—I feel vulnerable due to all the changes and challenges. This feeling of uncertainty is bringing out an edgier side to my personality. I have been saying inappropriate things and cursing a lot (don't judge me). I have surprised my husband time and time again, so let me just apologize now. And I promise to clean up my act . . . soon!

So, the title of my blog is pretty self-explanatory. After all the bug killing that I have endured; I faced a new challenge last night. It was my first night without my husband (so no, *the big cockroach* is not referencing him . . . see, inappropriate)!!!

After I finished my nightly routine (wash my face, brush my teeth with bottled water, moisturize, clean off my feet, gloss on a little Chapstick, and pop a cough drop in a mouth— maybe this is all *too much information* but hang in there with me, I am trying to set the stage) I settled into bed. As I reached for my Kindle, I saw the biggest cockroach I have ever seen! There he was, spying on me in the right-hand corner of my room, above the door! I'm not sure it was a cockroach . . . I just know it was a critter with black, long antennas, several legs and measured roughly three inches long and two inches wide . . . *Eeewwww*!!!

My thoughts began to race. Does this thing fly? Will it go away if I turn the lights out? Is it a vegetarian? Is it possible to sleep with this thing alive scurrying about my house? Well, I knew the answer to the last question . . . *No way!* So, I decided that I had to kill the big cockroach!

First, I attacked my nemesis with disinfectant spray, which kills viruses, bacteria, mold, and mildew. It should do some damage, right? Seriously, I sprayed and sprayed, and I think maybe one of its legs twitched a little. Frantically, I scanned the room until I spied my next weapon; an air freshener and room deodorizer. I threw it at the cockroach and made a direct hit to the middle of its body (two points). The cockroach fell to the ground, took off running and repeatedly tried to disappear under the bedroom door, but it was too big to fit.

I kept thinking, *"step on it Lesa!"* but for whatever reason,

I could not do it! After several attempts, the little demon finally squeezed under the door and took off running into the family room. I kept thinking, *My children are in danger*, so I need to kill this thing *now*! So, I took off my flip-flop, let out a loud scream and slammed my shoe down to smash it! It took me a couple of tries (fast little bugger), but I heard the loud crunch and was so proud of myself for killing it. My glory was short-lived. I realized that I had to pick up the *cucaracha* and flush it down the toilet!

Thank the Lord, there was a storm brewing outside my window. When I turned off the lights, the sound of rain drowned out my thoughts of the cockroach as well as the sounds of my loud screams and the death slap of my flip-flop. I'm hoping (praying) this was my first and only experience with a bug of this size.

Goodnight Friends!

1 Comment:

Timothy said . . .
Feisty? LOL . . . ah . . . understatement of the century! So everyone knows I think I might now be married to Sailor First Class Grimes . . . if you know what I mean ;-) I love you and am so proud of the fact that you didn't wake up Martita "The Bug Killer" Grimes to go after it! Yes, Lesa regularly tells Martita to kill bugs bigger than an ant . . . and like a good daughter she does it!

Thursday, June 18, 2009
Smile for the Camera!!

Today was supposed to be a *quiet* day for us . . . no plans except for a run in the morning with Scarlett and then off to the pool. We have been getting a lot of rain in the afternoons, so we planned to watch the movie *ET* and chill. Sidebar: This eighties classic is Lucie's favorite movie, which she doesn't understand is like twenty years old, so she's always asking people, "Have you seen *ET*? It is the best movie ever!"

Well, after our run and a hot breakfast of eggs and bacon, we got a call from our friends Jack and Beth who asked us to join them for a trip to the mall to get our kids' passport/visa/immigration pictures taken. This was on our *to do* list—so we said, "Sure."

We went to the pool for a quick dip, showered, and then we were off to the mall for our photo session. There are several stipulations to the passport photo: #1 Martita's hair has to be pulled back, #2 the photo has to be two inches by two inches, #3 the picture must have a white background, and #4 we need eight copies. Sounds easy enough, right? Well, Jack and Beth's adopted son, Ignacio went first. He sat there perfectly straight and smiled on cue. The photographer took one picture and boom . . . finished. Then it was Martita's turn . . .

Our girl does *not* take good pictures. She has a difficult time looking at the camera. She won't smile, and she doesn't sit still at *any time*! As you might have guessed; we had a few issues. The first few shots did not work out, then the camera ran out of battery (only in Nicaragua), so we waited for the photographer to come back with a charged camera. I took this opportunity to *coach* my girl. In my best Spanish I told Martita, "Love, you need to sit still, smile and look at me when he is taking the picture."

She replied, "*Si* Momma!" She always says, "*Si* Momma!" ;)

When the photographer was ready to snap another photo, Martita looked at me. I smiled and told her to smile, which she did but shut her eyes. This went on for the next several shots (all with my daughter's eyes closed). When I told her to open her eyes, she put her hands up to her face to open them, then the camera ran out of charge (*again*), and the photographer disappeared.

Now by this time, Lucie is losing it in the lobby, screaming for her Mommy, Scarlett is rolling her eyes and our friends must be thinking, "Why did we bring *them* along?"

Then it hit me . . . Martita smiled just like her Mommy—big grin and eyes closed! My little girl was listening so well and doing exactly what she was told to do. When the photographer returned, I said it was up to him, so I stepped back and stopped interfering. First shot, eyes open—no smile but she looked right at the camera. Success! Albeit, she looks like a criminal, I think the photos will work. Just goes to show you how smoothly things can go when I take a step back and hand over control. Another lesson learned.

We had a great lunch with our friends, did a little shopping and came home. After having a nice dinner with my girls; I am exhausted. It surprises me when I hear people say that there is nothing to do here. Maybe it's just *my* family, but we seem to fill the days with so much activity that I don't know what else we could handle.

Tomorrow is another *quiet* day . . . who knows what will come of it. I'm looking forward to another adventure!

Friday, June 19, 2009
Saying Goodbye . . .

Well, as you may have guessed . . . our relaxing day turned into a very busy one. We received a call from the director of the orphanage, Natalia, who told us the Davila children were leaving Puente de Amistad *today* to return to their family. There are five Davila kids; Yolanda, Ricardo, Kamiel, Maria, and Mario. Our family is very close to these kids, which is why I have very mixed emotions about this news. Yes, it's a blessing they're going home to their parents but how sad for everyone (including me) who loves these kids and have been part of their family since we started coming here.

The girls and I left this morning to spend time with all the Davila's. Maria and Mario have been favorites of ours from the beginning. My husband always wanted to adopt their five-year-old boy, Mario—who we met at age two. The children's mother does visit them every month, and they all look forward to seeing her. They love her very much. Their father lives in a neighboring city but does not come to visit often. They also have another three-year-old brother who lives with their mom. Their mom doesn't work, but takes care of six children ranging from three to twelve years old.

Currently, Mi Familia employees are reviewing all the *orphan* cases in Nicaragua to determine if the orphans are qualified to live at the orphanage. Kids (with families) who are staying at the orphanage for financial reasons are being sent home to their relatives. When the kids return home, the government will provide financial assistance to help care for the children. I think this program has merit. Kids should be with their biological families whenever possible. But in this case . . . is it possible? Is it the best solution for them?

For the Davila's . . . the situation is dire. Their mother doesn't have a job, or food to care for six kids, and there are no beds where her kids can sleep. Today, as the kids waited for their mother to show up, Mi Familia called and told Natalia that they could not be returned to their mom due to the lack of food and accommodations. It has been postponed until July 2nd. When the kids heard the news, they were devastated. They sobbed and were inconsolable. I held Maria as she cried while the girls and I repeatedly told her that we loved her. When Mario heard his mom wasn't coming, he started crying. Scarlett just held him and rubbed his back. I came back to check on her after about fifteen minutes, and Mario was asleep on Scarlett's lap. Little love.

We often ask visiting groups this question, "Would you rather live with your parents in *La Chureca* (the dump) where there is no food, toys, and beds and survive by pillaging through the trash or would you rather live without your parents in the orphanage where you could go to school, eat regularly, and flourish?"

Tim and I are always astounded by the responses. There was a sweet, nine-year-old girl Sydney on our last mission trip who told us she would live in the dump because being with her parents is all that mattered. Amazing, isn't it? This is how *all* the kids feel. It's the same answer, no matter which kid you ask. In our world of big houses, multiple cars, and 401K's . . . Can you imagine having to make this choice? Sadly, this is not a hypothetical question for the Davila family. In the end, they've chosen their parents.

I don't know how to feel about this. I don't know how to pray for these kids. I want them to stay healthy, to be loved daily, to go to school, to have a future. Do their parents have any idea what these kids are giving up to be with them? Do we appreciate the fact that our kids will never have to make this choice? I will have to say, "goodbye" and it won't be easy. I have a little more time to love on each of them and to tell them how special they are. I just pray it makes a difference and that their future is bright . . .

2 Comments:

Timothy said . . .

Well, as you might expect and as Lesa has written, this is a real heartbreaker for me. Mario is the one that came running to me as I got off the bus back in the spring and almost skidded out in the process as he rounded the corner. We have a special relationship, for sure. This is a perfect example of "getting your heart dirty." Baye, you mentioned in the body of your blog that you weren't sure how to pray . . . and then at the end, you state that you pray, "It makes a difference and that their future is bright." I think you know more about prayer than you thought. The time you have between now and July 2 is a complete blessing. And while I miss you a ton, you being there and at the orphanage, each and every week is a TOTAL blessing to us all. Love you

Saturday, June 20, 2009
I Seriously Am Not Making This Stuff Up!!!

Today is my Scarlett's Birthday! I started the morning off with our tradition of telling her about the day she was born. I included all the details—like how I knew I was in labor, how I pushed for what seemed like a lifetime, and then how this gorgeous baby girl came into the world with a crown of dark hair with red-tipped ends! All the nurses took pictures of her and said it looked like she had frosted hair. It is such a rarity in my family to have a child with dark hair. Scarlett is the first and only one so far. I loved her from the second she was born, and she continues to amaze me, her beauty (on the inside and out) her loving heart and her upbeat attitude.

My baby girl is twelve years old today (going on twenty) and she is a complete joy. Scarlett's birthday made me wonder about the birth story of our sweet Martita. Since I don't know her birth story, I will describe to her how her *Papi* and I felt when we first saw her. I'll explain how we knew she was meant to be with us. She is our second dark-haired child who we love so dearly. I hope that story will suffice and that she'll know that even though we aren't her birth parents, we chose her to be our daughter.

We planned to go to the beach since Scarlett loves the ocean. Pacific, here we come. Our good friend Natalia and her daughter, Antonia came with us. We were planning on going to a resort called *Montelemar* but it was a little too pricey, so we opted for a neighboring beach *Vistamar*. As I've described in past entries, the roads in Nicaragua put our potholes to shame! Bumps and brakes at every turn! There's no speed limit or limit to the craziness that occurs once you strap on your seatbelt. Strike that. There aren't any seatbelts! Praise the Lord; we made it to the beach safe and sound and enjoyed a day of fun in the sun.

However, on the way home our travels were a little more *eventful*. I promise I am not making this stuff up. We were on the road for about ten minutes (it's about an hour drive) when we passed a large herd of cattle on the road . . . again, this is pretty common. I think about thirty cows were moving in the same direction as us. Our cab driver, Norman honked the horn, moved over into the other lane (two-lane road), and we continued down the road passing cattle. We traveled at forty miles an hour and had passed about half the cattle when a huge black cow darted into our lane. The cow was so close to the passenger side (where I sat) I could literally reach out and touch him! Norman quickly jerked the wheel, and we swerved just before hitting the cow, I am still shocked that we didn't! I yelled out *Jesus!*

Lucie, Martita and Antonia were asleep but woke up suddenly to the swerving car and the people screaming inside.

I was just catching my breath when Norman suddenly jerked the wheel *again*, only this time we hit something! He slowly stopped the car and started to back up as we all screamed, "What happened?! What did we hit?!"

Norman stopped the car a few feet back and jumped out. He messed around with something as a few choice words flew out of his mouth. (FYI, I know all those choice Spanish words.) Then, Norman stood up holding (wait for it) a very large iguana by the neck. The lizard had blood on its face and did not look happy, but at least it was still alive. To repay Norman for running him over, the iguana pierced our cab driver's hands with its claws.

People were walking down the road surveying the scene, so Norman sparked a conversation with an onlooker and nonchalantly asked the woman if she wanted the iguana. She smiled, walked across the street and grabbed it! Antonia looked at me smiling. I was in total shock. What in the world was the lady going to do with an injured iguana? Not a great pet; this guy seemed a little too wild to tame. Antonia explained that iguana is a delicious meal for people here. I seriously, could not make this stuff up!

I began to wonder if I ever ate anything here that looked like an iguana. Do I really know what all the toppings on my last pizza were? What does it even taste like? I know I am getting out of my comfort zone and all but that's a little too much for me. Now that it's on my radar; I will definitely be on the look-out.

As we got back on the road towards home, I was a little shaken up about how close we came to hitting that cow. I couldn't stop thinking about what could have happened to the five of us sitting in the back seat without seat belts. What amazes me is how Natalia, Antonia, and Norman reacted like it was no big deal. Surprisingly, I too, was calmer than usual.

I want to tell you a little bit about Norman, our cab driver who we met shortly after we moved here. We had a couple of cab drivers before Norman but had issues with cost and timeliness, so we went on the hunt for someone who was a better fit for our family. We had a choice of either renting a car, which Ignacio's adoptive parents did, or using a cab to get around. I did not feel comfortable driving the streets alone with the girls in tow not knowing where to go or what I would do if we had car trouble. It's not cheap to rent a car, and I also liked the idea of having a local driver to watch out for us.

Norman came highly recommended and over a brief period of time, became part of our family. We call him almost every day to take us to the grocery store, restaurant or to the beach. He is always there for us. Every evening that he drops me off he says, "Ms. Lesa, you can call me no matter what time if you need any kind of help."

I sweetly refer to Norman as my *Nicaragua husband*. We are both happily married to other people, but he has taken such good care of us that I consider him family.

Today, I told Norman, *No more surprises please*, so I'm praying I have no more cow stories to tell you. I also hope there aren't any future iguana, cockroach or bug stories either. Been there; done that! Nicaragua continues to surprise me. There are so many things I experience here that remind me to stop and reflect on how different my life is in the States. What I will say is, even the *quiet days* are never dull here. Each day, I learn more about myself and my girls. I truly appreciate what an awesome experience this is for my family.

So today was an exciting birthday for my girl. As I told Scarlett how exciting it is to celebrate your birthday in Nicaragua, I realized that Lucie celebrated her birthday here (April 8th) as did I (May 16th). We pray that we will *not* be here to celebrate my husband's or Martita's birthdays, which are both in November!

Love and Blessings to you all—*buenos noches*!

1 Comment:

mawyer said . . .
Happy belated Birthday Scarlett! Sounds like you had a fun and very exciting day!
Love,
Tracy & Sydney

Sunday, June 21, 2009
Defiance . . .

Defiance can be a good thing . . . being defiant can reflect how strongly you believe in something or convey how solid your convictions are. However, when a kid (your kid) demonstrates defiance; it can be a challenge, which is putting it mildly. Our girl Martita is very defiant and today was tough.

We started Sunday off at one of my favorite places; the church at the orphanage. Since today is Father's Day in Nicaragua,

Pastor Martin gave a tribute to the fathers and their roles in our lives. It was a very emotional day; I miss my husband and wish he were with me. I'm so proud of the father Tim has become.

We Skyped with Tim earlier this morning, and he began the conversation by telling each one of his daughters why they were special and what he loved most about them. During my trip home, I had set up a Father's Day scavenger hunt for Tim, so when we spoke to him this morning, we gave him his first clue. He went on a wild chase running through the house, looking for his gifts while we all watched him on Skype. It was a great start to the day.

After church we visited the orphanage. As I've written before, the orphanage is my happy place, and when we visit there, Martita feels at home; which is a good thing. The challenge is that she doesn't listen to me there like she does when we are by ourselves. My youngest smiles when I correct her behavior, but then she continues doing what she wants to do. Albeit, we are in front of other people, I still discipline her and make sure that she understands that I am her mother. Usually, Martita's kind heart and wanting to please attitude allow us to work through our disagreements. Today, she did not back down.

We struggled throughout the morning, and the situation escalated later at home. Martita defied me at every opportunity refusing to listen. She was in time out for most the afternoon and while in time out—acted out. She cried and screamed when she was punished and sometimes refused to obey time out. When I sent her to her room, she punched out her window screen. I got to the point today where I ran out of consequences. It was a battle.

As I began to reflect upon my time at the orphanage, it struck me again that the children are very seldom reprimanded. The staff will tell the kids not to do something, but if they don't listen, the adults just laugh and shake their heads. I can't imagine how difficult it must be caring for forty children, so I completely understand their position. However, now I'm dealing with the consequences. Due to the lack of discipline, the children do not comprehend why they can't do what they want to do. The messages I send Martita are conflicting with how she was raised at the orphanage, so she is struggling with where she fits and how to behave.

Today, I got a taste of how difficult this transition will be, but I hope we made some progress. I have to show Martita that she is loved and that she is part of us. However, I also have to communicate what I expect of her as a member of our family. (I have to be tough now so that we can live in peace later.) Sometimes I want to pull my hair out as I question how well I'm doing as a parent. I know we'll be a much more united front when we're home with Tim, my partner. When I am at my wit's end, I just hold on to the thought that she is my beautiful little girl who loves to please (most of the time).

Defiance . . . it's a good thing, right?!

2 Comments:

ctGoodyear said . . .
Hang in there Sweetie. She'll come around. Love Mom & Tom
XOXOXO

Donna said . . .
Hi Lesa,
I have been away from the blog for a little while, but am now caught up (having smiled, laughed, and teared up through all the entries). It sounds like yesterday was a very challenging day, but you held your ground and survived! I hope today was a wonderful day for you and the girls and look forward to reading all about it! You are always in our prayers.
Donna

⟨ Chapter 10 ⟩

Jesus Take the Wheel

Monday, June 22, 2009
A Little Control Today . . .

I want to thank everyone who is reading my blog; you have no idea what your words of encouragement and support mean to me . . . so please, keep reading, keep praying and keep those comments coming. They are my lifeline!

Today the Consejo was *supposed* to meet, and as you may have guessed from all the CAPS, they did not meet today. So again, we find ourselves in a holding pattern. They could possibly meet sometime this week, but they promised to do so next Monday. The Consejo is not known for ever meeting when they're scheduled. But, I have learned that this is out of my control, and all we can do is . . . wait.

Well, I had bigger plans today besides waiting to see if the Consejo would meet. I had plans to take an extraordinary young man, Fernando to his new home. Here's the backstory: Fernando is seventeen years old and was recently asked to leave the orphanage (because of his age). I have known him since we first started visiting Puente de Amistad. This young man is an old soul with a gift for connecting with all types of people on many different levels. Sometimes, I forget how young he is when we chat. He genuinely wants to know all about you, your family and why you traveled to Nicaragua. He has such a vibrant spirit and loves God. He has touched many people.

Last spring when our team was here, Fernando made plans to go home to his broken family. His mother is a prostitute, and his father is non-existent. Fernando has several siblings who are also struggling. I met his younger fourteen-year-old sister who had just had a baby. Fernando wanted to go home and support his family any way he could.

Soon after Fernando went home, he realized the situation was dire. They had no food, and he could not attend school. I felt like someone had thrown a brick at me when I heard he was spotted begging for money on the streets of Managua. This young, kind and courageous teenager with so much potential was now in a seemingly hopeless situation. When Tim and I heard this news, we started researching options. The organization we work with, ORPHANetwork, assisted us in identifying places Fernando could go that would support him.

When I returned to Nicaragua, I asked Natalia (director of the orphanage) about Fernando's status, and she told me he was still on the streets. So, I contacted ORPHANetwork and discussed the situation. We had several conversations with Natalia, who approached Fernando and asked him if he would be interested in living at Casa Bernabe.

Casa Bernabe is the orphanage where I stayed during my first trip to Nicaragua. It has a remarkable school (one of the best in Nicaragua) where kids also learn trades like bike repair, agriculture and baking/cooking, to help prepare them for the outside world. We would love to see Fernando there; however, their director wanted to ensure they had enough room and that we could afford to send him. Well, we worked everything out and picked up Fernando to take him to his new home.

We met with Casa Bernabe's director, Jose, who explained all about the orphanage and the process to get Fernando settled. Since I had stayed there before, I was familiar with the routine and even knew many of the workers. We met with the psychologist who would assist Fernando during the transition, helping him get settled in his new surroundings. We got a list of things he needs for school (uniform, school supplies, etc.) and some things he wants (music, music, music). The girls and I will come back on Thursday to check on Fernando and bring him everything he needs.

Driving away was difficult. We said our goodbyes, and I watched Fernando from the rear-view mirror standing under a giant tree looking so small with his head down. I couldn't take my eyes off him as he slowly walked by himself towards his new home. I'll never forget that image. I kept imagining how scared he must be and how discouraged he must feel about his family and how he couldn't help them. His pain palpable, his dreams, shattered. The loss that this young man has endured so early in life is unimaginable.

Fernando is extremely apprehensive (understandably) about his new home. He doesn't know anyone and is essentially starting over. But we explained to him how incredible it is that he has new opportunities allowing him to focus on school and his future. Being there is also the best way for him to help his family long-term. I am so excited for him.

We shared Fernando's story with our friends, and a very dear friend of ours felt so devastated by his situation that she wanted to do something, so she went to a local food bank and donated food. Since she couldn't help Fernando directly, she would help someone else. How amazing is that? Isn't that what we should all do when we feel helpless? Make a difference in any way we can? Our sweet Fernando is helping people he doesn't even know!

Fernando certainly helped me today. He helped me feel like I was able to make something good happen by letting him know how much he is loved and that we are all pulling for him. Today was a gift—one that will keep on giving throughout Fernando's journey.

1 Comment:

Timothy said . . .
Hey Love . . . The other day I found myself describing the situation with Fernando and your ability to be engaged in his life. At the end of this conversation, I said, "It is such a blessing to have you in Nicaragua" . . . and then it struck me . . . WHAT DID I JUST SAY? You are on Day forty-five as of today, I have seen you five of those days which, leaves forty without you (not that I am counting)! And it is a BLESSING that you are in Nicaragua?!?!?! Let's see . . . all of the things I caught myself saying, "BLESSING about" involved someone else's life . . . all of the others? Not me. :-(Just a little self-centered eh? Hmmmm, maybe this is a lesson for us all. Getting involved in other people's lives is hard and involves sacrifice for sure . . . but it can be such a gift in the end. You know how I always talk about the fact that things involving God tends to be "logic upside down" . . . this is yet another case of it. I know that my gift isn't about the sacrifice of missing you BUT knowing the impact you are having on Fernando, our girls and the people you touch in Nica. Love you soooooo much. P.S. AND COME HOME SOON!

Tuesday, June 23, 2009
Feeling safe . . .

I am blogging right now with my dear friend, Optimus beside me. When the girls are in bed, and I turn the TV off and wind down at night, Optimus shows up to tuck me in, so he's here with me now. No need to raise your eyebrows friends, Optimus is a lizard. I must admit that I'm not 100 percent sure if it's actually Optimus . . . it could be one of our other three geckos but since

Optimus is named after Optimus Prime from the movie *Trans-formers*, he makes me feel safe. Bonus: The little green guy loves bugs, which makes me love him even more! I may be losing it . . . having a gecko as a security blanket is a little off, right?!

I, like most people, need to feel safe, so I can function. Albeit I'm living in a third-world country in a gated and guarded (yes, we have several guards on the premises) community, I do feel pretty secure here.

My friend, Rachel called me early this morning because she needed to talk to the condo owners and wanted me to watch her children. A man (Rachel didn't know) knocked on her door at 4:00 a.m., which really shook her up. She lives on the upper floor in one of the two bedroom units and has been here about a month longer than us. She never had a problem until now. She talked to the owners who recognized this man as one of the tenants and said they would handle the problem.

When things like this happen, I become hyper-aware of the situation I am in and how I need to always be on alert to ensure my children and I are safe.

We went to a local market to purchase some clothes for Fernando today. I knew we'd be safe with our cab driver and dear friend Norman who took us to the right place and did all the negotiating for us. He told me to leave my sunglasses in the car and to hold tight to my purse . . . hmmm, maybe not the safest situation. (Where's Optimus when I really need him?!)

I held on tight to my kids, and everything went very smoothly. The shop owners were very welcoming. They smiled, talked to us and of course, touched Lucie's hair! As we were leaving, Norman took Lucie's hand and walked her back to the car. We have been blessed with so many wonderful people here . . . people who take care of us. Norman is at the top of the list.

Nicaragua is an extremely impoverished country, which translates to a lot of crime. People are starving and struggling to survive, so some people steal to eat. That's why you have to be so careful to never be in the wrong place at the wrong time.

While theft is common in Nicaragua, I honestly feel safe. I take precautions and am always on guard (which I think is appropriate), but I do have a sense of security. Again, I think I'm ultimately safe because of the people I'm blessed with on this journey.

Tomorrow is another busy day for us, but I am hoping to have some one-on-one time with Lucie. We have a meeting at Mi Familia and some more shopping to do for Fernando. My apologies, I'm exhausted and not very witty tonight. I wish you all (my loved ones) a great evening and a fabulous day tomorrow. Please know how much we love and miss you all.

2 Comments:

Timothy said . . .
"With the Autobots (your husband) gone, we cannot return life to our planet." And fate has yielded its reward: a new world (a third world) to call home. We live among its people now, hiding in plain sight (at Condo Allyson), but watching over them in secret, waiting, protecting. I have witnessed their capacity for courage (while they wait for the Consejo to meet), and although we are worlds apart, like us, there's more to them than meets the eye. I am Optimus Prime (the gecko), and I send this message to any surviving Autobots (adoptive families) taking refuge among the stars (in Nicaragua). We are here. We are waiting.

—Optimus Prime

Okay, I am not sure who the person is that is losing it at this point! I love you and PLEASE PLEASE PLEASE stay safe. XOXOXOXOX

Signed,
Sam Witwicky

wuzupinNicaLesa said . . .

VERY witty my love but because I know you so well and KNOW that you never remember much about movies . . . I have to assume that my geeky husband got this from the Internet— which makes me laugh! I love you and would like to have my Autobot with me . . . PPPLLLEEEAAASSEEE!!!!

Wednesday, June 24, 2009
Dia De Lucie

We have been in Nicaragua for forty-two days (not that I'm counting). During this time, everyone (my husband, Scarlett and me) has had a *break* from the Nicaragua experience, everyone except Lucie. I know how I feel when I have been with the kids for an entire day and cannot wait for them to go to bed so I can have some time to myself. Lucie very seldom gets that kind of time, so I planned to take my Goose out for the day, no other kids to compete with, no communication issues, no sharing, just her and I. I would focus all my energy and love on her alone. We would do whatever she wants to do, go wherever she wants to go so today was *Dia de Lucie.*

We've been talking about our special day for about a week now. Lucie's favorite movie is *Transformers* (*ET* is a close second—the girl's a Spielberg fan), so when *Transformers 2* came out, I knew that seeing it would be on the top of her list. After Norman picked us up at eleven this morning, we dropped Scarlett and Martita with my friend Rachel, then Lucie and I went to Centro Metro Mall. This is the only place I know *Transformers 2* would be playing in English (with subtitles).

The movie didn't start until 2:30 p.m., so we had a lot of time to hang out. We went into lots of shops—some for Lucie, some for Mom and everywhere we went people stopped and stared at us. Usually, I am with a large group of people when I go to the mall, but since it was just the two of us, we noticed the attention a lot more today. Everyone we encountered was very friendly. They smiled at us as they'd compliment Lucie, "What beautiful hair you have" or "You have gorgeous eyes."

Keep in mind that earlier this week Lucie told me that she hated her hair and wanted to cut it all off. However, after hearing a few kind remarks from strangers, she decided that she didn't want to chop her hair after all. (Mommy is *very* happy about that!)

We ate lunch at McDonald's (yes, I ate at a fast food place); it was Lucie's day, and that's what she wanted. As we ate, Lucie would stop eating and look up at me. I would ask "What?" and she would say, "I'm so happy to be here with you Mommy."

Precious times . . . precious girl. After gorging our french fries, we watched the movie, which was nearly three hours long but kept us on the edge of our seats. During certain parts of the film, I thought Lucie was scared, so I held her hand, and she just smiled at me. She said she was cold (a couple of times) and wanted to sit in my lap. The chilly moments seemed to align with the scary parts of the movie. :)

Walking hand in hand with my Lucie is such a joy. I love the unique person she is and admire how she is never afraid to say what's on her mind. She truly has her own identity. I'm also proud of Lucie for being the most amazing big sister to Martita. Of course, they argue and struggle (as sisters may) to find their place, but Lucie is very patient with her younger sister. She communicates so well and shows her how things work, and loves to love her and care for her.

Lucie is only six months older than Martita, but since Martita is extremely behind in many areas (e.g., communication, emotional maturity), she often acts like she is much younger than Lucie. This is a challenge because Lucie expects a lot more from Martita at times, so her patience is a gift.

Sure, I think about everything that Tim and I are sacrificing to be here in Nicaragua, but sometimes I forget to think about the girls. Lucie was forced to make some significant sacrifices. We took her out of school before Lucie had time to finish and I know she misses her friends and activities at home. Before

Martita came along, Lucie was the baby of the family and had a lot more of her mommy's and daddy's time to herself. She put everything on hold for our Nicaragua adventure. So, here's to *Dia de* Lucie. I am so proud of the person you are becoming and treasure this day we spent together.

1 Comment:

Timothy said . . .

Viva *Dia de* Luuuuuuuuucie! I am so glad you guys had such a great day. Two things about what you said above . . . 1.) If Daddy was in Nica and I took her to *TRANSFORMERS 2,* I would have heard from Mommy about how it is PG-13, TOO scary and maybe you don't want to go to the mall because I might lose Lucie!!!! 2.) When you said, "how she is never afraid to SAY WHAT SHE LIKES/WANTS and has her own identity." Hmmmmm . . . wonder where she gets THAT TRAIT FROM?!? ;-) I am SO glad you guys had a great day together . . . yeah she is one sacrificial lamb for sure. I knew she was thriving when she left me that sweet message on my cell phone. She sounded like a different girl. Okay, *Dia de* Lucie is over . . . back to the real world girlfriend . . . give her a broom, the laundry, and the fly swatter . . . BACK TO WORK!!!! XOXOXOXOXO

Thursday, June 25, 2009
Dia De Norman

Today was another amazing day! And . . . the unexpected happened (again). This seems to be a recurring theme in Nicaragua (there's also the bugs, the electricity going out, my kids driving me crazy and the smothering heat).

We were awakened this morning by our new best friend, Jacklyn, who cleans our casita and washes our clothes. Why couldn't I have met Jacklyn on day one? I love her so much. Tim says that waking up to Jacklyn is *almost* as good as waking up to him. Usually, I would say that's true, but I'm missing my husband a lot right now . . . so it's a far second. Clean house, clean laundry, how could the day get any better?! But it did . . . Scarlett and I went for a run. Way to go Scarlett! She has been running with me in the mornings and is kicking butt! I'm proud of her and pumped for me as it is the *best* way to start the day!

Norman arrived at 11:30 a.m. and took us to Casa Bernabe for our meet-up with Fernando. During our cab ride, Norman told me his story. He had actually grown up at Casa Bernabe from the age of five until he was fourteen years old. Norman told me how happy he was there. He said everyone treated him well and that the school was great! He was looking forward to seeing it again. I asked him to talk to Fernando about his experience; I thought Norman's story would help him realize what a great opportunity he has.

When we arrived, Norman kept saying how much the place had changed. (It had been twenty years since he had been there.) We met up with Fernando, and visited for a while. He seems to be doing very well. He made a few friends and said his new home is relaxing and fun. We also took a tour of the campus. I wanted to see the place where I had initially stayed, which at the time, was being torn down and needed a lot of work.

Today the missionaries stay in a beautiful building that stands in place of the old dilapidated one I remember. All the rooms have air conditioning, hot water, and showers—*unbelievable!* I ran into a few friends, met a few new people and then walked back to the car. While we were saying goodbye to Fernando, I saw Norman talking to an older man. He was very animated, but I didn't know what he was saying.

When we finished saying our goodbyes, I looked over at Norman and signaled . . . *let's go* and he said, "Wait just a minute." He came over to me and asked for a pen and paper. Then he went back to the older man. We left about five minutes later, and on the drive home, Norman told me that this man was an old friend of his. The older man worked at the orphanage and helped raise Norman and his brother. Norman hadn't spoken to or seen him in twenty years, but the man remembered Norman immediately. He got all his contact information, and then his eyes welled up with tears as he said, "Thank you so much Lesa, I am very happy."

He kept smiling and thanking me all the way home. Norman connected with a man who helped raise him. *How awesome is that*?! Norman's mood was contagious; I was so thrilled to see him so happy. It was a very moving experience. I told Norman that he should spend time at Casa Bernabe sharing his story with the older boys and mentoring them since this place was so important to him. Now he could really make a difference for those children. *Amazing*!!!

Later that day at Puente de Amistad the celebration continued at our sweet Miguel going away party. He is being adopted by a couple who live on the French Riviera . . . Hello?! Natalia kept saying, "Don't forget me!" I think she is dreaming of visiting them very soon! ;) Lucie also had a lot to celebrate at the party, since she was the first child to get a piece of candy after smacking the *piñatas*. This is a big deal because Lucie has always been afraid of *diving in* with the rest of the kids. Rightly so, it's *kids gone wild in Nicaragua* when that *piñata* comes out, so our girl is definitely acclimating herself. We had a blast with the kids and said goodbye to both Miguel and our dear friend Amanda who is going back to the States tonight. We will miss them both.

Today was such an emotional day filled with love, tears, confetti, and surprises. As I reflect upon the past ten hours, I keep returning to Norman. I know today deeply impacted him. What blows my mind is how it all goes back to Fernando (who once again) is making a difference in someone else's life. It's amazing how God works!

1 Comment:

Timothy said . . .

Baye . . . what a great story. I remember when we first started going to Nicaragua we said there is something about that place. It is just crazy the way your days unfold. And the stories you are engaged in? JUST CRAZY.

I know we always talk about the way in which both of us will be changed by this whole experience—wondering how we can capture the things, activities, thoughts, etc., and implement them when our life is *normal* again. (And oh how I crave normal right about now!) How can we bring a little Nica back here? I am not sure why it always seems to be so fulfilling there but MAYBE, JUST MAYBE, it is because THERE we take the time to do things at a pace (which can be crazy sometimes) that allows us to take God in, observe what He is doing, and get on board HIS train, as opposed to always asking Him to get on ours. It took twenty years for Norman, in Nicaragua, to make a connection with this guy . . . and twenty years for THAT guy to make the connection with Norman. They had a special moment for sure. I guess if we figure some of this out, despite it having taken fifty plus years for me and thirty-three years for you ;-) . . . the key is that we ARE figuring it out and maybe we will be better for it!

P.S. Don't get any crazy ideas with Natalia about the French Riviera! I am almost positive the two of you going there to visit Miguel is not a good idea!! Although, the vision of you on the beach, sun tan lotion . . . ooops . . . never mind. XOXOXOXOXOX

Friday, June 26, 2009
Can I Come Back?

All signs this morning pointed to a fantastic day ahead, which took a nosedive to the most difficult one to date.

We got up early for a run because we were meeting our friends, Jack, Beth and Ignacio to take a trip to Granada today. They know the best breakfast place in the area and wanted to show us. Why they keep torturing themselves by bringing us along is a mystery to me. We met up at 8:30 a.m. to make the trip. Jack and Beth have this tiny, tiny car so Scarlett, Lucie, Martita, Ignacio, and I squeezed in the back seat for the hour-plus ride. Once we got there, the smell of waffles put smiles on all our faces, and we proceeded to have the most incredible breakfast! Blueberry waffles, banana pancakes, country sausage, bacon and the best coffee I ever had. It was delicious. We then attempted to work off some calories by walking the streets of Granada.

Granada is one of the big cities located outside of Managua and is home to many beautiful churches and parks. In the center of the city, local merchants gather to sell food and trinkets. The buildings are painted in bright colors, which add to the culture of this enchanting place. We felt a little more at home here as this is a popular tourist destination for North Americans and Europeans. It was comforting to hear English being spoken everywhere we went. We stopped at a couple of hotels to check out the rooms and make future plans.

I can't believe I didn't start my blog post with this information, but my husband is coming in two weeks for a short trip (three days), and we are going to head straight for Granada and stay in a lovely hotel to get away from Managua—*I am so looking forward to it*!!!

On our way home, Jack got pulled over by the police. This often happens, so we knew the drill. We sat in the car and pretended not to speak any Spanish. This has proven to be a good tactic—frustrate the police and they may let you go, but it didn't work out for us this time. They claimed that Jack had made an illegal turn, which was pretty amazing since we were traveling straight on the same road for about ten miles *before* we saw the police and another twenty miles *after*! Corruption!

When we got home, our cab driver, Norman was waiting to take us to Mi Familia. We rushed to go to the bathroom and stretch our legs. I gave the girls a serious talk about where we were going and what it entailed. It is so crucial for the girls to be well behaved at Mi Familia. It is a stressful time, and there never seems to be enough minutes to convey our frustrations, learn about the next steps, and get in the best favor possible to expedite the process. I explained this all to the girls and reminded them that our purpose for being here is not for all the fun in the sun, trips to Granada or even visiting the orphanage. The reason we're here is to adopt Martita. These meetings are critical for making that happen.

We were immediately seen by Diego when we got there (which is a miracle in itself). I left Scarlett, Lucie, and Martita in the main lobby. Manuel (our interpreter), Diego, and I went into the back office to discuss our case. As I explained why we needed to be seen as soon as possible, I heard my girls yelling and screaming from the lobby. (After I had explained to them how important it was to be quiet and well behaved.) I just wanted to cry. Then Diego told me that the Consejo was postponed until July 3rd and I just about lost it.

I kept a smile on my face, thanked Diego for his time and asked him to please keep us in consideration during the process. Immediately after, we had a meeting with our lawyer Amelia. When I saw the girls, I just frowned at them and said, "You are all in so much trouble."

We met Amelia outside the office, and she proceeded to explain all the potential issues that may come up and delay our case even longer. There may be problems with the birth certificate or another delay in the Consejo . . . I didn't really know how to respond except to say that we have done *everything* they have asked us, when they have requested, and that we deserve to be a priority case at this point. I tried to remind Ameila that her job as our attorney is to *help* us overcome these obstacles and not just tell me what can possibly go wrong. I already know that every part of the process can go wrong.

On the way home, I felt my anger and frustration bubbling

beneath my skin, but I knew I had to keep it together. I explained our situation to Norman, and all he could say was how sorry he was for our troubles. The girls were finally quiet. I think they are very intuitive and knew that they had overstepped their boundaries.

Martita was sent to her room as soon as we got home, and I asked the two older girls to decide what they felt was the best consequence for them. So, everyone is in time out and missing a movie or toy for the rest of the day. Consequences are supposed to work, right? I sometimes feel that it makes little or no difference.

I made dinner, cleaned the house and got ready for our trip to the orphanage tomorrow. Then I Skyped my husband. That's when I lost it. I explained what happened today and just cried and cried. I told him how frustrated I was that I have no control over the adoption process. I have no control over how our lawyer is falling short of her responsibilities and how our girls misbehaved. I told him that I'm done, and I want to come home. Tim talked to the girls and reinforced everything I had explained to them. He is such a great parent and partner.

I know that I have terrific kids, who for the most part, are very considerate and well behaved. However, it's the *perfect storm* here sometimes. I am feeling such a significant amount of pressure to keep this process moving so I can get us home. I had no idea this would be such a challenge, so when I need my girls to be on their best behavior, and I need to hear confirmation from Diego or Amelia, and none of that happens, I feel frustrated and alone.

When something needs to get done, I do it. I own my responsibilities, and if I fall short, then I have to deal with the consequences. There are no consequences here. I've done everything I am supposed to do, crossed every T dotted every I, and still haven't moved forward. The stress has got me in a choke hold; I can barely breathe.

I am so afraid to let my guard down and cry. I am terrified that if I allow myself to feel this pain that I won't be able to claw my way out of this dark pit and be positive. It really scares me. I'm trying so hard to be strong, to be patient, to be the best mom I can be, but I am really done with all of it right now. I don't care that the government here sucks, that the process is ridiculous or that it's someone else's fault. I just want to go home with my family.

In the middle of my breakdown, as I was cooking dinner, I spied an ant that I needed to kill. The little shit actually flew at me! Flying ants . . . you cannot be serious! I'm afraid to ask, *What else can happen?*

We still have such a long road ahead but at this very moment, I want to scream, "I don't want to do it anymore."

I know I have to stick it out, but this sucks. Someday I will look back at this experience and only remember the good times and appreciate how the difficult times made me a stronger person. But I'm in the middle of it and can't see my way out. I don't know how much more I can take.

I'm sorry to be such a downer, but I am feeling very lonesome and lost right now. I've already had two glasses of wine and peanut M&M's . . . what else can I indulge in? I will have a good night's sleep, and everything will look brighter in the morning, right? We are going to the orphanage where we will hop on a bus and hit the beach. I think that's exactly what I need, a fix with all my kids—they always give me strength.

Here's to a better and brighter tomorrow and to me coming back to myself.

2 Comments:

Timothy said . . .
Good Morning My Love . . . I have tried to type a comment here a few times and can't seem to come up with the words. I was witness to your frustration last night and feel more helpless than ever. I remember several weeks back when yet again, a setback had occurred and Jack (Ignacio's adoptive father) posted on Facebook the discouraging news. I knew

Jack was real, albeit a pastor (yeah that doesn't keep him from being a person folks) when he stated in the update that he didn't want to hear any, *Well it's all in God's timing crap* . . . he was *not in the mood.* I liked what he said THEN . . . I can relate to what he said NOW. So, folks on the blog, you can view this as "heresy" if you want, but here is how I feel right now. We are pissed off . . . REALLY pissed off. This is not about *doing God's work, winning favor with God,* or any of that other crap. This is about sorting through the bull that is Nicaragua . . . about sorting through cultural differences that are CRAZY . . . and about GETTING MY FAMILY HOME!!!! Enough is enough! Our lawyer, the people at Mia Familia, and everyone touching our case repeatedly saying as a flippin' excuse "It is in God's hands."

"What?" I say. That is a lame excuse . . . at some point, people have to understand that WE are the hands, arms, legs, feet, etc. OF God. We cannot and should not sit idly by when we see or witness injustices happening in the world. Unbelievable. SO, I was going to say, "Sorry for this rant" . . . but I apologize for nothing at this point. Baye . . . you have shown more strength in a dire situation/environment than I have ever seen. I admire you and love you deeply. Here's to a better day today and going forward. Keep the faith my love and know in the end you will find peace. I can't wait to see you soon. XOXOXOXOXOXOXOXOXOXO

Saturday, June 27, 2009
The Good, Bad, and Ugly

I hope that I didn't freak anyone out with my last blog, but I thank you for listening. Although we will continue to have some great times here in Nicaragua, the underlying stress and frustrations are real. When I actually write about (no filter) what I'm going through; it helps me work through my feelings. I'm sorry to have been so down last night; I'm trying so hard to be strong.

Another reason I am blogging this entire experience is to have an account for our Martita when she gets older. I want her to know the good, the bad, and the ugly.

The good—my beautiful girls (sometimes they're also the bad and the ugly) my supportive husband, the other adoptive families, the kids at the orphanage, the people of Nicaragua, and all the new experiences.

The bad—feeling alone without my husband here, the delays, the postponements, the bugs, the bugs, the bugs, no air conditioning, no dishwasher, no hot water, no washing machine, no dryer (the list goes on and on).

The ugly—the bugs, the heat, the adoption process and my mood from time to time.

So please be patient with me when I let off some steam. I have come back from my mini-breakdown, and with the support of my husband and friends, I will squeeze all the sunshine I can out of the next few weeks.

I have one quick story to tell you before I go. When we got home from the beach today, we were greeted by a ginormous moth (I could be completely wrong as this could be some other type of creature) in our kitchen. It was black and scary looking. The winged devil was flying about trying to get out of the house when it landed on the kitchen window, where it stayed for a while. After dinner, I always shut that window to prevent bugs from creeping in. While the girls were in the kitchen helping me clean up, I knew I had to close the window. As I predicted, the moth demon started to fly around. I encouraged Scarlett to pick it up by its wings and throw it outside. She looked at me like I had six heads!!!

Then it hit me . . . it was time to bring in the big guns, Martita; our bug killer! I called her over and explained the situation. She went after the demon and grabbed its wing, but the moth flew out of her hand. She was fearless in her pursuit. My little girl tried again and again. We all encouraged her, *You can do it Martita . . . get um*! Finally, she grabbed it and squeezed it hard in her little hand. She headed to the door to chuck it when the little bugger flew right back in! Lucie and Scarlett let out blood-curdling screams. Martita started jumping up and down. I'm sure she was wondering, "What is wrong with these crazy *gringos*?" I must admit that I, too, was totally freaked out at this point.

Amidst all the chaos, we lost the creature in the house. Finally, I spotted it on the dining room chair and pointed it out to my youngest daughter, *Get um!*

Such an ace; this time when Martita stepped out of the house, with the demon in hand, I closed the door to ensure it could not fly back in, however, my Martita was out there as well. So, we brought her back in, and the demon was out. Kudos to my Martita, the bug killer!

Here's to a great rest of the weekend, to a light heart, to a quick smile and to focus on the good, not the bad or the ugly.

1 Comment:

Timothy said . . .
After reading this blog I knew my Baye was at least partially back from the DARK SIDE!

YEAH!!!!! I can tell you're feeling more like yourself, any time you use our children to do tasks like killing bugs. Too bad Scarlett is getting old enough to be wise to your tactics! (Looking at you with six heads.) It was also interesting how calm and cool and collected everyone looked on Skype. I hope right? This after a long drive and day at the beach. Hmmmmm . . . Benadryl? Hope you had a nice relaxing evening of TV after the kids went to bed . . . LOL TEN MORE DAYS AND I AM NICA BOUND!!!!

Sunday, June 28, 2009
Relaxation

Happy Sunday! Sundays are my favorite days here in Nicaragua. Actually, I think Sunday is my favorite day of the week—period. Church with good friends, some alone time with God, lunch with my family, precious time with the kids from the orphanage and sometimes . . . a little relaxation. Relaxation is a goal I've recently strived to achieve here.

After church, we helped serve ice cream to the children from the orphanage and other community members. I told my girls that we would get ice cream together after we had lunch. Big gulps . . . Martita listened! Albeit she gave me quite the dirty look, she listened to Momma. I was so proud of Martita for passing the ice cream test. Since I forgot to pack our lunches today, Norman picked us up early, and we went out to eat as a family. It was *almost* like home (except we're missing one key person). After lunch, we did some grocery shopping and then came home for some . . . yes, *relaxation* just typing the word makes me feel better.

Once we got back to the condo it was time for the next *big* challenge; nap time . . . The three letter word poses a huge obstacle for us every day. Typically, when the word "nap" is uttered my youngest refuses to listen, fights me, and receives a consequence (losing privileges like pool time, TV, watching movies). Not today . . . Martita fell right asleep. I was so *relaxed* that I took a short nap myself.

After feeling refreshed after our siesta, we hit up the pool. We haven't been for several days due to our hectic schedule, so the girls were very excited to splash around for an hour before dinner. We went out to eat with our friends at a pizza place near the house. The food was great and the company was even better. Again, my Martita, Lucie, and Scarlett were so well-behaved. Seeing them relaxed and happy, makes me relaxed and happy.

What a great way to start the week especially since the Consejo is supposed to meet on Friday. (I was told they could even meet sooner.) The Consejo was originally *supposed* to meet last Monday, which was pushed to Friday, which didn't happen, so please pray for some good news. Once the Consejo meets, we'll still have more items to check off the list, but this meeting is pivotal, and if it happens we'll be celebrating. My husband will be here soon, and *I hope* we can celebrate this . . . together.

2 Comments:

Timothy said . . .

Funny that I was totally *relaxed* and *calm* as I was reading your blog . . . and then you seriously reminded me this is "Consejo Week" and I knotted up . . . UGH. Remember a few weeks back we were talking about the time I got my MBA and how I was going to find some *really cool things to do* with the hours I would get back . . . no more school-related studying, reading, etc. And I said during that conversation that this kind of feels the same way? One thing I don't want to try and fill in my/our daily routines will be *worrying about the flippin' Consejo*. I say we don't worry about a whole lot of anything once you guys get home. We should put a big sign over our bed, and the door outside that says, *Remember the Consejo*? WOW, we would be the happiest people . . . NO WORRIES! XOXOXOXOXO

mawyer said . . .

Lesa, *mi amiga*—I have just read the last four days of your blog (I am so far behind and am so sorry—the days for me have been flying by without a minute to think). I am praying for you guys and think of you every day. I love that you are so honest in your blogs and are sharing everything with those of us who can't be with you in Nica during this time. I so wish I was there the other day when you were *on the dark side*. I'm glad to see you had a relaxing day and enjoyed your Sunday. Also, glad to know that Tim will be off to see you in just a short time.
Love ya, T

(Chapter 11)

Focusing on the Lessons

Monday, June 29, 2009
What I Will Bring Home . . .

This blog is dedicated to the ones I love. I am in the middle of one of the most challenging experiences of my life and am *surrounded* by people who love me. I wake up every morning excited to start my day, wondering who I will see on Skype? Who will I talk to on the phone? That's because not a single day goes by that I don't feel supported by my friends and family.

How blessed am I?

Today I received several calls via Skype, which made my day. First on the line was my dear friend, Sue. She caught me up on what has been going on stateside, listened to my frustrations and helped me contemplate the challenges and rewards of being here. (Obviously, one of the best rewards will be hanging out with my friend again!) She made me laugh, and I felt closer to home.

Then I heard from my sweet Di and JJ. They are truly like family to us and have been taking good care of my husband in my absence. We made plans to get together after we return to the States; seeing them makes us all miss home so much. The girls and I felt loved and happy by the end of the conversation.

Next, I Skyped with my sister Vicki (for the first time). She couldn't get her sound to work for a while but fixed the bug, and we had a great conversation. It was so good to see her pretty face while reminiscing about our memorable visit last month. I saw my sweet niece Taylor and caught up on their lives. Albeit, my sister scored very low on my *How well do you know Lesa?* quiz on Facebook, she knows me better than most and always gives me the love and support I need.

I have to give a shout out to my good friend Tracy, my cheerleader, who always keeps in touch and prays for my family.

And to Donna, who is my dear friend who also takes care of my husband and is the best prayer warrior I know.

Way to go Mom for being Queen Skyper! I am so proud that she has overcome her technology challenges so that I can see her beautiful smile on a constant basis.

To my cousin Sandy, who is like a sister to me. She reads my blog to her co-workers every day, which makes me feel like she is sharing this experience with me. Oddly enough, although we're separated by hundreds of miles, I have never felt closer to her.

Then there are my friends here in Nicaragua (Beth, Jack, Rachel, John, Natalia, Gabriela . . . and of course all my kids) who are always there with a sympathetic ear and a warm hug. No matter what kind of day I'm having, they can always put a smile on my face. They help me remember what is really important.

Finally, to my main squeeze, my love, who never fails to call me (even when he's so tired). He has been my partner through this entire process—seeing him puts my day to rest. He listens and gives me a chance to share all my feelings. I know that he is my biggest fan. Tim, you are my greatest blessing.

Thank you, thank you, thank you dear ones for keeping in touch, commenting on my blog, sending emails and picking up the phone. I am also grateful for all the people who tell Tim they're sharing in our story through my blog and keeping me in their thoughts and prayers. Each and every one of you means the world to me. I could *not* do this without your love and support. You make the days go by faster and give me the security in knowing that I am supported through the good, the bad and the ugly.

My husband is always asking me what I will *take home* from this experience. This is a difficult question to answer but what I do know is this; my life is blessed with the most beautiful, loving and caring people. We often take these relationships for granted but I will not going forward. I *know* how much I am loved and supported. It's a pretty amazing gift to bring home, don't you think?

Tuesday, June 30, 2009
Debbie Downer

By the name of the title, you know where this blog is heading . . . Send in the wine, M&M's and reinforcements. We started off the day with a run, a delicious breakfast and some time at the pool. We decided to see *Transformers 2* again, since the first time it was just Lucie and I. Scarlett was a little green with envy after hearing her younger sister rehash the movie repeatedly, so we went to Metro Centro to see Optimus Prime (the Transformer not the lizard) and do a little shopping.

All was well until I heard from our friend Jack, who met with Diego at Mi Familia. Surprise, but not really a surprise, Diego told Jack that the Consejo would probably *not* meet this Friday. Apparently, for the Consejo to meet they must receive a final authorization, which they haven't received yet, which means it *probably* won't happen. Well, what I figured out is this: when they say, *for sure* it means maybe, and when they say, *probably* it means, never. So now, our *for sure* date is next week. Lord, how much longer will this Consejo be postponed?

Gotta love my friend Jack who is doing everything he can to spin this news positively. I, on the other hand, am not buying it. This is the fourth time they have postponed the Consejo for

June, which has carried over to July?! This government *never* does what they commit to, which leaves my family in limbo.

When did I turn into *Debbie Downer*?

At least I am doing much better than I was a few days ago, I haven't lost it again, but I am definitely not the woman I know and love. I remember that lady who my husband always described as the woman who *carries her own weather* or the one who *brings sunshine everywhere she goes*.

Where did Lesa go?

Well, this time I refuse to let *Debbie* win. It is only another seven-day delay, right? It will give us something to celebrate when my husband is here in eight more days. I told Scarlett we are going to the beach this week to celebrate the here (we're on an exotic vacation) and the now (we're not leaving anytime soon). Now that's a positive spin.

I know that once I get home, it will only be a matter of days until my life returns to *normal*. My routine will set in; I will have my friends back, be with my husband, live in my house . . . and get on with my life. In the meantime, I will enjoy our summer in Nicaragua, not part of the summer (like we initially thought), but the entire summer. I am trying, with all my might, to make my: "What I did on my summer vacation essay err blog" a diary of positive memories. (Can you tell I'm trying to talk myself into this?!)

Here's to a bright and sunny tomorrow and the return of the woman who carries her own weather.

2 Comments:

Timothy said . . .
Consejo—So what exactly IS the "Consejo?" I realize I have no grasp of the Spanish language so for me NOT to know what one is, is really not too strange. So, the geek in me decided . . . let's do a little web search and see what I can find out. The first Google return that I got was for a BLOG called "Consejo." I

thought HMMMMMM, interesting . . . and then when I clicked on it, I got a notice that said, "This Blog is for INVITED readers only." WOW . . . okay. The next click was from some frustrated person dealing with the "Consejo National Adoption Agency" . . . IN GUATEMALA! So here is what I have so far . . . Secret Society, International Society . . . I clicked on. Wiki says Consejo is the "first album" of some super Latino band! Okay, NOW THAT MAKES SENSE TO ME. At least in my own mind, I can see how a rock band is up partying all night, lots of groupie chicks, drinking . . . no wonder they can't keep a date! I decided to CLICK one more time . . . Consejo is also the hottest RAP and HIP HOP group in . . . CUBA! Ah ha! Ever since the Cuban missile crisis, we have been on a stand down with Cuba! So that explains it . . . the Consejo is not ALLOWED to meet for the best interests of the U.S.! It's an international political thing. I knew it HAD TO BE SOMETHING OF MAJOR INTERNATIONAL IMPORTANCE BECAUSE REALLY . . . OUR TWO DOGS, STELLA THE LAB, AND ESME THE BULLDOG COULD FIND A WAY TO DO AT LEAST A FEW THINGS THEY ARE SUPPOSED TO!!!! Okay my love, sorry for the rant. I saw the weather forecast for next week in Managua . . . hot and sunny. I knew when I saw that forecast that you must be living there! Kick Debbie Downer in the ass and tell her to go start a rap group . . . in some other country!!!! XOXOXOXOXOXO
Love you

ctGoodyear said . . .

Sweetie, you are doing great, if you have some downtime we all understand. I don't know too many people that could do what you're doing. Hopefully, we'll have it soon so we can Skype. I miss you so very much. Love, Mom XOXOXOXO

Wednesday, July 1, 2009
Typical Nicaragua Wacky Day!!!

Well, today was just . . . wacky. We started today with a run, which was accompanied by some interesting *visuals*. Our running route is up and down the road in front of our complex, which ends by the pool, where some horses are kept. Today, they were breeding the horses, so every time we got to the end of the road, we saw a huge white horse *mounting* a sweet little brown horse. We would make a loop, go down the road again and upon our return; they were still going at it! They bit each other and made loud noises. They did *not* sound happy. I didn't really know what to say to Scarlett, so I tried to be as casual as possible. Avoidance . . . is a great trait for a mother to have.

After about our third lap, Scarlett said how sorry she felt for the little horse that was being attacked by the big white one. My reaction . . . to say nothing and hope that was the end of the conversation. On the fifth turn, she informed me that only humans and dolphins take pleasure in intercourse. Okay, I must admit that I already knew this fact (what can I say, I'm married to a very intelligent and handsome nerd) but how in the world does my twelve-year-old know this?! I just smiled and said, "What a smart girl you are," praying this was finally the end of the conversation.

The wackiness continued after the run. The girls and I were pumped because I had spotted a nail shop on our way to the mall yesterday. I have been in search of a nail salon since the first day I got here. I have been getting my nails done since I was nineteen years old (don't judge me) and albeit, I'm in a third world country, I still need to get my nails done.

On our way to the nail salon, Norman started explaining the tragedy that had happened at 4:00 a.m. this morning. The mayor of Managua, Alexis Augrello, was found dead. He was shot. According to the news reports, he committed suicide. Many people here loved Alexis Augrello, which I think had more to do with his boxing career than his role as mayor, but the news was shocking to the people in Nicaragua.

My initial reaction was, *Should we be in the streets of Managua right now?* Although I think I would trample over children to get my nails done today, I don't want to risk my own girls' safety. Norman assured us that all was well, but I had him wait for us outside the nail salon, just in case we needed a quick get-away!

My translator, Manuel told me that the President of Nicaragua had declared a three-day mourning period, which means no government business during this time. Now I know that I am a compassionate human being but to be honest, my first thought was "Man, couldn't he have waited a few days until the Consejo met?" (Don't judge me!) So, only God knows when the next Consejo will happen.

Right before I started making dinner, our friends Jack and Beth called to ask if we wanted to go to TGIF's instead. All of us *gringos* in Nicaragua go to TGIF's to feel closer to home. They have kids' meals and food we recognize. I had a hamburger, which was *muy rico.* Yummm. We all laughed about our feelings over today's events and reminded ourselves to stay positive. I am so grateful for them.

Like I said just a *typical* wacky day in Nicaragua.

1 Comment:

Timothy said . . .

HA HA HA . . . okay this is a VERY funny blog at least the first part of it! There are so many things that I want to say about the whole horse thing . . . HA HA HA. So, I am both a nerd and immature, so I will save my comments for when I see you since this is a public forum (I am still cracking up!) And tell Scarlett that she is in BIG BIG TROUBLE WHEN I SEE HER! Here's to "Family Life" class in sixth grade, although I have a feeling this little tidbit of information is maybe coming from the Internet or a "peer" group? I know . . . let's blame Allie! :-) Anyway, glad you went to TGIFs for the *Rico* (Sauvé!) burger. It is amazing how *caballo* can be dressed up to taste like a "burger." (Here I go about the horse again!) As you can tell, I am just a little punchy this morning. I guess it is because last night was the first time that I didn't get to talk to you on Skype. Love you and see you soon!

Thursday, July 2, 2009
Short On Minutes . . .

If I were to write a handbook for Nicaragua newbies (not a terrible idea), this would be the chapter on how to navigate communication without losing your mind. I have a pre-paid phone here, which is based on how many minutes you have. Albeit, you need to have minutes there is no way of knowing when you are running out, so it's crazy! There are two types of phones here, Moviestar and Claro. Apparently, if you have Claro phone (which is what I have) and call someone who has Moviestar, your minutes get eaten up much faster. If you call Claro to Claro, the minutes are calculated strictly by the duration of the call (no penalties). If you have Claro and phone the States, it is less expensive—which is why I got Claro. So basically, unless you know what kind of phone all the people you call have, there is no way to know when you will run out of time.

Every once in a while I will get a text message informing me about a promotion. If you buy more than $15 in minutes; you receive double the minutes. Are those Claro minutes? Minutes to the States? Minutes to Moviestar? I always buy $20 worth of minutes at a time because I am convinced that if I pay more, I won't get more and because I have no way of knowing how much I am supposed to get. How could I ever complain? If I buy less than $20, I will be out of minutes and being out of minutes is not fun because you can't go anywhere, and you're forced to beg someone to make a call for you (using their minutes)! I seriously feel like I'm in the middle of a Seinfeld episode. ;)

Today I noticed that my phone calls have gotten very short. When I called my cab driver today, I said, "Norman, we need to go to the orphanage today at 10:30 a.m., does that work for you?"

He said, "Yes" and I said, "*Ciao*"—end of the conversation—two minutes.

When I saw him in person, I tried to be extra nice because I was so short and rude to him on the phone, which is how I'm communicating with everyone these days. When I need to talk to one of my friends at Condo Allyson, I call and say, "Hey, I'm coming over to talk to you" and hang up. (Need to save those minutes!) When someone calls me, I am just as short, even though it's *their* minutes; it's all so confusing that I just make it quick and get off the phone.

Not even Tim is immune to this. I can't help but think about the minutes (or lack thereof) during our entire conversation, I even forget to say, *I love you* sometimes, and end the conversation with "*Ciao.*"

I think I get this trait from my Mom (she says I blame all my bad qualities on her, but this really isn't bad per se) but I really don't like talking on the phone for any length of time. I am a face to face person. So, if you call me and I'm abrupt, please don't take offense.

I'm just always short on minutes! *Ciao*!

1 Comment:

CtGoodyear said . . .
That just figures it's all my fault. It's OK Sweetheart, I'll take the blame (credit) for being responsible for any or all of you. I love you so much. I miss you and am so proud of you.
Love Mom XOXOXOX

Sunday, July 5, 2009
Surprise!!!

As you may realize, it's been a few days since I blogged ... due to a fantastic surprise. Thursday night around 9:30 p.m. I got a call from our friend Jack telling me that his wife Beth was coming over to ask me a question. He didn't want me to be concerned that someone was knocking at my door so late. Well, when I opened the door, it was my handsome husband!!!

I just cried when I saw him. What an awesome surprise! He got a great deal on a weekend ticket and hopped on a plane that morning. I only have him for two days but he is coming back on Wednesday, so I am not *supposed* to cry. I have never been too good at doing what I'm *supposed* to do.

Tim and I had a great reunion—the girls were thrilled! Even though we talked on the phone every day and he reads my blog every day ... we stayed up for hours just talking and loving on each other. It is what we all desperately needed.

Friday

We had a great visit, which started off a little crazy. We watched Rachel's sons from 7:30 a.m. until 1:00 p.m. Rachel and her husband had their court date Friday, which makes for a long day, so we were glad to help out. All went well at court and Victoria is now officially their daughter! They have another week worth of paperwork to complete, (i.e., visa, passport, etc.) but they'll be going home in the next few days. I have mixed emotions about all of it. Of course, I wish it was us ;) but I am so happy for their family. Their situation is very different from ours. They came to Nicaragua to adopt, and Victoria was ready to be adopted. They met, agreed to move forward, and twelve weeks later they're bringing home their new daughter. Their adoption process took four months whereas, ours is three years and counting.

We started our day in true Grimes/Nica fashion with a run followed by a tasty breakfast. Then it was off to the park and the pool with the kids. We went to Esperanza for lunch, which is a coffee/cafe that has an incredible view overlooking the mountains. It really is so beautiful here. We ate warm panini's and swallowed the cheesy goodness down with iced coffees.

Since it was our friend, Beth's birthday on Friday, we offered to look after their son Ignacio, in the evening, so his parents could have a date night. We enjoyed a delicious evening at an Italian restaurant right down the street and were spoiled again with the view of the mountains, which we enjoyed over our brick-oven pizza.

Saturday

We rented a van and went to Los Cardones on the Fourth of July to celebrate our American independence (sort of ☺). Los Cardones is my favorite beach in Nicaragua. This little surfer's paradise resort is only seven months old and was created by a guy from Australia who came to Nicaragua to surf. He fell in love with the beach and built his home here. (Lucie, Martita, and I had visited this beach with our friends, but this is Tim and Scarlett's first trip here.)

The property is made up of eight bungalows that boast of gorgeous hard-wood floors, hammocks and ocean views. There's no electricity, but we decided we could rough it and booked a stay for an upcoming girls' trip (when Allie, my stepdaughter, joins us on July 15). I am hesitant to stay overnight without my husband, but I feel more comfortable after speaking with the owner. This beach is well protected, and I am looking forward to the experience with all my girls.

We enjoyed the day at the beach so much and had the sand in our toes to prove it! Our family did a lot of swimming, walking and shell gathering. The girls and I fought over our handsome boy whom we all adore. Tim is quite the lucky guy being surrounded by women who love him so much. We all soaked up this treasured time together.

Back to reality, we are still waiting for the Consejo to meet; I pray it's this week. We are all so ready for some progress. Once the Consejo meets, we should be about a month out from going home. Tim keeps saying August 10—that's when he thinks this will all be finished . . . I pray that he's right.

I just dropped my husband at the airport. We had a fantastic long weekend together. I am a little sad right now—writing—wishing my Baye was still here. However, he'll be back in only three days—that I know I can do. Just one day at a time.

2 Comments:

Timothy said . . .
So, a quick little correction to the story of my surprise. Lesa says, "all" she did was cry. Actually, she cried AFTER she called me a cuss word! LOL. She really did . . . but don't judge her! This was a fast trip for me but one of the best for sure. Watching my girls thriving in Nicaragua is well . . . unbelievable. They are such strong women . . . all of them and I have my wife to praise for that trait for sure. Seriously, Lesa's blog is a living document of her "carrying her own weather." She has found a way to turn a VERY challenging situation in a VERY challenging environment INTO this wonderful paradise.

The beach she took me to yesterday was . . . well really indescribable. We really could have been in Tahiti . . . no lie. But with huge and I mean huge world-class surfing waves . . . ten and twelve footers were standard fair. Great food, great scenery, cold *cervezas*, and four great women . . . could a man ask for anything more?!?!?! It is great to be back home in Virginia tonight but as the song says . . . I left my heart in Nica . . . or was that San Francisco? Mine is in Nica. Baye, see you in a few days! XOXOXOXOXO

Amy said . . .

How awesome!!!! I would have cussed, too. Lesa, I bet you went crazy. I know you must be so ready to come home. I sure miss you. WE will be praying that August 10 is the day. You are such a strong woman. I would really be having a hard time down there by myself.

We are so proud of you.

Love you!!!

Amy

❨ *Chapter 12* ❩

I Would Like to
Introduce to You . . .

Monday, July 6, 2009
All in a Name . . .

Well, the food and the stress have finally taken hold of me, physically. I am a little down and out today with some stomach issues and overall body aches—yuck. I thought first it was the stress of the Consejo meeting. I really hoped it was today, but as the hours go by without any news; we know it's not promising.

We spent the day with our friends, Jack, Beth, and Ignacio. We went to lunch and did a little shopping. They are so supportive in this process as they're feeling our pain as they go through it themselves. It's a blessing to have another family to discuss details, vent, and combine forces. Jack will be meeting with Mi Familia tomorrow morning, and I in the afternoon. Our goal is to communicate, yet once more, the negative impact these delays have on our families. Now that we have been delayed so many times, we are in jeopardy of missing the first part of the school year in the

U.S., which is *not* something I am willing to do. They say they are always considering the adoptive child's best interests, well how does missing the beginning of school (when she is already so far behind) benefit her? Frustrating to say the least . . . While there were many stresses today, we did not let the Consejo dictate our happiness.

In other news, Tim and I have been discussing a new name for Martita when the adoption is final. We want to be sure Martita keeps her identity, but we really want to add Grace as her middle name. We always describe Martita as our child from God, and since God's grace is getting us through this experience, it just clicks. Grace is also my favorite word in the English language; it's something we all need more of, in my opinion. We are excited to give Martita this additional name.

I talked to our girl today and explained that she has another name now as she officially becomes our daughter. Martita Grace Grimes. I talked to our girl today and told her that now, that since she is our daughter, she has two new names—Grace and Grimes. She practiced her full name a couple of times and beamed while saying it.

A few minutes later I asked her, "What is your name?" and she replied "Gracie!" She loves it, and so do we!

So, I would like to formally introduce you all to our daughter, Gracie Martita Grimes!!!

4 Comments:

Donna said . . .
I love it! Gracie Grimes! It has such a nice ring to it. She can practice writing it because you will be back before school starts. Keep the faith.

Donna #2 (McKinnon) said . . .
What a beautiful name—Gracie Martita Grimes! We are praying that adorable Gracie and her wonderful mom and sisters

will be home before school starts. Stay strong—your wonderful husband will be there soon, and you are more than half-way through the "NICA CHALLENGE." (I realize that's an understatement)!

Amy said . . .
I am in tears. What a perfect name for her. God's grace has been evident through this whole process. What a gift . . . and what a gift Gracie is to your family. We can't wait to see her!

ivaniam97 said . . .
Hi honey!
Been away for a little but love every bit of catching up. I love you so much, hang in there my love! I wish with all my heart that I would be able to come and spend some time with you in Nica but those darn flights out of Los Angeles are so expensive. I just want to say that I LOVE Gracie's name!!! It is absolutely beautiful!!!! Kisses to all the girls, praying you all come home SOON!
XOXO

Tuesday, July 7, 2009
Gracie . . .

I'm feeling much better today, physically. I am the kind of person who doesn't *allow* herself to be sick. Last night, Lucie said, "Mommy, you *will* be all better in the morning, I promise."

She was right. I think knowing my husband will be here tomorrow has sped up my recovery.

I know that I introduced you to Gracie Martita Grimes last night, but I want to give you some more insight. My time with her has given me the chance to *really* know who she is becoming. This experience with my daughter has been extremely challenging but also utterly rewarding. I have had the opportunity to see Gracie at her worst and at her best. I want to share some of those details with you.

When Gracie wakes up in the morning, she is so happy. She smiles, hugs me, and says, "Good morning Momma."

She *loves* her sisters and wants to do whatever they do. She is attached at the hip with them both. They watch movies, color, and swim together. She always wants to be with them. If we go somewhere and the girls are not with us, Gracie gets very upset and repeatedly asks, "*Donde esta* Lucie?" (Where is Lucie?)

The joy she brings us is indescribable. She just *fits*.

Our youngest daughter is happiest when she makes us happy. When we praise her, she literally *beams*! She has a beautiful smile and is easily pleased. Grace is quick to say, "I love you" and to hug anyone who is in need.

She is very friendly and says, "Hello" to everyone she meets, including people standing in line at the grocery store. Everyone is her friend. ;) She *loves* clothes and shoes (fits right in with Scarlett and me) and anything that is just *for her*, makes her feel special. She has the most contagious laugh. It starts in her toes and erupts into that gorgeous grin. She doesn't hold anything back. Honestly, she is one of the happiest kids I have ever met, most of the time.

Our Gracie is very strong-willed. If she wants to go somewhere, it is difficult to keep her from bolting. If Grace wants to do something and you deny her, she will make a hideous face at you and attempt to escape! When it's time for a nap or bedtime, she shoots me an *ugly look*. I think it's because she never wants to miss out on what's going on, which may be why it takes her a *long* time to fall asleep. She has a difficult time focusing when something is happening around her. Gracie can be very defiant, which can be a good thing and has tested me in ways I've never experienced as a parent.

I have heard so often within the Christian community that adopting a child is like giving birth to one; there is no difference.

Well, I could not disagree more. Adoption is difficult, and I did not give birth to Grace. She comes from another part of the world and has endured struggles that I couldn't imagine for any human being. Grace was raised by someone else during her formative years of development. She was abused, neglected, and almost starved before she arrived at the orphanage. Grace will suffer from the horrors she survived, for years to come. And it weighs on me. My little girl is confused and lost a lot of the time. She has special needs and is way behind socially and academically. She's different—so completely different from my other girls. Her needs, wants, and dreams look different. It's beyond challenging at times.

We are in the process of transforming a child in need of rescue into a daughter, who needs our love. But this is a process that takes time. I am learning that my love for Grace is very different from my love for my other girls. That doesn't mean our bond is less valuable or real, it's just so different.

Perhaps, what's most amazing is how Gracie has changed. The first time I met her, she didn't speak at all. She could only yell, point at what she wanted and cry if she didn't get it. Her appearance has also changed dramatically. Our girl was so malnourished when we first met. Gracie's body was covered in bug bites, and her head was covered in bald spots. I will always remember that moment when I held her; I could feel how much she needed me— how much she needed us. I felt such a strong connection with her and could visualize her as part of our family. But it's a process.

Every morning I wake up and make a conscious choice to love and accept Gracie as my daughter because she is not capable (at this time) to bond with me like she is my child. It's as if I'm pregnant with Grace and still have all the anxiety and questions that come with having another child. Will she ever bond with me? Will she bond with the girls?

When I think of our relationship, the word *shallow* comes to mind. When Gracie hugs me, it's no different from when she hugs a stranger. This cuts me deeply. It's painful and hard to say any of this out loud. I just have to trust that Gracie is our daughter and someday she will know that I am her Mom and that we are her family.

Some days it's difficult knowing the best way to love her because it's not the same. For example, Lucie crawls into my lap when she is sad, happy, or just tired. All I have to do is hold Lucie, and she just melts. No words need to be spoken; it's a love language. With Gracie, it's different because she doesn't initiate this type of affection. When I pull her into me, it's awkward and uncomfortable for both of us.

My Grace doesn't know what a family is . . . She's never had that refuge, so it's impossible for her to connect with us on that level. My challenge is finding ways to communicate my love and acceptance for her in different ways. I understand the *why* behind Grace's reluctance, but it doesn't make it any easier to love her as my daughter. It's hard. I know I will have to work on this for years to come, but I am sure that together as a family we will navigate this in our own way.

With God's grace and love, our girl will soon *officially* be our daughter. Sometimes I forget, with all the challenges and battles in Nicaragua that we are here for one sole purpose—to bring our girl home. With all the doubt and uncertainty, I do know in my soul that God has blessed us with Gracie, a child with the most beautiful heart. I look forward to creating precious memories with my daughter and helping her discover who she truly is. She's already an incredible kid who has overcome so much in her short five years. I look forward to seeing this blossoming girl grow into an incredible woman. We have traveled thousands of miles and uprooted our lives to endure this process. But make no mistake, this journey has been incredible.

Saturday, July 11, 2009
The Journey to Granada

We just got home from an overnight stay in Granada; it was magical. We've made several trips to Granada, and during every visit, we stop to admire the Hotel Plaza Colon that towers over the square. This time we booked a room there. The hotel is gorgeous, and our room had a balcony that overlooked the square. Beautiful. The girls had a separate room; and we brought our friend, Antonia, to help look after them for us.

We spent the first day walking around, getting to know the city. Ten minutes into our self-guided tour, we heard a loud "DONG!!!" noise. We looked back, and Gracie ran straight into a light post that was in the middle of the square! She hit her head *hard* and started to cry. This was a big deal because it takes a lot for our Gracie to cry. Antonia had been holding Gracie's hand and felt terrible about it, so naturally, we (jokingly) told her she was fired and gave her a hard time the rest of the trip. (Maybe that's why she asked me to take her straight home when we got back to Managua.) Antonia is the daughter of El Canyon's orphanage director, Natalia, which means she's basically part of our family. We love her dearly and feel comfortable treating her like one of us (AKA giving her a hard time). Later in the day, the girls went for a swim in the beautiful pool at the hotel and Tim, and I got ready for a night out. Yes, just my husband and I, out on the town without the girls.

We had a romantic dinner down the street. While out and about on the town, we enjoyed watching street entertainers dance, sing, and juggle fire (seriously). This was the first time I had been out walking around at night, which made me a little nervous. Tim kept saying, "Let's cross here" or "Okay, slow down a little," when we ran into anyone on the street.

Yes, I was a little nervous. When I explained my feelings to my husband, he said, "Don't worry, I took Tae Kwon Do ten years ago."

Great, still nervous! We stayed safe and really enjoyed our evening out. Back at the hotel, we took *hot* showers (so so nice), in our air-conditioned room, and slept on the most comfortable bed. P.S. I didn't see one bug in our room the *entire time we were there*!!! *Yyyyeeeessss*!!!

Today, (our second day of the trip) we met our friends, Jack and Beth along with Beth's Mom and sister at Kathy's Waffle House for breakfast. We arrived in a two-horse carriage after taking a tour of the city (definitely one of the highlights of our trip). After we loaded up on syrupy carbs, we took to the streets for some shopping. There was no shortage of vendors selling movies that are still out in the theaters. I never stopped to look before because I know this is totally illegal but of course, when Tim is here, we do things that I wouldn't usually do. (He is such a bad influence!) So, we bought the girls ten movies for $10. You wouldn't believe the quality, they are awesome. Now I'm hooked and planning to get more movies before we go home. (Don't judge me.) We should have plenty of entertainment to last us a few more weeks. Then it was time to head home with some tired girls and even more tired parents.

I promised Tim that we would not discuss the adoption during our time away. I wanted to escape the prison of Managua for a couple of days, but I couldn't help but think about the adoption, of course. When I sat out on the balcony at our hotel, I people watched for a long time. I was out there first thing this morning and saw the street vendors getting ready for their day. They cleaned the tables, swept the ground around them, and set out their food and items to sell. They all work so hard. They will work from morning until dark . . . every day. I saw locals walking through the square that may have been heading to work. I saw children playing and tourists bustling from place to place.

When I was out on the balcony, I reflected on how blessed I am to be here in this beautiful place with a family I adore. I am so grateful that my girls are healthy and strong; each with a promising future ahead of them. I guess what I'm trying to say is that we all are blessed. My life may be very different from the woman in the plaza selling food, probably easier in many ways, but I bet she has a family to love and is proud of her accomplishments. This lady also experiences happiness and fulfillment, just like me. We are all so different . . . but all so much the same.

Again, I made a commitment to myself to remember how blessed I am. I know that this time is only a moment in my life, a trial I know I can conquer. I will wake up each day being *grateful* for my life, not wondering why God isn't listening to my prayers because I know that He listens. There is no more feeling sorry for myself. It's time to pedal forward and enjoy the ride.

As I'm sure you can tell from this blog entry this trip did wonders for my attitude. Having my husband here *always* makes me feel secure and loved. The challenge will be keeping this attitude *after* he leaves. ;) Allie comes in tonight, and we are all so excited to have her here with us. Finally, we will all be together as a family. So, here's to another day of knowing how blessed I am. We must love the days of our journey without focusing too much on the destination.

1 Comment:

McKenzie said . . .
Wow. I am so glad you and Tim were able to get some time together.
Yes, we are blessed. Thanks for the reminder.
Miss you and love you.
Amy

Sunday, July 12, 2009
Fun in Leon

Today we were *finally* all together as a family . . . the four girls, my husband and me. As good as it was, we only had today to enjoy it. Tim leaves tomorrow morning, so we decided to venture out and explore a new place together, a city called Leon, which is about an hour drive from Managua. We asked some friends to join in the adventure as well.

I didn't realize that because it was Sunday, many of the shops were closed and the city was very quiet. It reminded me a little of Granada—clean streets, lots of shops, and less poverty. We saw some striking old churches including the San Francisco

Church, which is the oldest church in Latin America. We took lots of pictures, and our little friend Ignacio kept asking, "Why is Jesus dying on the cross?"

Communication is a challenge for his parents; they speak limited Spanish and Ignacio, very little English, but we did our best to explain. Gracie kept saying, "Shhhh, Momma, come and look," as showed me the statues. She was in awe.

Lunchtime! We talked to someone on the street who recommended a beautiful hotel that had fabulous food at affordable prices, so we went there. The hotel is two stories and is surrounded by plants and flowers. We walked into a grand lobby and followed the signs to the restaurant. It was gorgeous. The walls are made up of stone and decked out in pictures of locals. We sat the kids at a separate table and due to their *active personalities* we were immediately seated! ;) The food was excellent, and the company was even better.

We walked around the city a little more and went into a couple of open shops. Since I always go to church on Sunday, I didn't know that Sunday is *not* the day to explore. I really enjoyed spending time in Leon but missed my church in El Canyon and the people who go there, especially all the kids.

Having Allie here is a lot of fun. Gracie is spending a lot of time with her and even told some locals that Allie was her mother. She looks a lot more like Allie than me, that's for sure. When Gracie said this, I just smiled at her and asked, "Who's your Momma?" and she smiled that famous glowing grin and pointed at me.

Gracie is having a difficult time bonding with us, which makes sense since she's had no real family structure and her interactions consisted of revolving groups that visit the orphanage and then leave. She is so used to people coming and going that she quickly warms up to you, however, she doesn't understand or know how to truly bond with someone. It is a struggle that I know will take some time to conquer.

As we walked down the street people would stop and stare at us. Of course, most of the attention was directed toward Lucie.

I'm still amazed that people actually touch her hair when she walks by. Even very grim looking people smile at her and talk to her in Spanish. Lucie is getting a lot of attention that I am hoping will not have a long-term impact on her. "Rock Star" in Nicaragua does not translate to Rock Star at home! ;)

Tomorrow is a big day for us. We have a meeting at 8:30 a.m. with the Minister of Mi Familia. She is the one we are waiting on to call Diego who will authorize when the Consejo meets. Our understanding is that everything is ready and waiting for her call, so we asked to meet with her. We spent some time talking to Jack about what our approach should be. Again, we will plead for our case and our family while asking her to please sign off on our paperwork (which we believe she has authority to do) or to at least, make the call to Diego to arrange for the Consejo to meet.

In the past, these meetings at Mi Familia have been tough for me. I feel I have no control and am beyond frustrated by this process. It doesn't help that Tim is leaving tomorrow, which is hard too. Albeit he is planning on returning August 7, it's still nearly a month away. However, I'm trying not to think about it and focus on the positive things happening.

What's exciting is that I have Allie here for a week! This is a big deal for us since we (she and I) have never spent any time together without her Dad. As I mentioned before, being a stepmom is challenging. Allie was 11 when I came into her life and the transition was difficult, especially for her. Divorce is *never* easy and having Scarlett and I come into Allie's life while she was handling her parents' divorce was hard. It didn't make things any easier on her, that Tim and I had Lucie, shortly after we got married.

I often look back on that time and wish so many things had been different. Perhaps, if we had slowed the process down, it could have been easier for Allie to adjust. She has always known how much her Dad loves her, but she's not been 100 percent sure of me which is entirely understandable.

This time together will give us a chance to bond and provide a real opportunity for us to get to know each other better.

I hope that by the end of the week, she will have a better understanding of how much I love her and what she means to me. I also hope that she starts connecting with me on a level that doesn't always have to include her Dad. This being said, she has a wonderful Mom, and I want Allie to know that I will never try to replace that relationship. I just want her to know that I can be another family member who loves her unconditionally. So, here's to a fantastic week with Allie.

Once Allie leaves, there will only be three weeks left until my Baye comes back. I pray that our case moves forward, so I can focus on the adoption rather than counting the days until he returns. Most of all, I hope I can remember how blessed I am and to remember that this journey has given me so many opportunities that I wouldn't experience at home.

Love to you all—and again, thank you for taking this journey with me!!!

Chapter 13

Family Reunited

Monday, July 13, 2009
Normal kid . . . Normal Mommy

I met Rena today at 8:30 a.m. Rena, as you may recall, is the Minister of Mi Familia . . . the head *honcho* . . . *El Jefe* who sits at the head of the Consejo. I have been to the offices of Mi Familia probably twenty times in the past three years. The visits make me feel very uncomfortable. I walk into a room and meet people who have the authority to *allow* me to bring my daughter home. I have to be careful that I don't push too much or say the wrong thing. I find these meetings to be extremely stressful and leave feeling completely frustrated.

Today was a very different experience! I marched in that office with not only my husband but all my children. It was my first time at Mi Familia that I was there with my entire family; we were a united front, *familia unido*. It felt good and I felt strong. I wasn't nervous during the meeting, but I was apprehensive about the meeting's outcome.

Our understanding was that Rena had the authority to sign off on our adoption papers. (We found out this is not the case.) By law, we must go before the Consejo to receive our final approval. She did however, log on to a computer to find our specific case. Seriously, I was beginning to wonder if we existed in any computers! She read the letters we submitted last week outlining how important it is for our families to finish this process and get our children home to start school on time. She was very warm, professional, and assured us that the Consejo would meet this Friday.

I am sure you are probably thinking the same thing I am . . . *How many times have we heard that before?*

I think it's actually been six times that I've heard the *June* Consejo would be meeting. It is now the middle of July and still no Consejo. I also hate when they say, *Friday.* Why can't it be Wednesday or Thursday?! Why do I have to wait around all week for Friday to come, not get a call and then strategize/agonize over the weekend about what I will do Monday to make that week different from the last? However, I feel differently about this time; my family is giving me strength that I've never felt here before.

We are already planning our celebration dinner Friday night with our friends and will keep busy for the remainder of the week. So please keep all your body parts crossed and I'll keep you posted!

After our meeting, we all went to the airport to send my husband home, which I dreaded. I just wave, and cry, and wish he could stay with me. He gives me a feeling of calmness and security. I miss him so much when he's gone. He got into Dulles at midnight and has to go to work first thing in the morning. Tim lives in an empty house and works his tail off, so we can continue to live in Nicaragua. He has, and continues to do, so much for our family.

Tonight was also the goodbye dinner for our friend Rachel and her family. They go home tomorrow with their daughter, Victoria. I am so happy that they are going home, but it makes us a little sad to be left behind . . . still struggling.

When we first came to Condo Allyson in May, six adoptive families were living here, now there are only two families left. It is always sad to see our friends leave, which makes it difficult to keep going. During this goodbye Lucie was sadder than most of us because she is good friends with one of the boys that's leaving. She told me how much she would miss him.

Tonight, she came to me, gave me a big hug and said, "Mommy, I want to be a normal kid and I want you to be a normal Mommy, and I want to go home."

I just hugged her and told her I knew exactly what she meant and I, too, want to go home, but I reminded her that we are on an adventure . . . a special vacation that will be over soon. I hope I am telling my daughter the truth. I always need to remember that this is a challenge for my girls, too, not just me.

1 Comment:

CtGoodyear said . . .
Dear Lesa, I hope you are telling Lucie the truth also, but I know if it takes a little longer, you can all do it, and it will certainly be worth it to have our Gracie Martita home. I am so proud of you and wish I could do something to make it easier. Know that we love you and think of you every day.
Love Mom & Tom XOXOXOXO

Tuesday, July 14, 2009
Grimes Girls for the Win

Today Allie joined Scarlett and I for our morning running ritual, I love having them with me. It amazes me how the girls keep up the grueling pace while maintaining a positive attitude. Truth be told, I know they think I'm a slave driver because I push them to exercise while reminding them *how good* they will feel when it's all over.

We went to the orphanage today and had a great time with Natalia, the kids, and all the staff. Allie is so well loved by the kids there. She was greeted with love, hugs, and kisses from many of the kids. Allie is a beautiful, olive-skinned, nineteen-year-old woman. She has a gorgeous smile and is very easy going (most of the time). People often ask what nationality she is because of her skin tone. Many would assume she's Latina, Indian, Asian, however, she is caucasian with gorgeous colored skin. Because of this, many of the new children assumed she spoke Spanish. Allie struggled with Spanish in school and is about as proficient as her Dad. We laughed a lot about how everyone just talks to her in Spanish and expects her to answer. She just looks at them funny and looks at me to respond. ;)

When we served lunch, I noticed a lot of new faces at the table. Many of the children I know have been adopted or have gone home to their families. They've been replaced by new children who are struggling and need help. Even the newbies wear big smiles and give their love so freely. We met a newborn named Javon and his fifteen-year-old mom, Martina. She didn't know how to care for her baby, so she came to the orphanage for help. I have such mixed emotions about this newcomer. I am certain the right thing to do is to love Martina and her baby, but I can't help but feel protective of the older girls. I don't want them to make the same mistakes that Martina has. Being a teen mom in Nicaragua is extremely difficult because there are fewer jobs, and chances to educate yourself, especially when there is no father to help raise the baby. Hopefully, Martina's presence is a warning to the other girls as to what can happen if they don't make the right choices.

My girls and I did some good work today at Puente de Amistad. We helped Martina and her baby, assisted the psychologist Gabriela with some medical expenses, and we got in some time to love on and play with the kids. We also received encouragement and support from everyone regarding our own adoption. I was touched that so many people asked about the

Consejo and stopped to give us their best wishes and prayers. It was very uplifting to be there, and as always, I felt so loved.

Later that day, we had dinner with friends at our home and then started packing for our big beach trip tomorrow. Can I get a *woo hoo*!!! Of course, the evening didn't stay this mellow . . . I logged on to check my email and Facebook when all of a sudden, a *huge* cockroach ran between my legs (yes, right between my legs) and I screamed at the top of my lungs. All the girls were in their room watching a movie and came running out to see which creature had moved in.

The cockroach fell down the step and started running across the family room floor. It took me a couple of seconds to react, but it was already on the move. The creeper had crawled down the steps and onto the ceiling of the first floor. The girls stood back, just watching me as I pointed and screamed at our new tenant, "Look there, there he is!"

When they caught a glimpse of it, they screamed so loud I thought the mirror would crack. Allie said it was the biggest bug she had ever seen, so I handed her a tennis shoe and said, "Kill him."

She looked at me and said, "Are you seriously going to put this on me?"

Doesn't this sound like exactly something a nineteen-year-old would say? And I replied, "Yes, I have killed so many, can't you kill just this one?!"

And doesn't that sound exactly something a step-mom would say to lay as much guilt on her daughter as possible? Allie was so worried it would fly and attack her, but I assured her that was not possible (only Nicaraguan ants fly). She made me promise and then proceeded to kill the huge cockroach. She hit it with the tennis shoe, and it fell off the ceiling and onto the steps, but it was very much alive. Knowing that I would *never* sleep again if this creature were alive in the house, I went down the stairs and finished the job. Of course, I called in reinforcements (Gracie) to pick it up with a paper towel and throw it in the trash, while the girls screamed at the top of their lungs. But *we did it—together*!

I know you must be in awe of our bravery. :) I still wonder why the security guards with machine guns, don't come running at our door, when they hear the war raging inside here. Ummmm Heeelllooo, we are under attack! But again, this has happened several times, so they must be used to our screaming by now.

My heart is still racing over the entire experience, so I must settle down a bit before I sleep tonight. We have a big day tomorrow as we're leaving for Las Cordones in the morning for our Grimes girls' getaway! I am excited about our adventure but a little nervous as well. I want to ensure that we can function without electricity, or my husband. After all, we'll be on our own, away from Quinta Allyson but I know my girls, and I know myself, and I *think* we will make the most of this epic experience.

This means I will not be able to blog tomorrow, but I'll check back Thursday evening. I'm wishing you a day free of bugs and full of air-conditioning, love, and great memories. Thank you all again for your continued support and love and please, *please* pray that the Consejo meets this Friday!

Love and Blessings!!!

2 Comments:

Timothy said . . .
There are SO many things I want to post about this blog but really can't (I guess my mind is in the gutter!) What kind of impression are you making on our daughter Allie?! LOL. Does Sue Jones read this blog? She is much braver than me with the postings . . . Doug Hall? Steve Jones . . . are you guys out there? LOL Maybe I should direct them to the blog on Facebook! LOL

Amy said . . .
Way to go, Allie. I would have gladly killed that bug!!! If it had been a mouse, I would have wet my pants and screamed like a little girl.
WE will all be praying that BIG things happen Friday.

Thursday, July 16, 2009
The Crab Whisperer!

We are back from the beach . . . all a little sunburned and very relaxed. The girls were so tired when we got home that Lucie told me that it was past her bedtime, Scarlett *didn't* argue with me, and Gracie fell asleep reading a book. It was a great escape for us all. We are so enjoying Allie being here with us. She always makes us laugh, is so quick to look at the bright side of things and is so much like her father in many ways . . . let me explain.

Right before we left for the beach, we went on our morning run. This was Allie's fourth time running with us, and I think she is completely over it. She didn't talk at all, and when I asked her what was up, she told me her legs were so sore it was like knives were sticking through them (yes, this kind of detail is very much like her father). Then, the horse trainer asked if we wanted to ride one of the beautiful horses that are boarded there. Lucie and Gracie were more than willing. Scarlett tried but got too scared, (the horse was a mammoth that moved around a lot). I took her turn (and absolutely loved it) and when the trainer asked Allie if she wanted to ride she said, "Oh no, not me." I told the trainer she was scared in Spanish and when Allie asked me what I said, she replied, "I'm not scared, just didn't feel like it." (Tim Jr.)

Our friends went to the beach with us to spend the day. It was great fun, and Allie really connected with Beth's sister, Danell. She is a doll, and Allie and she spent hours talking. Scarlett and Lucie love love love the ocean and our Gracie, prefers to play with toys in the sand. Me? I love to find beautiful shells and wander over to the hammock . . . so relaxing. We all love beach time—in our own way.

Our friends left in the late afternoon, and it was just us girls. We spent the rest of the day on the beach, cracked open a few books, and just . . . relaxed. After we played all day, we retreated to our little house to shower and change for dinner. As I mentioned before, our little bungalow has no electricity and a modest shower.

All of the bungalows share two outhouses for a bathroom. Thank goodness they're only a short walk from our bungalow. The girls and I were excited to step out for the evening, so after getting showered and dressed we made our way to the cabana. The sun danced in the sky like a glowing beachball, and we made it out of the bungalow just in time to see it set. The evening was so tranquil and quiet. I took a photo in my brain of that sunset, which is something I will never forget.

In Nicaragua, nothing that sweet and peaceful lasts very long. As we ventured out, we noticed that we were not alone . . . there were crabs. I mean hundreds of crabs literally . . . walking (I don't know if they walk . . . I really don't know what to call it, but it's sideways and freaky!) I am not exaggerating. Where did they come from? We spent all day at the beach and once in a while would see a crab on the sand but as soon as the sun goes down . . . the crabs came out! They crawl out of tunnels from underground. They move fast, and they seem to be everywhere. Not sure what they are looking for, but they are moving fast to find it! We were all a little freaked out and made our way to the main area *very quickly*.

When I saw the owner, I told him about all the crabs we had just seen. I guess I thought this would be *news* to him, but he said, "That's nothing . . . wait until the sun goes all the way down, there will be many more."

Uhhhh!!!

I responded, "Well, I'm sure they don't go on the walking path."

And he said, "Yeah, they do, but you can just kick them out of your way."

Okay is this guy *serious*? I mean, does he realize I'm a girl? A girl from the United States who does *not* live on a beach and has really only seen crabs on a dinner plate? (Side note: My husband is so sexy when he eats crabs.) *plus*, I'm wearing flip flops for goodness sake! How is it possible to kick a crab in flip flops?!

Well, we saw a *gorgeous* sunset, ate some brick oven pizza for dinner and devoured some yummy dessert. Allie and I indulged in some local rum that was also yummy. We were ready to head back to our cute little house where the girls could unwind with a DVD, while Allie and I could sit and visit. As soon as we started to walk on the path, Scarlett shrieked. Lucie took one look at the ten crabs running across the walking path and freaked out (translation: she jumped into my arms, clinging for dear life while hysterically crying). Gracie looked at Lucie and started to cry while Allie and I resisted bolting to save ourselves! Mind you this was happening only about twenty feet from where we just ate dinner. There were still about ten people enjoying their meals as this scene played out. Lord knows what they were thinking.

Let's just say, the Grimes girls really wimped out. Our friend the owner, came to comfort us. He took one look at Lucie clinging to me and everyone else crying and immediately offered to walk us back to our bungalow. He kicked crabs out of the way as we moved along, albeit we're still just as distraught as before. We clung to the poor guy (yes, Allie and I too) and I guess I should have been embarrassed, but I was too scared! At this point, I wondered if this *beach getaway* was such a good idea and if I really can take care of my girls.

There's a set of stairs outside our bungalow that you have to climb to get to the front door. The owner assured us that crabs can't climb stairs, so we are good to go. Well, I didn't think ants could fly either, but they do. I'm not feeling too warm and fuzzy, but I know that I have to settle the girls down. I set up some movies, and they changed into their PJ's as they snuggled in to watch their shows with a flashlight. Allie and I went to sit on the patio. There was no place to relax in the little house, so it was either go to bed or chill outside. We bravely took our flashlights and ventured out. As we sat there, crabs came right up on the patio straight for us. Newsflash . . . crabs *do* climb stairs!

At first, Allie screamed a little and would shine the flashlight in their faces (again, I don't know . . . do crabs actually have faces? I swear they have little bitty eyes). Then she started to talk to them. I thought Allie was losing it, but, it actually seemed to work.

She would say things like, "Go away."

"Thank you."

"I see you over there."

"No, not that way." Farther!!"

She made me laugh so hard, I was crying but the crabs were *listening*!

After what seemed like hours of crab's play, I took the flashlight from Allie so we could actually have a conversation without her being on crab watch. It isn't easy to carry on a conversation with someone when they are preoccupied. Reluctantly, she agreed. Every once in a while, I would scan the stairs and patio for crabs. I was in mid-story when Allie grabbed the flashlight from me and shined it about two feet in front of us. Sure enough, a crab was making his way towards us.

She started screaming at the crab, "*No*—turn around—turn around *now*, that's right, go *that* way, keep going!"

How she knew that crab was there, I will never know. The girl's got a gift . . . a serious gift! I do not know what I would have done without my Crab Whisperer on this trip. Allie turned a scary situation into a very comical one that we all laughed and laughed about. I absolutely *love* having Allie here, she is a complete joy.

During our escapade to the beach, I didn't really have time to stress about the Consejo, so it was such a shock/relief/gasp when I got the call . . . The Consejo is meeting tomorrow! We are all so excited and very hopeful because once this happens, I will have a much better idea of when we can come home. Knowing that date will be such a comfort to our family. We are throwing out prayers for a wonderful day tomorrow and a reason to celebrate. This good news will give us another reason to visit Las Cardones again, but this time . . . I'm packing tennis shoes!

2 Comments:

Timothy said . . .

Since this VERY funny blog opened up with not one, but two *drive-bys* (for you older folks in the crowd) a drive-by is when you are slammed with something when you don't expect it. It's like walking on the street and getting shot when you haven't done anything! I feel an intense need to defend myself. YES, I understand the mature thing to do is to ignore the statements, but I am not always as mature as I should be. Allie, if I would have been there, I would have *felt the pain* in the shins. As mentioned, when Lesa is working out with people she has an *inner Jillian* (from *The Biggest Loser*) that surfaces quickly.

Now as for the horse riding thing . . . THAT comment about Allie is probably well deserved! I say this only because of a very long story that I will share with anyone that asks me/us. It has to do with Gray's Mountain Lodge, the Pion Palace and a big horse that cannot keep a saddle on straight . . . especially when Allie is on its back!

Finally, I am not sure what to say about the whole *me eating crab thing* other than when the Consejo meets today I will know to plan the BIG crab feast here in Virginia five to six weeks from TODAY!!!!!!! :-)

Friday, July 17, 2009
Consejo Met!!

Well, it actually happened . . . after ten weeks, the Consejo met and gave the final approval for our adoption!!! *Yyyeeeeaaaahhh-hhh*!!! It's impossible, really to put into words how I feel (insert all synonyms for happy here)! This has been a marathon of a journey for us. In August, it will be three years since we first turned in paperwork to adopt our Gracie. We still have a lot of work to do to get home, but this is a big step in the right direction.

I had some very close friends tell me that they felt very encouraged about this Consejo. They felt confident that this time, it would happen, and it did!!! I think I'm still a little in shock that it actually happened!

What a wondrous turn of events that started with a call around noon today from our friends Jack and Beth. They tortured me a little about giving me the good news but finally blurted out the blessed and best news of the day! I cried and congratulated them as well and then immediately called my husband. Tim answered the phone, I told him, "They met love, the Consejo actually met!"

Before I could give him any more details, he said, "Hold on love, someone is at the door." I heard him say, "Hey" it was our Pastor and friend.

Helloooo, can you believe the timing of that?! He was thrilled to hear the news and congratulated me on the phone, all I could do was cry! A few minutes later, I got a call from his wife, and again, I cried, and she cried. We laughed and were so excited! I love them, and I must admit that having a pastor be the one to visit my husband when he's home alone vs our pretty next-door neighbor, also makes me happy.

What a blessing you all are to me . . . to us! I have received so many calls, emails and Facebook messages; it is overwhelming and humbling. I do not deserve this amount of love and support, but I am thrilled to receive it. It makes me so happy to know that I am living a life surrounded by family and friends who take the time to make sure that I know how they feel, that they continue to encourage and love us through each step of this process . . . so thank you.

We spent most of today at the Galleria Mall. Allie, the girls, and I did a little victory shopping while spending some quality time together. The celebration continued that evening at dinner with our friends. Fun! We went to a lovely Italian restaurant. The server brought the kids some dough to play with to keep them busy, which they loved.

I realized this was probably the first time Gracie has seen dough, so I explained it to her quickly. The dough was already about halfway to her mouth when I told her, "No love, this is to play with, not to eat. It can make you sick, and you *do not eat it*!"

I turned to my friends to continue our conversation when I heard Scarlett yell "*No, Gracie, no!!!*"

Gracie had a defiant grimace on her face as she quickly chewed the dough. That could not have tasted good. I went over, forced the dough out of her mouth, which was not an easy task and took the squishy ball away from her. When I sat back down, I looked over at a grouchy Gracie who looked so dear with flour all over her face that we all started to laugh.

All day, I kept thinking that this was Gracie's day and felt terrible that she didn't really understand it. My husband told me that it wasn't just Gracie's day, but *our* day, and I agreed. This is a day we all needed badly, a day of good news, a day of celebration! How awesome to have Allie here to celebrate with us. She is our new good luck charm.

So, what happens next? The Consejo must give the offical word to the court that we have been approved. This is called our *declaration*. The government offices are closed Monday (because of a holiday on Sunday celebrating thirty years of independence, so I guess they need a day to recuperate), so the declaration should be completed next Tuesday.

Once the declaration is submitted, we wait for our court date. This can take one to four weeks. We just wait for the phone call, and then we show up at our court date and the judge signs the paperwork that legally makes Gracie our daughter. At this point, her name is formally changed, and she is given a new birth certificate.

Once that is complete, we have two more weeks to get her medical check-ups, visa, passport, and all other government documentation, and then we come home. So, we could be home as soon as mid-August, or, worst case scenario, late August. Just in time to get all my girls back for the beginning of the school year. How's that for timing?!

I am still digesting this good news. Still working through all the emotions but I know that my adventure here will soon be over, and I will be going home.

The girls and I are creating a *Consejo Dance* to celebrate this day! I look forward to dancing it for you all . . . soon.

3 Comments:

mawyer said . . .
We are so happy with this news—YEAH. We can't wait to see you back in VA with ALL the girls (and Tim). You are in our thoughts and prayers every day. Keep the updates coming!
Love,
T & S (Tracy & Syd)

P.S. Syd says, "*hola*" to Scarlett, Lucie, and Gracie :)

Donna said . . .
That's great news Lesa (and Tim)! We can't wait to see Gracie again! Looking forward to the *Consejo Dance* as well!
Donna McKinnon

CTGoodyear said . . .
Congratulations, we are so happy for all of you, and us. Sooooo Happy.
Love to you all Mom & Tom XOXOXOXO

Sunday, July 19, 2009
Adios Allie

Our Allie just left for the airport, and we are sad to see her go. It's been a wonderful week with her here and time just flew by. I am really proud of her because she flew here alone and is going home the same way. Since her flight is at eight this morning, she left for the airport at 5:45 a.m. It would have been a difficult task to get all the girls up and out the door on time. Not to mention my girls do not do well without a lot of sleep. I asked Allie how she felt about going alone with Norman and she said she was good to go. I gave Norman all the instructions to ensure Allie is all checked in, and okay before he leaves her at the airport. It's hard to say goodbye to our sweet girl.

Yesterday was our last day with Allie, so we made sure to squeeze in a lot of fun. The girls slept in. (I did *not* make them run in the morning! ;) We went to see the new *Harry Potter* movie (excellent) and had a great lunch at one of our favorite places, Esperanza. We love their pastries and panini's—yum! Norman, who speaks very little English says, "I likie panini." ;) We also went to another one of our favorite restaurants for dinner, Mia Luna, which is an Italian restaurant with an unbelievable view. We took a lot of pictures to capture our last night together while enjoying the scenic surroundings and delicious food.

While we had a lot of fun yesterday, the exhaustion began to set in, which surprised me. After all, the Consejo met, and we had the entire weekend to relax and celebrate, but I was restless and feeling a bit rundown. Although I was beyond tired, I kept waking up. I slept about four hours and felt like a truck ran me over. My nerves were shot, and my body ached.

I told my husband how I felt, and he said that it made perfect sense to him. Tim rationalized that I had been full of anticipation (as well as anxiety) for so long that I didn't realize the toll it was taking on my body. I think he's right. I think it had the same effect on the girls. Gracie was so defiant, (not listening well to any of us) Scarlett talked back to me most of the day, and Lucie often cried for no reason . . . *Ugh!!* Isn't it always like that though? When I'm having a tough day, every one of my kids decides, *Let's get Mommy* and boy, do they know how!

We have also been so busy with Allie. We really wanted

to make the most of our time together, so we spent most of our days showing her places we love and that she hasn't seen. So . . . it's been a crazy week. Strike that . . . a crazy ten weeks. Saturday was our 70th day in Nicaragua . . . I don't like counting each day, but I have the days numbered (every Saturday) to give me an idea of how long it has been. No wonder I'm a little tired.

Sunday is my favorite day of the week, but I'm feeling exhausted and sad to see Allie go. I woke up early to get her on her way and made a plan for the rest of the day. Our Sunday would consist of long naps, sitting by the pool, and taking time to reflect. It really amazes me how your body tells you when it can't do anymore, so I need to listen and rejuvenate.

Today is our day to relax . . . a day to remember and talk about all the fun we had with Allie. I am so pleased to say that having this time with her (without Tim) has really made us all closer. She saw me at my best and my worst, which I think helped us bond. She experienced our adoption process first-hand, which made her understand all that we are sacrificing to get our Gracie home.

Gracie is really the glue that connects all of our girls. Allie is Tim's daughter, Scarlett is mine, and Lucie is ours but having Gracie join our family is what binds all of us together: His, Her's, Our's and God's. How could we have had this experience without our beautiful Allie here? Our week was everything I hoped for, loaded with memories I will always cherish.

I hope you are all having a great weekend and a great summer.

Love and Blessings . . .

1 Comment:

Timothy said . . .
Rest love . . . it is well deserved. Thanks for being who you are and for what you do. I can't wait to see Allie and hear her thoughts. Love you Baye XOXOXOXOXOX

Sunday, July 19, 2009
30 Year Anniversary FSLN

Today, Nicaraguans took to the streets to celebrate the thirty-year anniversary of the Sandinista Revolution. Thousands of people gathered at the Plaza La Fe in Managua to commemorate the fall of the Somoza family dictatorship. The Somaza family's notorious reign included a history of executions, terrorism, and instilling fear. The Sandinistas (a group of workers, peasants and guerrillas) joined forces to defeat the Somoza family. (My husband knows a lot more about all this than I do.)

Since we arrived in Nicaragua, I've taken notice of the red and black flags and signs that read FSLN. This stands for *Frente Sandinista de Liberacion Nacional* or Sandinista National Liberation Front. However, the rally cry for FSLN has quieted over time. Over the years, the Sandinista government experienced its own share of failures. Now there are fewer people meeting in the square and more citizens celebrating quietly from their homes.

When you ask someone if they are Sandinista, most people answer with pride saying, "Yes, I am Sandinista, and this is a great celebration." However, this is not true for our friend Norman who does not identify with this group. Norman told me that years ago, the Sandinista police killed two of his uncles because they thought they were rebels. Due to this experience, Norman and his family do not identify as Sandinista.

In my lifetime I have never experienced anything like this and cannot imagine the U.S. as a dictatorship. I read about how the United States *assisted* Nicaragua. Looking back, was it the right thing to do? Politics are so complicated; there are so many decisions to be made that impact so many people.

Any political gathering in Nicaragua scares me; I know it's silly, but it's true. The girls and I did not leave the gates of our complex today. We played it safe and stayed home. My friend Jack, however, went to the square with a local to check out the event. He said there were a lot of people and it was awesome to experience. All day long, we heard loud music and guest speakers taking part in the ceremony from the city. Tomorrow all government offices will be closed to commemorate the anniversary.

I never paid very much attention in history. Actually, I'm not sure my history class would have ever discussed Nicaragua, but events like the Sandinista revolution affect us all. When I hear dictatorship, I know it's not good for the people but what about the alternative? Just look at the Sandinista revolution, what started as a revolt against injustice is now a government that is also tainted with corruption.

I'm sorry for going on and on about this topic, but I am fascinated to learn how the U.S. is viewed by the rest of the world, which begs the question. "How I am viewed when I walk down the street of this third world country?"

Well, today we had our own party. The girls and I made shell necklaces and put tattoos all over each other. There were no flags or speeches, but we celebrated being able to bring a Nicaragua girl home (soon) to the United States to join our family.

1 Comment:

Timothy said . . .
You did a GREAT job with your historical facts! Two things that I find fascinating about our world. First, what is so interesting is that world conflict, etc., usually starts with a single person with power (power be it, ego, weapon, etc.) that decides to flex a little muscle . . . and then all hell potentially breaks loose. Second, history has a habit of causing even the most democratic countries to flip flop. Case in point . . .

1937—U.S. puts Somoza in power.

1970s—Jimmy Carter supports the Sandinistas.

1980s—Ronald Reagan defies the Sandinistas (can you say Oliver North and Iran/Contra).

1990s-2005—U.S. likes "democracy" in Nicaragua.

2005—Sandinistas back in power . . . the Nica people vote their leader Ortega back in.

2009—Honduran President (a leftist) gets overthrown by a military coup, takes refuge in Nicaragua. While he is a leftist and the guy overthrowing is U.S. supported . . . we side with the leftist . . . the same side that Chavez (yes, the same guy that thinks the U.S. is part of Satan's army HA HA) and Castro are on . . . crazy crazy crazy world. On the one hand it's pretty wacky and on the other scary. Last week there was a front-page article in the Washington Post about Nicaragua. Seems the Iranians have built an Embassy in Managua . . . but no one can find it! Also reported that fifty Iranians have been given entrance to Nicaragua without passports . . . and no one can find them! Of course, *we* believe the Embassy (wherever it is) is a terrorist camp, and the fifty? Terrorists? The same day I read a quote by Mother Teresa that said, "If we have no peace, it is because we have forgotten that we belong to each other."

Well said . . . Making shell necklaces and tattoos seem like a very productive day compared to all of this stuff my love.

{ Chapter 14 }

One Step Forward . . .
Two Steps Back

Monday, July 20, 2009

Jinx . . .

Today started out so calm and peaceful that I actually thought: *What in the world will I be able to blog about tonight*? When will I learn *not* to ask that question?! ;)

We started our day with a run and then spent a little time at the pool. We visited with some friends and then went home for lunch and a quick shower. Norman picked us up at 1:00 p.m. for my nail appointment. This is only the second time that I have gotten my nails done since I've been in Nicaragua. (This is a big sacrifice for me.) The nail place I found here is so different from the nail salons in the States. There's no frills or fancy instruments (like nail clippers, cleaners or dryers)—they simply fill your nails, apply one coat of paint and voila . . . you're finished. Albeit, it's not what I am used to, I get by.

After getting my nails done; we had one more stop, the grocery store on the way home. The girls were so well behaved (this, in retrospect, should have been my first clue that something wasn't right). Lucie asked me if we were going home and I explained we needed groceries but would head back right after.

As we pulled into the parking lot of *La Union* (grocery store), Scarlett asked Lucie, "What's wrong with you? Aren't you feeling good?" I looked in the back seat, and Lucie had her hand over her mouth (not a good sign) and before I could tell Norman to stop the car . . . Lucie puked through her hand, all over herself. Norman stopped the car, but since we're in the middle of the street, we couldn't exit. I am trying to think about how to say, "pull over" in Spanish but I was at a loss for words.

Lucie continues to throw-up all over the back seat and into her activity bag, which contained coloring books, crayons, DVDs, etc. Gracie starts crying and is desperately trying to open her door, which is locked, and she is yelling *"abre la puerta"* in English open the door!

I finally use sign language and limited Spanish as I'm telling Norman to pull into a parking space. Then, I grab Lucie out of the car as she continues to puke. Now Gracie is mimicking her big sister making all the throw-up noises, but not actually vomiting. This is making me want to toss my cookies!

When Lucie appeared to be finished, I used every anti-bacterial wipe I had in my purse to clean her up. I kept apologizing to Norman—his car was destroyed. I helped clean up the best that I could, and he kept repeating, "No problem, I will go to the car wash, and everything will be fine."

Poor guy. Norman tells me how he and his wife want to have five children (all girls). He thinks girls make a happy home. Well, after these months with us, I think he very well may change his mind.

Funny thing about Lucie, she never says, "Mom, I'm not feeling well" or "My tummy hurts a little" or even "I am getting ready to puke."

She doesn't say *anything*! It amazes me how fast it comes on and if I don't ask her directly, "How are you?" she will never tell me.

I need to remember this about my girl and notice her, *I'm going to get sick all over the place* clues . . .

We headed into the grocery store, and I rushed around because I knew Norman wanted to drop us off and clean his car. We were frantically combing the isles when Lucie told me she needed to go to the bathroom. Here was a golden opportunity to ask her how she felt but instead my reply was, "Scarlett, honey please take your sister to the bathroom."

Lord, what was I thinking?

I was at the check-out counter, getting ready to pay when the girls finally came out of the bathroom. I was worried about them and waved them down to where I was. When Lucie got to me, she looked a little pale, and I asked her, "How are you feeling love?" and she replied by throwing up all over the floor! Why she couldn't puke in the bathroom is a good question, but she has always preferred to be with me when she's sick—lucky me.

Okay, so now I had to pay for my groceries. The check-out lady asked me if I wanted some coupon deal and gave me all the details while the bagger continued to sack my groceries. Can't they see what's going on? They were not phased in the slightest. I took Lucie's hand and started to walk her outside, leaving my groceries behind, she threw up a couple more times before we got out the door, and finished when we were outside. As soon as she was done, she clapped her hands together (this is Lucie's language for *pick me up*) and because she was so pitiful, I immediately did so. Now, at this point, there is puke all over her clothes, in her hair and now on me. My sweet, pitiful girl, I don't know if there is a worse feeling for a mom than knowing your child is sick.

The bagger showed up outside with our groceries. (I didn't know that I actually had paid for them already). I searched my bags, found some baby wipes and cleaned my girl up the best I could. We got back in the cab, which actually didn't smell too bad and went directly home. Lucie and I took a shower, and she went to bed . . .

She's feeling much better, ate some dinner and is sleeping, so I think the worst is over. Scarlett and I replayed the entire scenario this evening and shared a chuckle. Does it mean that I'm a good mother because I can laugh at my children getting sick? Remembering Gracie trying desperately to get out of the car and pulling on the door handle makes me laugh so hard. She was freaking out, and I thought it was hilarious. Am I totally losing my mind because I find this all so funny? Is it time to go home?

Well, it's actually surprising that this is our first sickness (and hopefully the last) since our stay in Nicaragua. I think we are all exhausted and it reminds me of how blessed we are to have had good health during this journey. So no, I will never ask myself again, *What will I be able to blog about tonight?* Because in my world, something *always* happens!

P.S. Just getting ready to publish this post and my girl just got sick again. Please pray for her speedy recovery.

Love and Blessings . . .

1 Comment:

Amy said . . .
Oh my gosh. That is terrible. I was holding back a bit of laughter though, picturing Gracie mimicking her sister. I am so sorry. There is nothing worse than puking kids in a car or store.
Hang in there.

Thursday, July 23, 2009
Catching Up . . .

I'm so sorry, I haven't blogged the last two nights . . . we lost our power two nights in a row. There was no Internet, and I had some hot, sweaty, cranky girls to handle (including myself) so let me catch you up to speed.

First of all, Lucie is feeling great. She was sick for the day and then throughout the night but woke up very hungry. She ate two pieces of French toast and had a big lunch *and* dinner. My girl was brave and is completely cured. ;) We laid low that day and stayed in the house. The girls caught up on their sleep, and I caught up on all my paperwork. I think we all needed a rest day.

Yesterday the Grimes girls were ready to rock again. We had lunch with our friends at one of our favorite places, La Mercado (they serve hummus and delicious drinks). After lunch, we headed to Mi Familia to pick up our declaration. Our declaration is a letter stating that we are officially approved through Mi Familia, and this document along with our birth certificates and marriage certificates are presented to the court. Our lawyer confirms this will be presented today, then the judge reviews our case file and sets a court date.

We ran around to get a couple of signatures on the documents and then met with our lawyer, Amelia. Honestly, Amelia has been a disappointment in many ways. Every time I meet with her, she gives me worst-case scenarios, never commits to anything and I usually feel worse than before I saw her. She has also been sick for many weeks, which has affected her timeliness.

We are concerned about Amelia and about our cases, so we started the meeting inquiring about her health and asked straight-up if we need to get a new lawyer. She assured us that she was fine and that she was dedicated to getting our adoptions finalized. She also told us that it is possible to have us home within twenty days, which she has been able to achieve for some of her clients. She didn't make any promises, but it sounds very confident that we could be home in about a month!!! *Yyyeeesss*!!! So, we will wait (we're pros at this) and make follow-up calls, but we are making progress!

My kids sat at a different table the entire time we met with Amelia and were so well behaved. It was a blessing. I must admit,

I questioned if these kids were truly mine! Did I give them Tylenol PM and not remember it? Their behavior had me relaxed and at ease. It was the best meeting I have ever had with our lawyer. I have such peace in my heart right now. It feels so good to know I am coming home soon.

We got home around 7:00 p.m., so I rushed to feed my kids and then Skyped my husband; we got to talk to Allie, too. We miss her so much and told her how we want her back here to hang and go to the beach with us. It's weird going to these places without her now. We also caught up on what she's doing. It's a long story with lots of details, but our oldest *wants* to go back to college! She was at the house talking to her Dad about it. We are over the moon about this and have given her a few tasks to prepare. I think she is very serious about doing well and I am so excited about her future.

Allie has had her share of struggles. She was ten when her parents got divorced, was an only child who now has to share her Dad with four other women. Despite her challenges, she is coming into her own and is truly one of the most loving people I know. Allie *loves* being part of our family and makes us all complete. I am very proud of her.

My husband gave us some *great* news; he is coming on Sunday and staying until the following Saturday. This is his longest visit to date, so we are making some fun plans for his arrival. Having Tim here makes life so much easier for me. I have my partner to talk to, someone to help with the kids, and I sleep so much better when he is here. Yeah! I won't give any more details of what else I enjoy when he is here . . . his Mom reads my blog (Hi Mimi) but you all catch my drift!! ;) I'm a happy girl!

In other exciting news, we are leaving this morning for another overnight trip to Las Cordones, just the girls and I. We're looking forward to more time on the beach, splashing in the surf and collecting shells as we kick back on our mini-holiday away from Managua. We're bringing our tennis shoes this time to prep for the invasion of the crabs!

Wishing you all a great couple of days . . . I will blog when we return . . . tomorrow night.

Love and Blessings . . .

1 Comment:

Timothy said . . .
MiMi . . . what Lesa is referring to is that I make her coffee every morning ;-)

Friday, July 24, 2009
Our final trip to Las Cardones

The Grimes girls hit the beach for one last hoorah at Las Cardones. This trip went by very quickly and was full of laugh out loud moments. Since it was just the girls and I (no friends, no Allie and no hubby), I was a little worried about entertaining all three of them on my own. This time, we stayed in the *Suite*, which is the best casita at Las Cardones. It sits on the beach, so you can see the ocean, hear the waves and feel the cool breeze. I didn't want to move from this postcard, I wanted to sit in the rocking chair and take a couple of breaths, but the girls were anxious to get on the beach . . . relaxation, had to wait.

The ocean was a brownish/bronze color. I have never seen that before. I kept asking everyone I saw, "What's up with the beach?"

The only logical answer I received was that it was an algae issue!

Eww! All of us girls looked at each other and said, "Daddy needs to be here." ;)

Tim works with algae in his job, so he would know what it was. I married such a nerd, but boy do I love him! We also saw a dead dolphin on the beach, so we ventured down the shore where the ocean was white and spent our time there.

We arrived with two DVD players, two DS's (both fully charged), coloring books, school books, and Sudoku. But once

I convinced the girls that it was *relaxation time*, within twenty minutes they were (yes, you guessed it) bored. So, I tucked each one into a hammock, (myself included) and had a good half hour of bliss!

Our day went by quickly, and before we knew it, it was time for showers and dinner. Since we conquered (sort of) our crab fear last trip, we were much braver this time. There were still a few screams when a critter ran out in front of us, but the volume and shrill factor of our voices were much lower (myself included). We still were afraid to go to the outhouse at night and use the shower but hey, not too bad for four girls on their own.

Whatever Lucie had, I think I caught. I didn't sleep well and had an upset stomach, but I woke up feeling glad to be at the beach. We had a great breakfast, enjoyed another long walk/swim and went shell hunting before it was time to pack up, shower, and have lunch. I was a little concerned that both Lucie and Gracie didn't eat well. We had a scare with Gracie at dinner the previous night. She *inhaled* her spaghetti and started to choke. I told her to raise her arms up, and she let out the loudest and deepest burp I have ever heard. I actually thought she was about to get sick and rushed her from the dining area (again, we were the center of attention) to a sandy section a few feet away.

I held Gracie's head down and told Scarlett to keep the flashlight on me (to help monitor the crab situation) and waited for Gracie to get sick. She looked at me strangely, as I am sure she thought, "What is this crazy lady doing?" Seriously—I thought something serious was wrong but nope . . . just the biggest, loudest burp that has ever come from a four-year-old!! Scarlett laughed so hard she cried, which made me have the giggles. Man, what a bunch we are. I am surprised we haven't been banned from this resort!

Well, Gracie never did get sick, but my Lucie did *again* on the way home from the beach. This time I was prepared, I continuously asked her how she was feeling and when she finally said, "not so good," Norman skidded to a stop that about gave me whiplash (poor guy) and I got her out of the cab.

I think the term, *not so good* is pretty universal in any language. I took one of the beach buckets out of the trunk for her to hold. I sat next to her the rest of the way home. I got a cool, wet anti-bacterial wipe from my purse, and rubbed her forehead with it. I told her this is what my Mom used to do when I wasn't feeling well, and Lucie replied, "I miss Grandma." Little Bug.

So do I. We were very close to home when Lucie finally lost her cookies. Thank goodness because my stomach wasn't doing too well, especially when Lucie looked in the bucket to *examine* the contents (she so gets that from her father).

So, we are settled. Lucie is completely herself again, and I am chalking it all up to car sickness. We are not allowed to be sick, especially since my husband will be here on Sunday. From here on out we're on a strict regimen of vitamins, naps, and we're staying home tomorrow. I am actually really looking forward to a day with nothing to do. The beach was calming and so beautiful. We will miss it.

Our declarations were delivered to the courthouse this morning, so we hope to hear about our court date next week. I hope we get some great news while my husband is here, so he can celebrate with us. Hey, we may celebrate *even if* we don't get any good news next week. I know I already said this many times before, but all is well when Tim is here. I am so looking forward to having him with us.

Happy weekend my loved ones. I hope you are all healthy and enjoying your family time . . . Love and Blessings to you all.

2 Comments:

Donna said . . .
Have a great week Lesa and Tim! It sounds like you are on the home stretch—we look forward to seeing the whole family at DCC soon!
Donna, Matt, and Meagan

Saturday, July 25, 2009
Here's to Tomorrow . . .

Today was one of those days when I didn't want to read any more books to my children, do anyone's hair, tie any shoes, make any more meals, or clean up after anyone. I was short-tempered, sad, and angry. I don't know what happened to make me lose it today, but I did. I told the girls that I was tired of being dumped on and taken advantage of and I needed some alone time, which lasted for about five minutes, and it wasn't long enough.

You have to understand that I am with the girls 24/7. Our house is so small that even if they are in their room, I can hear everything. There's no saying, "Go outside and play" because that's not safe.

I can't take a hot bath to relax because there's no hot water and there are way too many bugs. Our routine has changed so dramatically. It isn't easy for the girls either since they have such limited activities they have to repeat day after day. How many times can you watch the same movie on a small DVD player? How many hours can you be with both of your sisters without any alone time? It's not easy. I kept telling myself that my husband will be here soon, I will be home relatively soon, and all will be well. But sometimes, no matter what I say to myself . . . it doesn't help. I'm sure the girls are also wondering when things will be normal for them again.

I killed my normal 100 bugs today, and Lucie still isn't feeling well, which is upsetting. Being in a third world county, I can't take our health lightly, and it worries me that we don't have a doctor on hand. What if something is really wrong with her? I am so ready to go home. I thought I was doing so well, knowing how far we have come and how close we are to the finish but today . . . is not a good day.

We went for our run this morning, and it started to rain on us. I know Scarlett was thinking, "Great, we're finished" but I kept running and didn't speak to her the entire time.

I kept my silence to ensure I didn't take any of my frustration and worry out on her. I kept thinking that soon, I would feel better. I would feel refreshed, but it didn't happen. We finished our run and came home, and I got a Skype call from my dear friend, Sue. At first, I wasn't going to answer because I didn't think I was in the mood to be pleasant to anyone, but I am so glad I picked up. Sue always makes me laugh and is such a good listener. It was exactly what I needed at the time. I miss my girlfriends so much. I miss being able to talk about life and hear what's going on with them.

Our conversation was cut short because Lucie didn't feel well, so we parked ourselves in the bathroom. Lucie was very upset. She is tired of being sick, which is totally understandable. Is there anything worse than your kids being sick? She didn't vomit, after all, took a long nap and felt much better when she woke up. My husband thinks she has a parasite; he is probably right. Okay, as tough as this experience has been, we have been blessed with good health until this point. You never appreciate the blessings, until they are taken away, so having my girl wake up happy and healthy was my saving grace. It puts everything else into perspective.

The girls knew I wasn't having a good day and played very well together. Gracie is learning to play by herself, which is a new experience for her. Scarlett was a Godsend—cleaning the dishes and rubbing my feet! ;) We had a much better afternoon than morning.

Now the girls are in bed, I am watching a movie and relaxing with a couple of beers. Maybe Lucie was right, her Mom loves beer! My husband will be here tomorrow night, and I won't have to sleep alone for another week. This is something I never knew would upset me . . . sleeping alone. I, of course, love having my husband close to me but as the years continue, now I *need* my husband next to me. I don't sleep well otherwise. I used to travel all the time by myself, sleep by myself and never had any issues but now I sleep much better with my husband sleeping beside me.

I know that I am not Wonder Woman, and I will have days like today, but it's tough for me to handle. Feeling sorry for myself and wishing something (like I want to be home now) that I know isn't possible, makes me feel weak and vulnerable. This has honestly been a roller coaster ride for me in so many ways. I can't appreciate the good without the bad, but the bad is not fun either. Could I just get to the top of the mountain already? The view from the valley is really getting on my nerves.

So, here's to tomorrow: a day of happiness, a day to rejoice, a day of knowing how blessed I am and enjoying every moment.

1 Comment:

ivaniam97 said . . .
I'm so sorry honey. Please know it's totally okay you're feeling this way. I still think you're the bravest girl I know!!!
xoxo

Sunday, July 26, 2009
Are We Truly Making An Impact?

I am doing *much* better today. Sunday to the rescue! There is something about Sunday that always lifts my spirit. We returned to the orphanage, after being away for a few days, so it was really wonderful to see the kids and catch up with our friend Amanda. Amanda is twenty-three years old, originally from Atlanta, and has a heart for mission work. She recently spent a few weeks in the Dominican Republic and just returned to Nicaragua. She told us all about the kids she met who were former gang members and prostitutes. Now, these young girls and boys are changing their lives *and* the lives of other children by sharing their stories. Amanda is an inspiration to us all. She told me that it gives her hope to see what these kids are doing. I hope our time at the orphanage is really making an impact on the kids in Nicaragua.

Sometimes, loving these kids is a complicated business. Just when you get close to one of them, they check-out, either physically or emotionally. Some of the kids go back to their families and are abused, while other children are sent home to parents who can't feed them, so they're forced to become beggars, prostitutes, and thieves. Some kids check-out while they're still living at the orphanage. They become *hard* because of their circumstances. It is understandable, all of it, really. These kids turn off their emotions and shut people out to protect themselves after being abandoned by the ones they love.

Thankfully, the worst-case scenarios are not always the case. Many of the children leave to start a brand new life with a loving family, which as you know brings my heart so much hope. Still, we often think that loving these kids will change their lives and sometimes, it doesn't change their life the way we pictured. I think of Fernando and his struggles after returning home. I hope his new beginning at Casa Bernabe will give him a second chance to finish school and start over. I pray that his future is a bright one.

One thing I know for sure is that these children are making a difference in *my* life. They bring me such joy and make me feel so close to God. Their hugs, stories, challenges, and laughter move me more than I could ever express. They show me that we are all the same and that love is really all that matters. It gives me a purpose because I know that with these interactions, lives are being impacted positively. Including mine.

One of my favorite kids (I know I shouldn't have favorites, but I do!!) is Esaul. He is only four years old and so articulate. He is always saying, "Lesa, Lesa, *mire*" (watch me) and does the funniest things.

He has a beautiful smile, and I am crazy about him. I haven't seen him for a few days and was so happy to see his sweet grin today. He got up at church and sang a solo in front of the crowd. He did a *great* job, and I took lots of pictures and some video. I know he knows how much I love him and how proud I am of him. I hope this will make a difference in his life.

Making an impact isn't just about the kids that live here but also about my own girls. When I watch them (really observe them) loving the kids at Puente de Amistad, I see the change in their faces and personalities. I love watching how they talk to them, interact with them, and learn from them. When Allie first came here two years ago, she was a typical teenager with an attitude. She really didn't like me that much and was very resistant to the entire process. We basically forced her to come, knowing that the experience would be life-changing. She resisted. This didn't last long.

Soon Nicaragua and these precious kids wiggled their way into her heart, and she began to change. She opened up and loved completely; it truly changed her life, which I believe has helped make her the person she is today. I see the spark in both Scarlett and Lucie every day—how they, too, have opened up and shared themselves completely. They understand how little these kids have and how happy they are—it's a valuable lesson. These kids have impacted my entire family.

So, I guess I have answered my own question. Yes, we honestly can and are making an impact.

Tonight, we picked up my husband from the airport. He actually surprised us, since his flight got in early, so when we were trying to figure out what gate he was at, he was walking straight towards us! I was so so happy to see him. Oh, how my heart swells up when I kiss and hold on to him. The girls were so excited to see him they started telling stories over each other, trying to catch him up on what's been going on. During the cab ride home, they sang songs that even Gracie knew. It felt so good to have us all together again.

We have almost an entire week with Tim, so you better believe we are making some plans. We hope to hear about our court date by mid-week, so we may go to San Juan del Sur for the next couple of days. It's a tough time because we don't want to be too far away if something comes up, but we want to make the most of our time with him as well.

I'm happy to report today was much better—today, I was present and genuinely enjoyed my girls and my babies at the orphanage. Being a mom today was an absolute blessing.

1 Comment:

mawyer said . . .
Lesa,
Here's to a better day—so glad your day was better, and Tim is there now. Love and prayers are with you all.
Love, T

Tuesday, July 28, 2009
The Latino Hairdresser

Now I know I go on and on about how happy I am to have Tim with me, but it's also pretty fantastic to have him here so I can ditch him to cheat on Jackie. (Well, that should raise a few eyebrows.) Jackie is my hairdresser from home whom I adore, but I desperately need to do *something* with my hair. It has been way too long since I colored the beast and I was looking pretty bad. My friend, Beth had seen a male stylist at the mall, Metro Centro, and was pleased with her hair, so with his card in hand, we left for the mall first thing in the morning.

I had told my girlfriend Sue, about getting my hair done and that having Tim here would allow me the time to do it. I was excited. Sue, the good friend that she is, warned me that the Latino hairdresser *may not* know how to handle thin, fine, blond hair and could leave the color on too long and burn my hair. She suggested I cheat on Jackie with Tim. However, that's not going to work because firstly, there's no blond hair color at the grocery store and secondly, my husband has never colored hair. With our luck, it would be a massive fail, which means I would look bad *and* be mad at my husband. ;) So, I opted to cheat on Jackie with the Latino hairdresser. Scandalous, I know.

The man my friend Beth suggested, wasn't working but there was another stylist, Dory who *knew how* to highlight. There was a guy behind the counter who spoke pretty good English, but we still struggled through the conversation. Yes, I was a little nervous. I ended the conversation by saying how different my hair is. "It doesn't need a lot of time for color, much less than most of your clients."

Everyone was shaking their heads. The universal language for *yes, we understand,* or they could also mean, *yeah, yeah, lady— we have no idea what you are saying but how hard can it be?*

The man of the hour, my husband, took my noisy children away while I got my hair done. Dory was much slower than Jackie back home. She took a lot of time putting the foil in my hair. I thought, "she's going to have to wash my hair as soon as she's finished." Her phone kept ringing, and she talked on it the entire time she did my hair. This is quite the task considering foiling takes two hands and some *focus* to use the right amount of color! When she finished, she whispered to me (so she didn't disturb the person she was talking to on the phone) "*un poquito*" or just a minute and left.

I kept telling myself . . . "Lesa, you have been waiting so long to get your hair done . . . this is your time to relax . . . so relax . . . she knows what she's doing . . . she is a professional . . . of course, she is paying attention . . . burning hair is cause for termination, etc."

I kept looking at my watch, and about ten minutes later, she showed up. She was off the phone, and I took a deep breath to relax. She checked a few foils and *again* said, "*un poquito*" so I told her again that my hair is very different and doesn't need a lot of time. She shook her head, smiled and left. Another ten minutes go by, and I'm thinking that I'm going to pull the foils out and wash my own hair. Who cares if they think I'm a crazy *gringo*, I'll never see them again! Right on cue, Dory shows up and is satisfied with how everything looks, so she starts to take my foils out.

I was then led to the sink where another lady washed my hair with *warm water!* It felt incredible. I was so relaxed and loving it! Then, she called Dory over, and they started to ramble in Spanish very quickly, and I couldn't pick up a word, and all of a sudden, I panicked, *Please God—tell me that I don't have lice!*

Well, everyone kept smiling at me. Good sign, right?! Then they told me that they were putting some extra conditioner on me. Is that because my hair was falling out? I told the anxious voice in my head to shut it, sat back and enjoyed every moment of the scalp massage. Who cares if my hair is burnt, falling out or dark brown? This feels *so* good!

Dory put me back in the chair and started to comb it out. All my hair looked intact, I couldn't tell what the color was, but I enjoyed being pampered. She cut my bangs (they were so long) and trimmed the ends. Then, she blow-dried my hair, and it was *gorgeous!!!* She dried my hair straight; it was so healthy looking and blond (Buh-bye dark brown roots and grey hairs!) My family gave me *mucho* compliments, and I was one happy camper!

We met our cab driver (affectionately known as my Nicaraguan husband) to go home, and he kept staring at me before I got into the car. Norman said, "*muy differente*" very different, and when I got in the back seat, he adjusted his rear-view mirror so he could get a better look. My husband was laughing and egging Norman on about how good my hair looked. ;) Come on Norman, don't be making these comments *in front* of my husband, right?! ;)

We met our friends, Jack, Beth, and Ignacio for dinner at a fabulous Italian restaurant and had a great time. Being around Ignacio, the son they are adopting, always reminds us how different boys are than girls. He makes farting noises with his armpits, burps a lot and can't sit still for two-seconds but he makes us laugh and fills our hearts with pure joy. We love our friends.

Now it's time to pack for our trip to San Juan del Sur, which is a gorgeous beach/resort located very close to Costa Rica. Everyone here raves about how beautiful it is, and so we are very excited to experience it for ourselves. So, it's off to San Juan del Sur for two nights. I will blog when I get home and let you all know how it was.

Have an awesome week—love and blessings to you all . . .

1 Comment:

Amy said . . .

Lesa, you are so brave. NO WAY would I have let them touch my hair. So glad it turned out ok. I know you must be enjoying Tim.

Do you have a date for your return, yet?? We are getting excited.

Part III

─⁓─

August, 2009 . . .

My One-Way Ticket

$\left\{ Chapter\ 15 \right\}$

Living in Paradise

Saturday, August 1, 2009
San Juan de Paradise

What an awesome week in San Juan de Paradise! I have so much to tell you all, and I will try to include all of the juicy details. As you know, my husband arrived on Sunday night, we spent Monday at the hairdresser and then we started to make plans for our San Juan del Sur trip. We researched some hotels online, and while we didn't know anything about where to stay, we came up with our own criteria:

- Does it have a swimming pool?
- Is it within close proximity to a beach?
- Does it have a restaurant/bar?

Our search brought us to a resort called *Piedras y Olas*, translation: Pelican's Eyes. This hotel has AC, two restaurants, and three pools, which sounds like paradise to me. We are still awaiting news on our court date, but our lawyer seems to think we won't hear anything until the end of the week. Since I'd prefer waiting on our court date with an ocean-view, we booked a room and told our lawyer we'd be leaving town for a few days. We gave Norman (our friend and cab driver) a call, and we were all set. Next stop Pelican's Eyes!

We left early in the morning and while I thought we had plenty of time, having four girls in the house means we're scrambling for every minute. We ran around like crazy people trying to get all our stuff in the car and be on our way. Hectic! Scarlett is always such a big help. She offered to pack for the girls and herself. I may have put a little too much faith in my first-born because when we arrived at the resort and unpacked our bags, we realized the girls didn't have swimsuits *and* we had left the bag containing all the electronics (DVD, DS's) at home. Scarlett was extremely apologetic. She is so completely fired. Good thing she's cute, that's all I have to say.

As we neared the resort, we saw a bunch of houses on the hillside and Norman said, "Wow, look at those homes!"

I thought what a dream it would be to stay there. Well, that's where we stayed! The resort is made up of *gorgeous* casitas lined up on a hillside, over-looking the Pacific Ocean (It was absolutely breath-taking). We checked in, unpacked and then headed straight for the pool. No surprise that we were (again) the center of attention due to the fact our kids were swimming in their clothes while being completely loud and obnoxious. Seriously, how many times do I have to explain what keeping a low profile means?

While my girls swam and disrupted everyone else at the pool, my husband and I laid out on some *very* comfortable chaise lounges in our swimsuits and pretended not to know the orphans swimming in their clothes. My husband had ordered me a drink, and when the cabana boy brought over the Mango Margarita, I responded, "Shut up, it's gorgeous!"

For whatever reason, this caused me having a complete breakdown. I looked at Tim and said, "I have been living in a hell hole for three months." I cried . . . tears of complete joy, and Tim said I was having an *episode* or an *exorcism*.

All the memories of the past few months; ants crawling up my legs as I tried to pee, being fearful to drink because of the ice, lying on broken chairs at our pool, and making all my own food because I'm afraid of how things are cleaned and cooked, vanished with one sip of my Mango Margarita. A Spanish speaking cabana boy, a yummy drink, sunshine, looking at the ocean, and having my very handsome husband lying right next to me . . . Bliss.

Well, we laughed about this for a long time as we continued to enjoy the sun and drinks. Laughing through tears is my most treasured emotion. We had a wonderful, delicious dinner at the restaurant and the girls were almost as happy as we were. (They were experiencing electronics' withdrawal, which takes a couple of days of getting used to.) We went back to our gorgeous home and put the girls to bed. When they were all tucked in, Tim and I sat on our private patio located outside our bedroom to enjoy the view and the peace. We were talking and relaxing when the wind kicked up, and the door to the patio closed shut.

We looked at each other and I said, "Well, we better be sure we aren't locked out." So, with a big smile on his face, Tim got up to check the door . . . and his smile disappeared.

Seriously, why do these things happen to us? We tried the door a few times, and yes, it was still locked. Tim called Scarlett's name a couple of times (their bedroom is right below ours on the first floor), but we didn't hear a peep from the girls, so we started brainstorming our options. There was an adjacent tile roof that Tim could climb out on but only by holding onto a pipe that did not look or feel very sturdy. I had visions of Tim falling and us spending the rest of our San Juan del Sur vacation at a Nicaraguan hospital, so I grabbed my beer bottle and started banging on the wall *screaming*, "Scarlett" over and over again. Still, no response.

Well, Tim decided he could scale down the side of the house (he used to climb mountains you know) and save us from spending the night on rocking chairs. I encouraged him from the sidelines, "You got this Baye!" "You are such a stud, I know this will work!"

He put one leg over the banister, nailed his *cajones*, and with a grunt brought his leg right back over the patio. It was the shortest-lived rescue attempt I have ever seen. So now I'm thinking, maybe it would be easier for me to do it. Before we had a chance to come up with Plan B, Lucie walks into our bedroom with Scarlett following behind her, looking for us. I started to bang on the door, and she let us in! We were saved by Lucie!!

Lucie was very upset she explained that Scarlett had heard her name being called and woke her up asking, "Hey Lucie—do you hear that?"

Lucie replied, "yes" and then they were both afraid that someone they didn't know was calling her name, which makes zero sense but after some serious coaxing from her big sister, Lucie (who by the way is six years *younger* than her older sister) mustered the courage to leave their bedroom (with Scarlett safely behind her) and explored the house trying to find where the voices were coming from. When she got to our bedroom door, Lucie started knocking (she didn't want to interrupt our *sexy time* she calls it . . . yes, she is well trained) and finally entered to find us stranded on the balcony. After a lot of hugs and reassurance, my children went back to sleep, and we unlocked every door in the house!

After spending the night in this beautiful place, we decided to upgrade our stay from two nights to three nights. I have never been able to extend a vacation like this and was so thrilled to do so. We had to go home after three nights because Tim was leaving for home (Virginia) early Saturday morning. We started our second day with a horseback ride on the beach.

After a lovely breakfast, a Jeep picked us up from the hotel, and we made our way into town. It was a short ride, and soon we were all on our horses ready to go. Tim and Scarlett rode on their own, Lucie was led by one of the guides and Gracie rode with me. We did a little trotting, but mostly walked and enjoyed the ride. We saw some monkeys playing in the trees, and a lot of locals out and about. It was an awesome experience that made everyone feel a little more secure with horses by the time we finished. We were all sore, and while Lucie asked to ride again the next day, we decided to try some other excursions.

We ventured into town after our ride to purchase some bathing suits for the girls. I was afraid they may not *want* us to stay another night if we didn't, and I really couldn't continue to deny knowing them at this point. We found some swim gear right away and then explored for a while. Even though San Juan del Sur has a lot of surfing shops and numerous hotels, you'll still find a lot of locals hanging about. We saw kids attending school, merchants selling their wares and boats cruising along the shore. The city is a solid mix of local customs and tourism.

It was such a treat to stay at this resort, dine at the restaurant and enjoy some of the luxuries, we've missed dearly. The resort's chef was a gift from the hunger gods; we looked forward to every meal. Fresh fish, decadent pastries—I wanted to devour it all. I even feel comfortable eating my leafy greens and veggies with all our meals.

Tim is really racking up the points on this trip. He booked me a massage at Casita Tranquila, so I left the girls in his care and headed off in search of more bliss. It was *fabulous* and only cost me forty dollars for an hour! As I walked back to the restaurant to purchase a couple of beers (to bring back to our house) I met the owner of the resort, Chris, very nice guy with a great story. We chatted for a while. I also met a big group of people as they were checking in on the last night of a mission trip. They had spent their time building a school while helping out some of the locals, so they were eager to shower and have a delicious dinner.

This resort caters to a lot of missionary guests and uses a percentage of its revenue to support the community. They employ 250 locals, give back to the schools and aid local charities. Isn't that wonderful? This place is not only meaningful to its guests, but to the world around it.

I headed back to the casita to check on my family. Due to the lack of electronics, Tim had to be creative while watching the girls. Since the electricity went out, there was no TV, so he invented some *Nicaraguan games* to play with Lucie and Scarlett. Gracie was napping (thank goodness and was not included in this). *Nicaraguan games* included balancing clothes on your head, walking upstairs, touching the bedroom door, and heading back down again. The first person to complete the obstacle won, and if you dropped anything, there was a five-second penalty. Now, when I heard how my husband spent his *quality* time with our children, I began to understand why all the things that happen to us, happen to us. We deserve them! ;) They had a blast together, and I had some *awesome* relaxation time to myself.

There was so much to explore at the resort, including an animal rescue habitation with monkeys (on site). Albeit I told all my children (including my forty-nine-year-old son AKA, husband who acts ten most of the time) *not* to touch the monkeys, they were petting and hugging them and not wanting to leave. (All of this happened when Mom wasn't around.) We also adopted a kitty cat while we were there. We fed the furry prince at mealtimes, and he slept at our house and jumped on my lap every chance he got. We met some great people, had fabulous food and drinks, and did *not* want to leave. It was the best time, ever.

San Juan de Paradise was a sip of heaven for us all . . .

1 Comment:

mawyer said . . .

Lesa,

Saw the photos Tim posted on your trip—looks awesome! Glad you guys had a great time (even if you did lock yourself out . . . hee hee hee!)

Counting the days until you come home! Love ya, T

Monday, August 3, 2009
Two Weeks to Go!!!

I have been cursed with blog issues. I attempted to blog two nights ago, and the electricity went out for six hours. Then, last night I was almost finished with my blog . . . and the power went out again! I was hoping it had somehow posted . . . but no such luck. Sorry for the delay, but I'm back.

The last couple of days have been busy. When the electricity goes out here, which is often, it reminds me of the conveniences I *do* have here that I also take for granted (lights, fans, and the microwave). I was cooking dinner for the girls when the electricity went out, and panic settled in with a barrage of questions: When will it come back on Mommy? How will we see? What will we do for dinner? How can we sleep? Panic! I went through the house, lit candles, opened all the windows, and prayed the lights would come back on soon. I warmed mac-and-cheese in the oven with some chicken fingers. The girls praised me for how *rico,* yummy dinner was. It never fails . . . I spend an hour preparing roasted chicken and vegetables and don't hear a peep from the girls, but when mac-and-cheese comes out to play, I'm a goddess with an apron.

The electricity didn't turn on until 11:30 p.m. I was asleep and awoke to the lights shining and fans whirring, so at least for the majority of the night, we slept in comfort.

Our mac and cheese dinner was slightly less exotic than the previous night's meal. I'm just going to come right out and say it, I ate a lizard!!! (But I'm blaming Tim for the whole experience.) My husband had been asking Norman about iguana (as a dish). After all, the giant prehistoric-looking reptile is considered to be a delicacy here. Who knew?! Sure, we see them running around all the time, and I blogged about how we ran one over, but to *eat* it? This is where my husband and I differ . . . greatly. Tim wanted to see what it tasted like. I, on the other hand, don't need or want that experience to write to you all about but somehow, I find myself doing it!

Norman who is such a dear friend to us wanted to make this happen for Tim, so he bought, and killed an iguana. His wife Susanna made iguana stew and brought it over for us to eat. She made homemade tortillas, and the stew looked really good (if only I could pretend there wasn't an iguana in it) so of course, my husband dug in. Immediately, he started to rant and rave about how good it was. Then it was my turn . . . and I had nowhere to escape, I had to try it. So, I put some on a tortilla and took my first bite. I actually crunched down on what felt like several bones in my mouth. (I was finished experimenting!). I started to push the food around on my plate and then my little savior, Gracie came over and said, "Yum iguana" and I fed her the rest of my food. Tim also examined my plate, looked at the bones and informed me that I had the rib cage of the iguana . . . eeeeewwwww! This is my luck. Everyone said it tasted like chicken, not so much for me.

My husband went home Saturday morning—early. I have been in a daze ever since. I am trying to wrap my head around the fact that we are going home in two weeks. Isn't it funny how sometimes it can take days for things actually to sink in? Over the past three months, we've built a new life for ourselves, which includes a community of people we love. It is a process for me to say, *Goodbye*. There are places I still want to go, people, I want to spend time with, and things I want to do before we leave. I know this time will fly by and I want to be sure to get as much in as we can!

We went to church yesterday and made some plans with Natalia and the kids. Leaving these kids will be . . . I honestly, can't even think about it. Every time I go to Puente de Amistad, I am greeted with hugs and stories. Inside those walls is love, pure love. All of the children hold such a special place in my heart. Being here, in Nicaragua, has given me the opportunity to take care of them, to know how each one of them is doing, to see them often, and notice the little things about them that change. I won't be able to do that when I go home. Letting go of those kids is the hardest thing for me. I always strive to make sure that each kid knows that I love and cherish them so for the next few days, I will take time to tell each one how I feel and let them know I will be praying for them. I know they'll ask, "When are you coming back?" How can I answer them?

Today, I am so thrilled by the notion of going home that I honestly have no desire to return anytime soon, but I think that after some time, I will feel differently. Yesterday, Lucie said to me, "Mommy, I want to come back after we leave in two or three months and I want to stay for one week and then go back home!" ;)

I think she is afraid that we will be stuck here, I share that sentiment. But after some time, I too will be asking when I can come back. When will I return to Nicaragua? Right now, the answer is, *I don't know*, and the tears will fall.

Today starts the *next to last* week here in Nicaragua. We have dinner with the girls from the orphanage tonight and a court date tomorrow. Gracie has two doctor appointments on Wednesday. Thursday is our party at the orphanage and Friday, we are hoping to head to Granada to eat at Kathy's Waffle House one last time. It's a busy week, and I know as time goes on, it will get even more hectic. We have piles of paperwork and appointments to attend to, so it will be crazy busy. But when I think of having all of us *home* . . . I know this will all be worth it.

2 Comments:

ivaniam97 said . . .
PRAISE GOD YOU WILL ALL BE HOME SOON!!! LOVE YOU ALL AND I REALLY HOPE WE GET TO SEE EACH OTHER IN A FEW WEEKS. I'M SO HAPPY FOR YOU!!!
XOXOXO

Timothy said . . .
My wife is a complete stud . . . not only has she thrived in Nica for three months, but she has done so with a big smile on her

face and with a big heart. Oh yeah, and she did eat iguana too! Love you Baye . . .

Monday, August 3, 2009
Susanna's New Career . . .

I had a difficult time sleeping last night, as I'm nervous about the next few days. I'm having flashbacks of years spent submitting paperwork while not having the *new and updated* form, or having the wrong translation or falling behind on the new requirements. Ugh. I kept thinking, *What am I missing?*

I woke up early and started going through paperwork—checking and re-checking. When the girls got up, they all smelled like disinfectant spray. Apparently one of them had a smelly number two, and the girls went crazy with the spray. Not a pleasant odor first thing in the morning but I *guess* disinfectant spray is better than the alternative.

We went for our run and enjoyed some time at the pool. We haven't been there since Allie was here. There was nobody else there, so we had some relaxation time. Gracie used to be a good swimmer, but for whatever reason, she is growing more and more afraid of the pool. She cried every time we encouraged her to swim. A few times I wanted to stick her head under the water so I couldn't hear her crying (Is that a bad thing? Don't judge me!)

I talked to my friend Jack about twenty times today as we tried to work out all the details of the next couple of days. Then, I called to make doctor's appointments for both Gracie and Ignacio, and of course, the receptionist didn't speak any English, but we got through it. I don't know whether my Spanish is improving . . . or other people are growing more tolerant. Either way, I am making it work.

Tomorrow is our court date! I am still in shock! We have our clothes picked out, and the camera is charged. They asked us to bring our passports and $625. They say that nothing else is

needed, but I am bringing every piece of paperwork I ever submitted so if they ask me for *anything*, I'm armed. The court is in
another city, which is about an hour drive from here. Depending
on how backed up the courthouse is, we may have to wait about
three hours before our case is heard. Our lawyer told us that last
month the judge didn't show, so she had to drive around the city
looking for him and bring him to court. (Only in Nicaragua!)
The Grimes' clan is ready for a long day; the DVD's all charged,
snacks packed, and I am definitely taking one of my little pills
(maybe two) to get me through the day. (Again, no judging!)

Today, we went to the orphanage and picked up the older
girls to go see the movie, *My Sister's Keeper*. We packed twelve
of us in one cab! We left when the girls were out of school, which
happened to be during rush hour traffic, so it was a very *long*
drive to the mall. *Mucho* traffic. We had dinner at the food court,
shared stories and laughed, it was a lot of fun. We want to do a
few more excursions with the kids before we leave. I love spending time with them.

On Sunday, when Norman, picked us up from church, he
brought his wife, Susanna, with him. She only spent about thirty
minutes at the orphanage but fell in love with all the kids. Norman's wife has had issues getting pregnant but longs for kids in
her life. She told me that she wants to work at the orphanage. She
doesn't want to be paid, she just wants to help (even though her
family is struggling). I am so inspired by Norman and Susanna.

They have a very small house and have a difficult time
making ends meet. Susanna just started a new job on Monday
(the day after she was at the orphanage) a paying job in an office
that she has been trying to get for a long time. I talked to Natalia,
the director of the orphanage, and explained Susanna's passion
for kids after which, Norman and Natalia had a long talk. I just
learned this evening that Susanna starts work at the orphanage
on Wednesday! I just know this will change their lives and bring
them the happiness they haven't experienced. Someday, they
may even adopt a child. Amazing how God works, right?! These

are the moments I feel I was meant to be here. These are the times I can see the impact we're making with my heart.

So, it's late, and I am heading to bed. I am *sure* that tomorrow will be a day of adventure—stay tuned for details. Have a great day tomorrow and God bless.

2 Comments:

Donna said . . .
Wow! I love how God works. Lesa, thanks again for taking the time to share with all of us. Just can't wait for you all to get back home but have to admit that I'll miss reading about your adventures! Wishing you the best tomorrow.
Donna

mawyer said . . .
Hey Lesa—love you and hope your day today was amazing! Can't wait to hear. See you SOON!
Love and hugs,
Tracy

Tuesday, August 4, 2009
It's Official . . . Gracie is Ours!!!

What a *fantastic, marvelous* day! As I'm sure you would guess, it was loaded with laughs and tears. I survived today with only one pill. I took that little bad boy right before we left the house when I realized the dress Lucie was wearing showed her new temporary tattoo (a giant cockroach) on my little girl's chest—so attractive. I scrubbed until her skin was red and she started to cry, so I opted to put a little cover up on it to mask the blue, green and black colors.

We left the house at 7:00 a.m. with our friends, Jack, Beth, and Ignacio in tow. It took us about an hour to get to court and then we waited another thirty minutes for our lawyer to show up, which she did. Yes! We headed to the courthouse right on time for our 8:30 a.m. appointment.

The courthouse was nothing like I expected. How long do I have to live here to understand that what I think things should be like in my head are definitely *not* how they are in Nicaragua? The courthouse was an old building (I mean about to fall down) with two plastic chairs, an open office, no air conditioning, and several employees. The judge was there but the second in command (not sure what his title is) had not shown up yet. So, we waited. After about thirty minutes, Gracie started to hold her private area (working on that) and told me she had to go to the bathroom. We were given instructions as to where it was, and I started to worry as we headed toward the end of the building. The bathroom light didn't work—so we had to keep the door open. There was no toilet paper, and the toilet wouldn't flush so we added to what was already deposited there. I know, eeewww! I pulled out my tissue and my anti-bacterial wipes, and we were set.

We went back to join the others. When there are only two chairs and four kids, that's a bad math problem. As soon as one child sits, the other one *has* to as well. Thank goodness my pill was working, I kept a cool head and gave each kid five minutes a piece on the chair and then it was time to switch. My non-medicated self would have made them all sit on the floor, and I would use all the chairs for myself, but I was in a generous and relaxed frame of mind.

We waited about one and a half hours before our guy showed up and then they called our name to go see the judge. Again, no *courtroom*, no black robe, and just two chairs. I really wanted all my girls to experience this moment (What in the world was I thinking and when will I learn?!) So, we all filed into the courtroom—Gracie, Scarlett, Lucie, Manuel (translator), Amelia (lawyer), her son (lawyer assistant) a representative from the Consejo, and me.

The judge was checking everyone's names and had to make a correction to our form to include both Lucie and Scarlett. As we waited, the judge started to ask Gracie some questions. I had been prepared for this. I was told that the questions would include: Do you love your Mommy? What is your name? Do you love your sisters—your Daddy? Do you want to live in the United States? Well, for whatever reason, the judge didn't ask any of these questions but only one question in Spanish . . . "Martita, do you know any words in English?"

She shook her head *yes* and he asked, "What words do you know?"

Gracie started to smile and began singing . . . yes, *singing* the song from the movie *Annie*, *Tomorrow, tomorrow I love you, tomorrow, you're only a day away* . . .

Well, everyone started to laugh, which just encouraged our little singer to continue (did I mention that Gracie sings about as well as Lucie dances?!) so, she took a deep breath and belted out, "Tomorrow . . . " and then she farted (yes, you are reading this correctly) loudly!!!

Lucie immediately yelled, "Oh no, Martita farted!!!"

She plugged her nose with her hand and waved her other hand in front of her face. Now to Lucie's defense, this is what we all do when Martita passes gas, but I looked at her and said, "Lucie, sssshhhh."

And she replied, "Mommy, nobody here speaks English except Manuel."

Well, of course, Manuel translated it all (even though it wasn't necessary) and I attempted to explain that plugging your nose and waving your hand is pretty universal in all languages. I think the word *fart* is also pretty universal. Well, we had the room hysterically laughing. I had completely given up at this point and enjoyed the moment with everyone else.

Our form was revised, and the judge explained to me that when you adopt a child from Nicaragua, their records are completely destroyed—it is as if she was born into my family. He explained that it would be important to continue to tell Gracie about her heritage—to give her a positive image of Nicaragua.

Then he said, "Congratulations, Grace Martita Grimes is officially your child."

I started to cry and then hugged and kissed the judge (I'm a
touchy, feely kind of gal) and kept crying and thanking everyone.
Three years, almost to the date and she is finally *ours!*

Our friends, Jack, Beth, and Ignacio went in after we finished.
Ignacio is quite the character, so it wasn't a surprise that he too acted
up, just like our girls. When they finished, the judge told Jack that
Gracie and Ignacio are two peas in a pod (or the Nicaraguan version)
and we all laughed and agreed. Then we all signed the documents
and floated out of the room (it felt like it anyway). It was 3:00 p.m.
by the time we got home . . . it has been a *long* and *wonderful* day.

And the joy poured in from all corners of the globe . . . all
day long! I received so many calls from our friends (in Nica and in
the U.S.) congratulating us. I'm tearing up as I type this . . . What a
blessing to have these dear and precious friends in Nicaragua and
then to have such an amazingly supportive group back home. This
has been a rough road . . . a long road, but I have had so many
blessings throughout this journey. The people who have given me
the support and love to carry me through this process are *amazing!*

Tim booked our tickets, and we are going home in nine
days. Nine days. It's just enough time to finish all our paperwork, pack, and say, *Goodbye.* Why does it always seem that time
drags when you're trying to reach a milestone but then when it's
in your grasp, you nearly miss it because everything is in fast
forward?! As my husband said to me today, "Love, you can now
see the finish line."

He's right, and I am so ready to cross it!

3 Comments:

Timothy said . . .
The very first thing I am going to say is DITTO on how amazing
God is . . . we have and continue to be completely and totally

blessed as a family. I can truly say if you want to know God exists
. . . look around and watch Him work . . . that is evidence enough
. . . at least for us. The SECOND thing I will say is that I am proud
the Grimes' family continues to make its mark on Nicaragua!
Gracie and her antics in the courtroom today PROVES that she
is part of our wacky family and is meant to impact her world as
a Grimes! This is one of the funniest stories yet! LOL LOL LOL.

mawyer said . . .
Lesa,
I am soooooo happy that the end of your long, wonderful,
sometimes bumpy road, the journey is coming to an end—or
is it just the beginning of yet another journey . . . bringing your
new girl home to VA? I cannot wait to continue to experience
this journey with you as your friend as you get to experience
all the joy and love that Gracie will bring to you—thank God
for having this plan for you and your family! Love and hugs, T

ivaniam97 said . . .
I'm in NC needed to catch up on the last few days . . . must
redo my make-up once again. I laughed and cried a lot while
reading this one :) I just love Gracie!!! SOOO SOOO HAPPY
FOR YOU *AMIGA*!!!!!!!
XOXO

⟨ Chapter 16 ⟩

Last-Minute Details

Thursday, August 6, 2009
No More Waiting . . .

What a day! We had our run this morning, enjoyed a great breakfast and then headed to our doctor's appointment for Gracie. Before our daughter (love the sound of that) can get her visa to enter the United States, she has to have all her vaccinations. There are only three doctors that are approved through the Embassy, so I made an appointment with the first one on the list. We arrived and were disappointed when we got there. We brought our interpreter, Manuel, with us and apparently, I had misunderstood the receptionist when I made the appointment. I had to have Gracie's passport before I could see the doctor. This is a long and pointless story, but the bottom line is that I could not understand the woman on the phone and albeit, I kept saying, "Please talk slowly my Spanish is not good" she continued to rattle a million words a minute.

We decided to leave that office and go to the second doctor on the list. We called our lawyer Amelia, and she made an appointment for us and worked out a great deal . . . nice work Amelia.

Gracie had to get two shots; right before the doctor gave them to her, she looked up at me and said, "I'm sorry Mommy."

It broke my heart in half. I did my best to explain to my youngest that she didn't do anything wrong but that she needed the shots to keep her healthy. Little bug. I had to hold her face to look at me, and we started to sing her favorite song (yes, Tomorrow, tomorrow, I love you tomorrow) to keep her mind off what was going on. Gracie didn't cry, and she was very proud of herself.

When we went to the waiting room to get the girls . . . Gracie started to tell them how brave she was, and Lucie burst out crying. For heaven's sake, right? When I asked her what was wrong, Lucie said that she wasn't brave because she always cries when she gets shots. I wanted to say, "That's right . . . you are a big baby and still suck your thumb." (Remember, Mother of the year) but instead, I said, "You are so brave, and you are the one who has taught Gracie to be so brave and look how good she did."

I'm good . . . right?!?!

So, it was off to McDonald's for a celebration (not my idea but they have a great play area for the kids). We then had our friends drop us off at the mall to do a little present shopping. Seriously, what do you give the people you love and who have selflessly supported you through this entire process? I am at a loss. Shopping didn't really help either. We spent a couple of hours there and headed home.

I went to the office to speak to our landlord and told him that we would be checking out on the twelfth. We worked out our payments and made an appointment for our final walk-through of the condo. I also made reservations at a hotel that is across the street from the airport for our last night in Nicaragua. Exciting!

Tomorrow we head to Immigration for Gracie's passport. Apparently, they have stopped making passports (on the front page of the newspaper yesterday) because they ran out of materials. They claim it will be December before they make any more . . . only in Nica, so tomorrow should be quite interesting. I have learned that instead of panicking, I will show up and do what I can to make it work.

We will be home in a week! In the meantime, we're making progress and having fun along the way. I love that we are being so productive, *awesome*. I have spent the majority of my time in this country . . . waiting . . . now I am actually doing things and seeing a clear path home. *I love it!*

Thursday, August 6, 2009
Nicaragua Embassy . . . Here We Come!

Well, today sucked. I don't know a better word to describe it. I knew it would be a tough day, but tough turned into horrific! We left for the Immigration office at 8:30 a.m. There was no air conditioning, and it got very uncomfortable. There were plenty of seats, so the girls were very well-behaved, playing games and coloring. We stood in many lines. There was one line to complete the forms, a different line to meet with the manager for approval, then off to another line to wait for final approval. We jumped through all the necessary *hoops* and finally made it to the final approval window. Phew! I kept fixing Gracie's hair for her passport picture, but there were bigger problems that needed fixing . . .

Apparently, there was an issue with our Power of Attorney, which we need because my husband is at home and not present. Our Power of Attorney has Gracie's name *before* we changed it on her new birth certificate. While it displays her original name and the revised name the guy behind the window still wouldn't accept it. He left us to discuss the matter with his supervisor and after fifteen minutes came back with the same answer: *This won't work.*

Manuel assured me we would work it all out and walked me to the other side of the building where we met with the head supervisor. I might add the supervisor is a woman with a permanent frown. Our meeting was short and to the point. She wasn't changing the answer. We had to revise our Power of Attorney.

Well, we told our lawyer Amelia the news, and she was furious. She told me the Immigration office is like a stop light—green (meaning go sometimes) and red (no go). When we started to discuss our options, I learned that each one seemed complicated and time-consuming, which begged the question, "How can we get all these things done before my flight on Thursday?!"

Amelia's response was, "Change your flight."

I stood up and literally growled *loudly* and walked out of the building (yup that happened). I am still a little shocked at my reaction, but I was so angry... so frustrated. After five hours of waiting in lines, sweating, and having to appease my children, I was *not* in a good mood. I finally thought all was going well and then, this. I spent a few minutes crying and yelling. This was Amelia's job... to be sure the forms were completed correctly and when her response was to just "change my flight," I lost it. This is not an option for me. Finally, I pulled myself together and walked back in. I called my husband, and he helped me find a solution (just like he always does).

Here's the plan: Tim heads to the Nicaraguan Embassy (in the US) first thing tomorrow morning. He is bringing our friend Edwardo, who speaks fluent Spanish, with him. I sent Tim a letter from our lawyer that explains what we need. Tim will sign it and bring it with him. They will create a revised Power of Attorney, stamp it, and then Tim will have to figure out a way to get it to me, here in Nicaragua, by Monday. This would be very easy in the States, but the mail process here is archaic. He's planning on making several copies and sending them via FEDEX, UPS, DHL, messenger pigeon, any possible way to ensure it reaches us on time.

The plot thickens . . . Monday is a holiday here, not an actual holiday but an extension of a previous holiday in July (seriously), so we miss another delivery day. When I get the document, I have to return to Immigration and repeat the same process again. They will have the passport ready for me the next day, Wednesday. I have to then go to the doctor with Gracie's passport to release her records and take all the documents to the U.S. Embassy at 10:30 a.m. They will then submit my paperwork for her visa, which I cannot pick up until 8:00 a.m. Thursday, and then head straight to the airport to make our 12:00 p.m. flight!

It's tight . . . nothing else can go wrong . . . and I am a little stressed.

I was feeling so optimistic about our situation—feeling so confident that everything would go smoothly—now, this. We were supposed to go to the orphanage today for a goodbye party, but I was *not* up to it, so it's postponed until tomorrow. I know that this may seem silly to everyone. It's only a short delay, right? I can't explain how challenging it is for me to hang on and be positive right now when I'm battling an overwhelming urge to tell everyone to go fly a kite (that's putting it nicely)!

Blessings, I am so thankful for my husband right now. When I called to lay this all on him, he *never* hesitated to do precisely what he needed to do to get us home. And what would I do without our friends who dropped everything and rescheduled their day to help? I am so blessed and supported.

Not a lot of laughs today, just a lot of tears. Tomorrow will bring more answers and hopefully give us a clearer understanding of where we are. Please keep us in your prayers that I handle this situation, whatever it may be, with grace and patience and that I resist the urge to growl and throw temper tantrums in public. Please pray that my children continue to thrive, and my husband knows how much I love and appreciate him. Here's to a better day tomorrow.

1 Comment:

mawyer said . . .
Here's to a better day today—please know you guys and this process are in my prayers. We are all supporting you, 100 percent. Stay strong my friend.
Love and Hugs, T

Friday, August 7, 2009
Fiesta De Adios Para Gracie

I woke up this morning with a call from my husband at 6:30 a.m. He was at the Nicaraguan Embassy with our friend Edwardo to get an updated Power of Attorney. Tim wanted to confirm Gracie's birthday, my social security number, etc. Of course, my husband completed every task that needed to be done. He promised me that he would have the documents for me—if he had to fly down himself! I like my husband, I like him a lot. We talked throughout the morning regarding the details.

What blows our minds is how amazing our friends are. Edwardo dropped everything, on such short notice, to accompany Tim to the Embassy. And you'll never believe what happened next?! We reached out to a friend at ORPHANetwork and discovered that he is coming to Nicaragua on Monday! Instead of taking a chance on the postal system, our friend will deliver the goods to me. This is our saving grace! Hand delivered documents . . . from a trusted friend . . . it doesn't get any better than that. Thank you for all the support and prayers; they're working.

Scarlett asked me today, "Mommy—when will we know if we can go home on Thursday?"

And my answer was, "Thursday at around 10:00 a.m."

We are cutting it a little close, right?!?! ;)

Today was Gracie's goodbye party at the orphanage. Jack and Beth bought the biggest *piñata* I have ever seen! It was a giant, yellow, smiley face with a party hat on top. We filled it with twenty bags of candy and headed to the orphanage. We brought seventy-five donuts, lots of soda, and of course, Mr. Smiley.

Going to the orphanage is *always* a blessing. After my day yesterday, I was not in the mood to celebrate, but I always feel like I'm exactly where I'm supposed to be when I'm there with my kids. They were excited about the party but were sad that we're going home next week. Leaving these kids is the hardest thing to do . . . I know I will see them soon, but I want to be with them often, so they will know how much I love them.

Now it was time for sweet Gracie to say goodbye. She doesn't fully understand what is happening, but I know that the staff and these children *are also* her family. Natalia wrote a letter to Gracie explaining her life at the orphanage. The letter described when Gracie arrived as well as what her likes/dislikes and mannerisms were like as a child. She ended the letter giving Gracie advice to listen to her parents, live life to its fullest and love God. Natalia read it to me, and I cried. Our girl was loved, and the people here have made her the beautiful girl she is today.

We will see everyone again on Sunday . . . but today was bittersweet—a celebration wrapped in a goodbye.

3 Comments:

Timothy said . . .
Leave it to Natalia. I hope she understands how much of a gift she is to between thirty and fifty kids. She really is the Mom to all of them. She is a quirky and LOVING human . . . someone that God has to smile at constantly. AND she likes Tona (my favorite Nica Beer) so she is pretty darn good in my book as well!

Donna said . . .
Lesa,
We are so excited for you, Tim, and the girls! You are in our prayers—that all will go off without a hitch this week. We can't wait to see the happy family soon!
Donna McKinnon

Saturday, August 8, 2009
Unconditional Giving

I want to start off my blog by thanking all of you, who read this and who continue to support and love my family and I. *You* have made all the difference in this *adventure* of ours. I still can't believe that our time here is coming to an end. Today Scarlett said that we will never live here again. We will return to visit but never live here. We won't frequent the places we treasure or be with the people who we've come to depend on and love. It has been a once in a lifetime opportunity for us—one that we hold sacred. Scarlett has such love for this country and the people. She has been so strongly impacted by this experience that I hope it helps her become an even stronger and more passionate adult.

We took our last visit to Granada today. We love this city. It is a vibrant scene of community and culture—so full of life and activity. We also feel at home with all the *gringos* around. :) We had breakfast at our favorite place, Kathy's Waffle House and ate too many pancakes and waffles! Lucie always orders their chocolate milk, which is heaven in a glass and everybody had a taste this morning. Our friends accompanied us on our last trip. We spent our time shopping for gifts while enjoying the morning in this beautiful city.

We are also filling our days, packing and sorting through everything to decide what to bring home. We plan to give everything away (e.g., the dishes, bedding, fans, games, and clothing). We will travel home much lighter than when we came, except of course for the additional child we're adding to our family.

In prepping for our departure, we're deciding what to do with each item (i.e., determining who we should give it to). I want to share with you that the process of giving my things away is causing me to reflect on my attitude towards unconditional giving. I always have considered myself a giving person, but I must admit that I have my limitations. I want to help—I want to give but still on *my* terms. I am ashamed of this.

Here's the scenario, Jacklyn is a cleaning lady that I've hired to clean our place and do laundry three times a week. She has been so good to us. My only regret is that I didn't meet her on the first day we arrived. Jacklyn is a lovely lady who I know needs the work, which is why I purposely over-pay her, and I am always thankful for her help. When we are away from the house on a trip, and I don't need her, I still pay her as if she was here working.

Yesterday, I explained to her that we are leaving and that her last day would be Wednesday. Jacklyn started to ask me to give her things around the house. She wanted the cleaning products and our fans. I explained that we are giving everything to the people at the orphanage. She responded by saying that she really needed one of our fans. I told her that I would think about it. And I have. I have thought over and over about who is most deserving. Is it the staff and children at the orphanage? Or Norman, my cab driver who has been *so* good to us? Jacklyn? Since I am being honest, I don't want to give her anything because she asked for it. I know my attitude isn't right and I am struggling with these feelings. I still don't know what I want to do, or more importantly, what is the best thing to do. Why is being good so hard sometimes?

I feel the same way when I am feeling unappreciated. There have been so many times that I have given to Natalia and the kids at the orphanage and never been thanked. Recently, we took several of the older girls and Natalia to a movie and dinner. It was expensive, due to the number of people, but I enjoyed doing it. I enjoyed giving until the end of the night when no one thanked me. I was a little resentful because of this, and I don't like feeling this way. Isn't giving supposed to be unconditional, regardless if you're being thanked? Natalia has a heart of gold and I know she appreciates me so why does hearing it mean so much? Why does this have such an impact on me? I will continue to work on my unconditional giving that focuses on other peoples' needs and not my own.

Today was a great day overall. The fact that we'll be home soon is settling in, and I'm jazzed about it. While I'm looking forward to boarding that plane; I'm not looking forward to our last day at the orphanage, which makes me very sad. I'm *never* good at saying goodbye and even catch myself lying about how long I'll be gone. (The kids will ask me when I'm coming back, and I will answer, "In a couple of months." Then I'll excuse myself to cry and cry some more.) Scarlett always contradicts me and says, "We aren't coming back for a long time."

Thank you Scarlett, can you go away now?

I find it strange to have such sorrow about leaving when it has been the one prayer I have asked for every day I've been here. So many times, I have wished and prayed to get on a plane and go home. It's funny how you can want something so badly, but then when you receive it, you can only see the good things happening that contradict the thing you prayed so hard for in the first place.

Being present. Not worrying. I am finally getting what I want, and now I'm crying about leaving? I realize that no matter where I am, who I am with, and what I'm doing, it is my present. It's what's happening to me at this moment, and I need to grab it, feel it, and enjoy it because tomorrow is never a promise to anyone.

So, I am off to bed to get a good night's rest, praying that I keep it together (or fake it pretty well) for our goodbyes, and focus on living in the moment and enjoying it all.

Love and Blessings . . . Happy Weekend!

1 Comment:

Timothy said . . .

So as a *guy*/husband, I totally want to jump in and try to solve this issue of the fan . . . but I have learned at my old age that sometimes, especially when your wife is being sweet and pouring her heart out to everyone . . . that silence and using my "listening ears" is the best solution overall. If the only issues you are dealing with is trying not to break the heart of a kid at the orphanage or trying to do the right thing with people like Jacklyn (remember, the right thing sometimes is NOT to give the handout) . . . then you are pretty strong in my book. And smack Scarlett in the forehead for me . . . tell her to stop trying to keep us honest! :-) Baye, thanks for being who you are and writing this blog. In fact, thanks for writing the blog every day (except when your husband came to town and distracted you!) I know it meant a lot to me, and I am sure to everyone reading it! This has truly been an adventure of a lifetime for you and the girls (okay so maybe Scarlett is right on this one!) I am blessed to have been able to watch this one play out. Love you . . .

Sunday, August 9, 2009
La Casa De Norman y Susanna

I know my Sunday obsession is a reoccurring theme in this blog, but I just love Sundays! I wish you could see the kids' laughing faces and feel the energy in this church. It's transformational. This sacred time allows me to focus on what's going on in my head, meditate on Pastor Martin's message, which always seems to put the things I'm focusing on in my head into perspective. Today when I sat in church, I wrote some notes about how I was feeling:

Today I am sad and happy. My adventure here in Nicaragua has come to an end. It seems like so long since I have been home, but I cannot believe it has gone by so fast. Why can't I appreciate every moment? If I did, I wouldn't feel this way—I would be ready for the next day.

Pastor Martin preached about Matthew 6:25 today, which happens to be about worrying. The underlying message of the scripture is: "When we worry about tomorrow—we miss out on today! Therefore, do not worry about tomorrow, for tomorrow will worry about itself. Each day has enough trouble on its own."

Amen.

This was the message I needed to hear. These last few days have been a struggle, so focusing on our time here . . . enjoying our time here, is exactly what I am going to do.

After church, our cab driver and dear friend, Norman invited us to his home for lunch. His wife, Susanna cooked for us while Norman gave us the tour of their home. He was excited to show us around and told me their house was small but full of love . . . and he was exactly right. Norman and Susanna live in a very modest abode, which is about the size of our downstairs townhouse. I would guess a total of 700 square feet. It was spotless and decorated with wedding photos and homemade pictures. The main area had a small kitchen, a sitting area and off to the left was a TV and shelves. They had plastic chairs and no fans (hello Norman, you are getting *all* our fans)!

Norman has about a quarter acre of land. They have two gardens, a laundry area and room to build on to their house, which they plan to do as their family grows. They have a sweet dog and two birds that we met and played with. Susanna cooked a *fantastic* lunch. We had fish, chicken, and the best rice I have ever had (Lucie ate all of hers and half of mine), plantains and tomatoes from their garden. It was *muy rico!*

After lunch, Norman had presents for all of us. He gave the girls bracelets with their names on them. He gave Lucie the movies, *Transformers I* and *II*, and I received a small keychain that says, *Nicaragua* on it. He wanted us to have these keepsakes so we won't forget him. Scarlett had me tell Norman that even if we didn't have anything from him, we would always remember him. How true is that?!

We talked, laughed and got to know Susanna better. We shared stories about our family back home, which includes two dogs. Norman asked Scarlett to show them what our dog Esme looks like and Scarlett immediately transformed her face to look just like our bulldog. It was hilarious. We spend almost every day with Norman but spending this quality time together, we really have gotten to know each other very well.

Norman told us that when he builds on to his home, our family can stay with him when we come back to visit Nicaragua. What a generous and kind human being. Lucie had a great idea—she could fly by herself (like Scarlett does when she goes to California to visit her dad) to Nicaragua and stay in this new casita. ;)

We had one of the best afternoons ever today. I know Tim would have loved to have shared this with us, but I'm grateful that I have this special day to tell him (and you) about. Norman started off as our cab driver, became our friend, and now he is a special part of our family. What a blessing he is to us all.

2 Comments:

Timothy said . . .
I MISS NORMAN!!!! And tell Lucie that if she doesn't listen to her Momma this week, we are going to ship her off all right . . . but it might not be to her buddy Norman's house! WOW, what a special afternoon. I think Norman might be our best friend in Nica. Okay . . . eighty-seven hours and thirty-two minutes more (NOT THAT I AM COUNTING!) XOXOXOXOX

mawyer said . . .
So much love you're getting and giving—you are so special Lesa—throughout this journey, you have given so much of yourself not only to those you are touching in Nica but those of us who are following your journey with you. Every time I read your blog I find myself laughing with you, crying with you, and just feeling like somehow what you're going through is helping me get through some of my own things. THANK YOU for sharing this with us. I cannot wait for you to be home and have Gracie, Lucie, and Scarlett all home together. Enjoy your last few days there (until next time). Love and hugs, T

Chapter 17

The Light at the End
of the Tunnel

Monday, August 10, 2009
The End is Near . . .

Okay, the title of this blog is a little depressing, right? Instead of feeling happy and excited, I am full of anxiety and stress. I am so ready for tomorrow to be here, but I'm also terrified that it is here. Already?! This is where we're at: My husband sent the documents we needed via two different methods. First, he sent them to my lawyer's city using DHL. However, after speaking with my translator, I discovered that she did not even attempt to acquire the documents. Amelia was apparently out of town and returning today, which is so crazy to me, she knew this was the plan. She is *so fired*!

Plan B, (the Hail Mary), our friend Bobby is flying into Managua at 12:30 a.m. tomorrow morning, a couple of hours from now and Norman will drive to the airport to meet him.

Now, this sounds like a great way to get the documents to us, but Norman has never met Bobby, and I am a little concerned that they won't hook up. I described to Norman what Bobby looks like I told him that he has red hair, thinking this was the only thing I needed to say. I mean seriously, I think Bobby is the only redhead in Nicaragua. But Norman continued to ask for details. "Is he tall?"

My reply—yes, much taller than you. ;) (Norman's head comes to my shoulders.) I told Norman that Bobby wears glasses, but Norman (obviously not satisfied) asked if he had dark skin! Scarlett chimed in and said he had the same color skin that she does, and I repeated again, "Norman, Bobby has *red hair!!!*"

So, I am praying they meet. And I asked Norman to call me as soon as he had the documents in hand.

Assuming we get the documents, we are slated to leave at 7:30 a.m. with Norman to pick up our translator, Manuel. Apparently, the documents have to be certified and notarized (albeit they came from the Nicaraguan Embassy), so our first stop after picking up Manuel, is to go to the bank and get this done. Then we are off to the Immigration office to meet with Amelia.

Amelia has been sick a lot lately, and has a doctor's appointment tomorrow morning but is planning to meet us after. Manuel attempted to meet her tonight to pick up the documents, but she would not release them to him. She wants to be there. So hopefully, she will be in and out of the doctor's to meet us soon after we arrive.

Then, as long as the documents are in order, we will request the passport. Usually, this takes twenty-four hours, but we are hoping and praying we'll get it tomorrow afternoon. By this time, we'll be off to the doctor's office to pick up his report and then head back to the U.S. Embassy to request our visa. It's all a little too much for me . . . one snafu and the dominoes will tumble, so all I can do is continue to pray that all will be fine.

My stomach is in knots, and I am running on nervous energy. I haven't slept well, and as hard as I try to put this out of my mind, the details are a bloody horror movie running through my brain. What I do know is that my family has done everything we have been asked to do and all we can do now is wait and see how it plays out. I also know that even if we run into a snag along the way, we will be home, and soon. Pastor Martin's words keep chiming in my head, "Don't worry, it's all in God's time" that gives me the peace and patience I so desperately need right now.

This evening, we babysat Ignacio; he is such a ball of energy! It just amazes me how different boys are from girls. The first thing he did was lock the girls' bedroom door (he was outside of the room) and shut it closed. This has never happened before, so I pulled out my massive keychain and tried every key . . . of course, none of them worked, so we went to the office and asked for help. This also gave me the opportunity to talk to the owner and explain our issues with the process.

I told her that tomorrow I *should* know when we will move out. Craziness. She unlocked the door, and we were back in business. We watched *Transformers* and every couple of seconds (not exaggerating) Ignacio asked, "Is that a Transformer? Why doesn't he transform now? What are they saying? Where is the airplane? What's his name? Why do Transformers exist?" We were exhausted from watching the movie, but we really enjoyed our time with this little guy. We will miss our friends very much when we leave.

We spent most of today packing and getting ready for tomorrow (because today is a holiday, everything was closed). Since the mall, movie theater and most restaurants weren't open, we were forced to focus on the big day ahead.

Love and Blessings . . .

Tuesday, August 11, 2009
Don't Ask . . . Because I Don't Know!!

The day started with a phone call from Norman at 1:30 a.m. letting me know that he had our documents, which he got from our friend Bobby at the airport. (*Score!*) When my phone rang, I thought it was my alarm and turned it off . . . realized the time and took the next call from Norman. ;)

So, the day started off great, one thing checked off the list. Norman picked us up at 7:30 a.m. (Did the guy sleep at all last night?) And I immediately called Manuel to tell him we were on the way. Good thing I called because I woke him up (he seriously said to me that his watch had stopped working). We had to pick him up close to his house because he was running late. So already, we were behind schedule. (And I forgot my pills at home.) We picked him up and headed to some sort of office that authenticates documents. Yes, even though the papers are from the Nicaraguan Embassy, they still needed authentication. Don't ask, because I don't know!

Amelia, our lawyer, met us there. Phew, another giant hurdle accomplished. The authentication process was so quick I thought that we were doing pretty well according to our schedule. My plan (I live by planning) was to be at the Immigration office early so we could pick up Gracie's passport in the afternoon and possibly head to the U.S. Embassy and be done.

Once Amelia looked over the documents, she told Manuel that the title of the document was incorrect. Apparently, it needs to read *Special Document* and ours read *Document of Correction*. She blamed Manuel because he didn't send the document to her for final approval before sending it to me. My question, "Why are you saying this now? Why didn't she say something last Friday?"

After further review of the document, she found another *error*. (At this point huge knots are growing in my stomach, and I want to pull a Lucie and throw up in public.) It stated that Gracie was born on November 20th in Managua and she was actually born in a different city. She told Manuel this was a *major issue* and if they caught the discrepancy another document would need to be sent. This was not news that I wanted to hear.

Instead of going to the Immigration office, we went to a building across the street where there were several lawyers with typewriters that could make an addendum for you right on the spot. We sat down and waited for an hour, while a lawyer typed a document that amended the title of our Power of Attorney. This was a tough hour for me. The girls were restless, we had not had breakfast yet, and it was hot and sticky, which makes for cranky ladies. We were also on a very busy street, so the entire time I was worried about one of the girls walking away or getting abducted. Norman was a Godsend as he always is. He played with the girls and kept a watchful eye on them while I tried to figure out what was taking so damn long and getting us way off schedule.

Apparently, I've passed the *Debbie Downer* torch to Amelia, who was extremely negative during this entire ordeal. She only spoke to Manuel (never me) and complained about how my negative energy was making her lose sleep! Apparently, when I lost my mind in the Immigration office last Friday, that upset her. My response . . . I have lost sleep for days . . . and this is *her* issue . . . *her* error, and how does she expect me to respond? She was apparently mad at me because she kept her back to me the entire time we were there. I was so close to slapping the back of her head and *hard.* I could visualize her head snapping up and down. No permanent damage, but at least a hard enough hit for her to know that I deserve respect and she needs to do a better job!

Once the attorney finished making the addendum, we headed over to Immigration. Amelia kept assuring me that they would catch the error of the city Gracie was born. If they did find that tiny mistake, then they probably wouldn't accept the addendum. Who is paying this woman anyway? Negative Amelia has become the ultimate *Debbie Downer* (in this blog anyway).

It is maddening to spend four hours in an office waiting to stand in one line to finally talk to someone, who then sends you to another line again and again. Not to mention I have three girls who I need to look after and appease all the while trying to keep my head from spinning completely around. The girls kept asking, "How much longer Mommy?"

"What is he doing?"

"When can we go home?"

And my answer to every question was, "Don't ask me love, I have no idea."

We spent a half an hour in one line then sent to another and another. Repeat. Every time we changed lines, I would say, "Ay ay ay!!!" My interpreter told me I was stressing him out, so I turned to the one person in my life who *always* listens and *always* has my back . . . my husband.

Many of you know my husband as a very mild-mannered guy . . . and he is . . . until he gets angry. It takes a lot, but when he does . . . watch out! When I called Tim and told him what was going on, he started to tell me how ridiculous this entire process was, how upset he was, and he used the F-word about ten times! I found this refreshing. My husband was saying exactly what I was feeling but couldn't utter aloud. It feels so good when someone gets fired up and has your back. I got off the phone and told Manuel how upset Tim was, and this made him even more stressed. ;)

We *finally* met with the boss lady. Remember the lady with the permanent frown who turned us down on Friday? Both Manuel and I were freaking out while she read through our documents. She asked us a couple of questions and started signing her name on every page! When we left the office, Manuel and I were both crying and hugging each other. What a relief! Our passport was approved! We still had a few more checkpoints that we sweated through, and nothing went as planned, but bottom line . . . success! We still had a lot of *Plan Cs* to come up with, but I am so happy to have this one step *finished*!

I called my husband and knew he was still agitated, so I said, "Hey love, I have some good news and some bad news. What do you want to hear first?"

His reply was, "What is it?!"

I gave him the good news. Yes, we have been approved! Then the bad news, they said we couldn't pick up the passport until Thursday, so we definitely would not make our flight. Well, he really didn't respond well. I was so happy that we were finally through with the Immigration office, but he was still very distraught. So, I told him I would be home soon to Skype him. (This way I could help him see the positive side—like he always does for me.)

Now there is really only one thing that I *know* will instantaneously improve my husband's mood, (seriously Mimi if you are reading this . . . stop now) flashing him. Any time he is really upset about something, I flash him, and he smiles. Then he laughs, usually asks for another peek and then is truly happy. Happy to the core! It still works like a charm as I have had to use this trick several times. So, when I Skyped him at home and knew his mood was still pissy, I flashed him, he smiled, and all was well. He asked me to do it again, which I did but I heard a very suspicious noise when I lifted my shirt up. I told him I that I thought we were being monitored and some type of alarm had gone off! I started to freak out. Finally, my husband confessed that he was taking a *snapshot*! Hellooo, I think you need my permission for that!!! ;)

So, all is well with the Grimes family. We are behind schedule but *so happy* to have finished this part of the process. Tim strongly suggested that we move out of the condo tomorrow, as we originally planned and stay at a nice hotel. I followed his advice, made reservations and we are moving out tomorrow! *Yes*!!!! I am packing like a crazy woman and getting bags and bags of stuff to give away. It's a good feeling. We will be staying at the Intercontinental, which is right across the street from the mall and if we are here a few more days, we will have easy access to entertainment.

Happy days are here again! We are so close . . .

Tomorrow we will return to the Immigration office to *hopefully* pick up Gracie's passport. Keep us in your prayers. Love and miss you all and soon, soon, we will be home!

2 Comments:

Timothy said . . .
Hmmmm . . . okay so what do I say at this point . . . "guilty as charged?" Sometimes a man has to do what a man has to do! My wife knows me very, very well . . . I have a few

"weaknesses," and she can leverage it at any time. But here is my question . . . I am ALMOST fifty years old, and both my wife and I are still concerned about what my Mom is going to think? My Dad, I am sure is going "good for you son . . . good for you" LOL. Okay, love all you guys and always know when you see me in the future . . . if I am angry at something . . . at some point that day I will be a very happy boy!

ivaniam97 said . . .
HAHAHAHA . . . YOU TWO CRACK ME THE HECK UP! LOVE YOU TWO!!!!! I'M SO P'D OFF FOR YOU LESA, I WISH I WAS THERE WITH YOU ON THAT DAY! I WOULD HAVE GIVEN THEM A PIECE OF MY MIND, *LATINA* STYLE!!!!!!!!!!!!!!!!!!!.

Thursday, August 13, 2009
I Need More Tissue!!

Well, it has been a very loco couple of days. Sorry I didn't blog last night, but we are now in a hotel that charges for every minute I'm on the Internet, so I have to ration the minutes. I only have a two-hour window to check my email, logon to Facebook and Skype (Sorry Baye)!

Today is Thursday, so let's get back to Wednesday. Wednesday started with an early 6:00 a.m. start to finish packing and check out by noon. Here's what surprised me the most:

1. I cannot believe how much stuff we have accumulated in the past three months.

2. How sad I was to say goodbye to our home of three months.

When we packed to come here, I had sheets, pillows, dishes, pans, and towels. All of that is staying here, so I assumed that I would have very little to bring home, which is *not* the case for us. I guess since we have an additional child that makes for more stuff.;) Hauling our over-stuffed suitcases out of the house was no easy task! Norman came to the condo at 7:30 a.m. to take two carloads of stuff to his home (we gave him all our fans, kitchenware, bed clothes, towels, etc.) Then he took another load to the orphanage. By the time he got back to the house, we were running short on minutes.

We had to get to Immigration before noon to see if there was any way we could pick up Gracie's passport a day early which of course did *not* happen . . . they told us to come back the next day. We also had to check out of the condo by noon, so when Norman arrived, he came to the rescue once again! We left to pick up his wife, Susanna, checked into the hotel, and left the kids with her. Norman and I went back to the condo, filled his car with luggage and checked out.

After three months of basically hell in a small, bug-infested house, I cried when it was time to say, *goodbye.* I stopped to look at the street that Scarlett and I had turned into our morning run ritual, and admire the walls in our house that were decorated with hand-made pictures from my girls. I peeked in the small bathroom where I had spent many days getting ready (where you can't shut the door unless you are in the shower) and thought . . . Wow, I am going to miss this place. I said goodbye to every room and to each of the condo guards. Then, in a matter of minutes, we were on our way to our new home . . . The Intercontinental.

We arrived at the hotel with ten bags of luggage; I hoped that our room was large enough to fit all of it. When we pulled up, two bellmen opened my car door and asked how they could help. I had seven bags taken to storage, and three brought to our room. I had a man open my door and Norman, as usual, jumped in to carry any bags I had in hand. I stopped walking and relished the moment. I looked around and told the men surrounding me, "Now this is exactly what I need . . . to be surrounded by men who want to help me."

Nice!

The sheets aren't even cold at Condo Allyson, and already we're loving our new digs! It has hot water . . . *Yes*! Clean carpet, *very* comfortable beds, sheets, blankets, room service, and a mini—*bar!!!* ;) I'm happy! We spent a couple of hours relaxing and then started to get ready for our big *Goodbye Dinner* that we had planned.

Tonight's dinner was our opportunity to thank the people who have been so inspirational and loving to our Gracie and to us. We decided to co-host the meal with the friends since Ignacio and Gracie grew up together. There were about twenty people there, which was the perfect number of folks to share all the stories from this adventure. We laughed and talked and then finally, said goodbye. I know I will see everyone again soon, but these people have been my family here, and it's hard to leave them. Let's be honest, I cry at Hallmark commercials, (do they even have those anymore??? I have TIVO) almost every movie I watch and sometimes . . . for no reason at all, so I was a mess last night.

Today, Thursday, was yet another busy and emotional day. It was our day at the Immigration office. They had turned us down yesterday when we attempted to get Gracie's passport early, so today . . . today we *needed* to get Gracie's passport, or we would be here until at least Monday. I haven't been sleeping well, and my stomach was doing backflips, but I really felt confident that we would be walking out with Gracie's passport. We got to the office an hour before we were supposed to be there and walked into a room full of Nicaraguans. I was the tallest and whitest girl in the building (actually, probably in the entire country). It was total chaos. There were about twelve different lines, and I had no idea where to go or what to do (stomach out of control by this point).

Norman took my paperwork and started to weave through the crowd. He came back a couple of minutes later and said, "Don't worry Lesa . . . sit and wait."

I did as my dear friend told me and seriously, ten minutes later I hear, "Gracie Grimes. Gracie Grimes."

I went up to the window and handed my passport to the guy. He looked at me, examined my passport and then handed mine *and* Gracie's passport back to me. *Can you believe it?!?!?! I have Gracie's passport!!!* I did the *Happy Dance* right there and then (a lot of hip shaking and arm waving with a big smile on my face). When the girls saw me, they all joined in the *Happy Dance* so did Norman! (Well, he just shook his head and laughed at all of us.) I started to cry then and didn't stop for about twenty minutes. Tears of total *joy*!

After talking to my husband, we headed to the doctor's office for Gracie's health certificate and then to the U.S. Embassy for her visa. We were at the Embassy for about two hours, completing paperwork, answering questions and making more payments. Apparently adopting a child in Nicaragua isn't free. This was something I heard them say over and over again, "It doesn't cost anything to adopt a child in Nicaragua." . . . ha! :)

The girls were pretty much out of control, but I didn't care too much. I was in a very weird mood today. I smiled a lot but didn't pull any punches. For example, when our coordinator at the immigration office told me, "There could be a problem with the computer and we may not get your visa in time for your flight tomorrow."

I replied, with a big smile on my face, "There will *not* be any issues, that I am sure of."

My husband thinks that I am scaring everyone here and they are going to be sure to get me out of their country . . . fine by me. ;) The final step is going to the Embassy tomorrow to pick up Gracie's visa. If there aren't any issues, we will have everything we need to go home. *Yes*!!!

We ended our day today with a delicious Mexican meal with our dear friends. It was our last evening with them, and again, I cried and cried when we said goodbye. Ignacio has become a very close friend of my girls, and both Jack and Beth have been there for me through it all. I will miss them all terribly.

It has been a *very* emotional couple of days. I look forward to finishing things up tomorrow without having issues. I'm excited to enjoy our last day in Nicaragua. We plan to take a late afternoon flight Saturday, which will get us home early Sunday morning. We will spend my favorite day, Sunday in our PJ's resting and embracing the fact that we are home . . . sounds like paradise to me.

Here's to a *great* day tomorrow—Love you all so much—Blessings, Blessings, Blessings!

Friday, August 14, 2009
Adios Nicaragua

Yes, it's official . . . tonight is our last night in Nicaragua! Did I mention I am *so ready* to go home? This gorgeous hotel has its perks, but one room for three nights with four girls . . . not so good. I can't go to the bathroom, shower, or sleep by myself. My only time of peace is when everyone is sleeping. Scarlett will not go to sleep until I do . . . so I never have a second to myself. When I am at my breaking point, I roam the halls in front of our room and listen to the piped in music (it's in English) and breathe deeply and slowly. ;)

Today we were able to pick up Gracie's visa. *So exciting*! We told our lawyer that we were leaving today (and the Embassy) because we didn't want any more delays. We arrived right at 10:00 a.m., and I decided to leave Scarlett and Lucie with Norman while Gracie and I ran in. I told him it would be five minutes and he was happy to have some company. I left everything in the car, including my phone because they don't allow you to bring anything in. Norman showed me where to go when I was finished and where he would be parked. We were all set.

Gracie and I were literally in there for ten minutes. We went right through security. We were handed our package and ready to go. When we came out of the Embassy—there were several men petitioning something. I don't know what, but I was approached by them asking me to sign their documents. I kept saying, "No" and continued to look for Norman. We waited a few minutes, and I wondered what was taking him so long. Cabs circled, and the drivers repeatedly asked me if I needed a ride as minutes passed. I was very nervous at this point, I only had my wallet and Gracie's paperwork. Then I started to panic! Where were my girls? I knew in my heart they were fine, but I was an emotional mess. (I thought I was done losing it!)

I have been so frustrated and emotional these last few days, but when it was finally over, I wasn't relieved, I was freaking out. Scared to be standing on this corner and scared not knowing where my kids are . . .

To make a long story, short . . . Norman had taken the girls to the park (Scarlett's idea) for a quick five minutes that turned into thirty. My lawyer, Amelia drove by and saw me stranded, so she called Norman for me and took me to where he was. All was well in the end, but I must say, my nerves are *shot*!

I have not been feeling well at all these last few days, and it just keeps getting a little worse every day. I think it is nerves, and a big parasite living in my tummy. Seriously, I don't know what it is, but I want it to go away. We took it easy and went to the pool today. We planned to walk across the street and see the movie, *GI Joe* but were told that it was in Spanish, so we moved on to *Plan B*. We bought popcorn and candy at the theater and walked back to our room to watch a movie. It was fun. We ordered room service for dinner, and the girls loved sitting on our beds eating their meal. I mean, who doesn't like room service? It doesn't get any better than that. Tomorrow, we are saying goodbye to Norman at 11:00 a.m. Then Natalia and Amanda will pick us up and take us to the airport. I still can't believe that we are leaving . . .

I want to thank you all for reading my blog—for loving me, for forgiving me—for not judging me. Having empathy for the journey, we have been navigating this summer. Having you all with me through this process has made it the best experience possible because I know I wasn't alone. You will never know what your calls, comments, emails, and messages have meant to me. Thank you from the bottom of my heart.

To our friends in this beautiful country of Nicaragua, thank you for the hospitality. Thank you for sharing your country with us and making such an impact on every member of my family. This has been a journey; one that has been so completely out of my comfort zone. What I know for sure is stepping (or in this case leaping) out of my comfort zone *always* has the most incredible payoff. I am a changed woman—a better woman because of my time here. I leave for home with my beautiful daughters and a new family. I know we will be challenged in the months and years to come, but I am so truly grateful and humbled to have had this experience and to bring Gracie home with us.

With gratitude and love, Lesa

Epilogue

May 2018

My original plan was to continue my blog once I got home but I was busy surviving motherhood (a.k.a. raising four daughters). So, the blog took a backseat. I was very sick upon my return to the States. I had several infections and was down and out for a while, but that didn't keep me from celebrating! Shortly after we arrived in Virginia, we spent our weekends introducing our new daughter to our friends and family. It was a joyous time.

Life after Nicaragua has been full of *Happy Dances* and rip out my hair moments. Gracie was much further behind than we ever thought possible. We got her going in occupational therapy, but learning has been a challenge for her. This is because Gracie's early years were void of nutrition, love, and support. We have spent a lot of time trying to determine what her development issues are.

We made it back to the States in time for school. Gracie started kindergarten immediately and then repeated it the following year. We had her in ESL (English as a Second Language) for two years to give her more assistance. We also enrolled her in private tutoring to help her catch up.

Gracie was first diagnosed as, *Other Health Impairment*, which means they knew she had special needs but didn't know what they were. We were so fortunate to have a supportive school system that diligently worked with us to give her the help she needed.

Although Gracie struggled with her classes and making friends, she is one of the happiest people I know. She laughs at anything remotely funny and always has us laughing with her. While we love our girl dearly, it has been a struggle to get her fully acclimated. She has attachment issues, because of the neglect she experienced as a baby (i.e., being abandoned and abused). Her early childhood lacked stability and was void of parental connections due to the revolving door of people in her life. As a result, Gracie struggled to bond with us as her family.

On one occasion, my Dad and stepmom, Debra, came to visit for a week, and Gracie loved having them with us. When it was time for them to leave, Gracie wanted to go with them. She told me, "Mommy, I want to live with them, not you."

Heartbreaking. This happened several times, and I realized that Gracie wasn't connecting with us like she should be. It was completely understandable, but it took us several years for her to comprehend that we *are* her family and that her permanent home is with us.

Where are we now? Gracie is fourteen years old. She is in seventh grade but is functioning at a second-grade level. Four years ago, we moved to Phoenix, Arizona and struggled to find a school that could provide Gracie what she needs, until this year. Grace is now in a classroom with all special needs children and is doing very well. She is finally getting some confidence and is excited about learning. She has a low IQ—52—and they believe that the gap will increase over the next few years. We have never cared about labels, but it is important for us to understand her abilities and how best to get her the services she needs.

Gracie is a lover of life. She is an incredible sister and treats everyone with love and respect. She has bonded with us after a few years and I no longer think she would want to leave with any visitor that stays with us. She's our girl and our family. Gracie's sisters are also thriving. Lucie is a sophomore in high school and is a gifted student. She loves playing on her lacrosse team, and video games are also her jam. Our Lucie continues to be of great support to her sister.

Scarlett is in college studying Sound Engineering and working at a production company. She speaks excellent Spanish and is passionate about human rights . . . for all people. We kind of saw that coming. ☺

Allie is now married to Adam and they have three kids; Kayla, Hunter, and Monroe. They live in Northern Virginia. We see her and her beautiful family every chance we get. She is happy and doing wonderfully.

My daughter, Grace has also taught me the most important lesson, the definition of happiness. As parents, we often think that our children need to be college graduates, have great jobs and be financially independent to be happy. But that could not be further from the truth. Happiness for Gracie means having a loving family, feeling proud of her accomplishments and looking forward to a bright future. She has all of those things, and I believe her future is very bright! I'm not sure what it will look like, and it may not mirror what other people have, but never-the-less, we know it will be meaningful just as her whole life has been.

I have been trying to turn my blog into a book for several years, ten years in fact. Life has gotten in the way, and the longer it took, the more hesitant I was to publish it. But the reason I am releasing it now is that I want to share the incredible story of how one lost child in Nicaragua has changed the lives of her family, friends and countless people that we haven't even met. We continue to support Puente de Amistad and work with organizations that are doing service projects for the orphanage.

It's not easy . . . as a matter of fact, some days are downright daunting, but with each challenge, I see my family becoming more and more committed to each other. I witness my girls growing in their capacity to love others. Gracie was the missing piece. She is God's glue that connects us, and I want everyone to know that our crazy (maybe even dysfunctional) blended family is all I ever wanted in life.

Adopting a child is a huge responsibility, and it affects every member of your family. It's hard work and is thankless most of the time. When I read back on this story, I realize that all the things I struggled with in Nicaragua (i.e., the delays, feeling helpless, things not going as planned) continue in my life raising Gracie. However, if I could rewrite this story, I wouldn't change a thing. Without the challenges, there would be no reason to do *Happy Dances*. Working through the trials helps us become the people God designed us to be. And as my daughter Grace continues to remind us, "The sun will come out tomorrow."

Thank you for sharing in our love story.

Love and Blessings,

Lesa

About the Author

Lesa Scarlett-Grimes' first loves are her husband and children. Fashion and travel come second, and a good tequila brings up the rear. (Don't judge her.) She values her relationship with God and is grateful for all of the blessings and hardships she's endured, as she feels they are often one of the same. Lesa is the mom of four daughters (Allie, Scarlett, Lucie, and Grace) and describes her family as "blended, complicated and wonderful." She is thriving in her marriage to her best friend, Tim whom she lovingly refers to as Baye. Lesa graduated from Northwest Missouri State with a Bachelors Degree and spent twenty-six years in the telecommunications business. She retired from the industry as an executive before starting a new career as a stylist. This working mom does not function without a to-do list, which feels incomplete if she's not training for a marathon or involved in some type of service project. She has a passion for helping others, especially children. Her most epic adventure to date was moving to Nicaragua without a return ticket home, and that's where her memoir begins.